Adam Nathan

Silverlight 1.0

UNLEASHED

SAMS | 800 East 96th Street, Indianapolis, Indiana 46240 USA

Silverlight 1.0 Unleashed

ISBN-13: 978-0-672-33007-0

ISBN-10: 0-672-33007-5

Library of Congress Cataloging-in-Publication Data

Nathan, Adam.

  Silverlight 1.0 unleashed / Adam Nathan.

     p. cm.

  ISBN 0-672-33007-5

  1. Silverlight (Electronic resource) 2. Multimedia systems. 3. Web sites–Design. 4. Application software–Development. I. Title.

  QA76.575.N387 2008

  006.7–dc22

2007037266

Printed in the United States of America

First Printing: October 2007

Trademarks

All terms mentioned in this book that are known to be trademarks or service marks have been appropriately capitalized. Sams Publishing cannot attest to the accuracy of this information. Use of a term in this book should not be regarded as affecting the validity of any trademark or service mark.

Warning and Disclaimer

Every effort has been made to make this book as complete and as accurate as possible, but no warranty or fitness is implied. The information provided is on an "as is" basis. The author and the publisher shall have neither liability nor responsibility to any person or entity with respect to any loss or damages arising from the information contained in this book.

Bulk Sales

Sams Publishing offers excellent discounts on this book when ordered in quantity for bulk purchases or special sales. For more information, please contact

U.S. Corporate and Government Sales
1-800-382-3419

corpsales@pearsontechgroup.com

For sales outside of the U.S., please contact

International Sales
international@pearsoned.com

 The Safari® Enabled icon on the cover of your favorite technology book means the book is available through Safari Bookshelf. When you buy this book, you get free access to the online edition for 45 days.

Safari Bookshelf is an electronic reference library that lets you easily search thousands of technical books, find code samples, download chapters, and access technical information whenever and wherever you need it.

To gain 45-day Safari Enabled access to this book:

▶ Go to http://www.samspublishing.com/safarienabled
▶ Complete the brief registration form
▶ Enter the coupon code **JEMM-ADIL-ILMS-WTLM-MFGJ**

If you have difficulty registering on Safari Bookshelf or accessing the online edition, please e-mail customer-service@safaribooksonline.com.

Editor-in-Chief
Karen Gettman

Acquisitions Editor
Neil Rowe

Development Editor
Mark Renfrow

Managing Editor
Gina Kanouse

Project Editor
Betsy Harris

Copy Editor
Rhonda Tinch-Mize

Indexer
Erika Millen

Proofreader
Kathy Bidwell

Technical Editor
Dave Relyea

Publishing Coordinator
Cindy Teeters

Book Designer
Gary Adair

Compositor
codeMantra

Contents at a Glance

Table of Contents

About the Author

Adam Nathan is a senior software development engineer for Microsoft and the founding developer of Popfly, Microsoft's first product built with Silverlight. He is the author of the best-selling *Windows Presentation Foundation Unleashed* (Sams, 2006), *.NET and COM: The Complete Interoperability Guide* (Sams, 2002), a coauthor of *ASP.NET: Tips, Tutorials, and Code* (Sams, 2001), and a contributor to books such as *.NET Framework Standard Library Annotated Reference, Vol. 2* (Addison-Wesley, 2005) and *Windows Developer Power Tools* (O'Reilly, 2006).

Adam regularly speaks at development conferences and to internal groups within Microsoft about a variety of .NET topics. Having started his career on Microsoft's Common Language Runtime team in 1999, Adam has been at the core of .NET technologies since the very beginning. Adam is also the creator of popular tools and websites for .NET developers, such as PINVOKE.NET (and its Visual Studio add-in). You can find him online at www.adamnathan.net.

Dedication

To Lindsay and Tyler.

Acknowledgments

As always, I give the most thanks to my wife, Lindsay, for her never-ending patience and support. I keep saying that I'm never going to write another book, but somehow I end up getting convinced to write one anyway! And yet, despite all my flaws, we're still married. Her thoughtfulness and dedication are remarkable and are just two of the many lessons I've learned from her. Without her, none of this would be possible.

Although most of the process of writing a book is very solitary, this book came together because of the work of many talented and hardworking people. I'd like to take a moment to thank some of them by name. Dave Relyea from the Silverlight team did a fantastic job as the technical editor for this book. Many other Microsoft co-workers graciously agreed to review chapters as I wrote them. I'd like to especially thank Tim Rice, who provided a huge amount of valuable feedback on technical details, grammar, and everything else imaginable. Without Dave and Tim's help, this book wouldn't have turned out nearly as good as it did. I'd also like to thank Andy Sterland, Patrick Wong, and Vinay Deo. I thank Paramesh Vaidyanathan for giving me permission to write this book in the first place, and Scott Guthrie for his support.

I'd like to sincerely thank the folks at Sams—especially Neil Rowe—because I couldn't have asked for a better publishing team. They gave me the complete freedom to write the kind of book I wanted to write. And, as with my *WPF Unleashed* book, they recognized the importance of full color printing and didn't even question doing it!

Finally, I thank *you* for picking up a copy of this book and reading at least this far! I hope you continue reading and find the journey of exploring Silverlight as enjoyable as I have!

We Want to Hear from You!

As the reader of this book, you are our most important critic and commentator. We value your opinion and want to know what we're doing right, what we could do better, what areas you'd like to see us publish in, and any other words of wisdom you're willing to pass our way.

As an Executive Editor for Sams, I welcome your comments. You can fax, email, or write me directly to let me know what you did or didn't like about this book—as well as what we can do to make our books stronger.

Please note that I cannot help you with technical problems related to the topic of this book, and that due to the high volume of mail I receive, I might not be able to reply to every message.

When you write, please be sure to include this book's title and author as well as your name and phone or fax number. I will carefully review your comments and share them with the author and editors who worked on the book.

Email: feedback@samspublishing.com

Mail: Neil Rowe, Executive Editor
Sams Publishing
800 East 96th Street
Indianapolis, IN 46240 USA

Introduction

Thank you for picking up *Silverlight 1.0 Unleashed*! Silverlight is changing the way many people think about designing and developing websites or web applications, and this book helps you take advantage of everything Silverlight enables. Silverlight makes it easier than ever to create rich web-based content or applications. And given that it's possible to use Silverlight without expensive development or design tools, learning Silverlight is a wonderful way for everyone from hobbyists to professionals to create compelling software.

As Silverlight was developed, it was obvious that a new wave of books would appear in the marketplace. But it wasn't clear to me that these Silverlight books would have the right balance to guide people through the technology while showing practical ways to exploit it. Therefore, I wrote *Silverlight 1.0 Unleashed* with the following goals in mind:

▶ To provide a solid grounding in the underlying concepts in a practical and approachable fashion

▶ To answer the questions most people have when learning the technology, and to show how commonly desired tasks are accomplished

▶ To be an authoritative source, thanks to input from members of the Silverlight team who designed, implemented, and tested the technology

▶ To be clear about where the technology falls short, rather than selling the technology as the answer to all problems

▶ To be an easily navigated reference that you can constantly come back to

I hope you find this book to exhibit all these attributes.

Who Should Read This Book?

This book is for software developers and designers who are interested in creating compelling web-based content, applications, or controls. This book contains a lot of content to help you get the most out of Silverlight, regardless of your prior experience with other technologies. And even if you are already well versed in Silverlight, I'm confident that this book still has something to teach you. At the very least, it should be an invaluable reference for your bookshelf.

To summarize, this book

- Covers everything you need to know about Extensible Application Markup Language (XAML) in Silverlight

- Examines the Silverlight feature areas in incredible depth: graphics, text, audio, video, animation, ink, events, and more

- Demonstrates how to create reusable controls and perform common tasks (such as drag-and-drop) using basic building blocks

- Explains how to download assets asynchronously to maximize your user experience

- Demonstrates how to create hybrid applications that mix Silverlight content with HTML or Flash content in powerful ways

- Highlights features scheduled for future versions of Silverlight while showing how to achieve your desired results with the current version

Examples in this book appear in XAML, HTML, and JavaScript. You do not need to be familiar with these languages in order to understand this book.

By focusing on version 1.0, this book clearly shows what you can and can't accomplish with the first version of Silverlight. If you are interested in learning about future Silverlight features in more depth, *Windows Presentation Foundation (WPF) Unleashed* provides a good preview of the direction Silverlight is heading (which is to more closely resemble the feature set of WPF).

Software Requirements

Three pieces of software are required to use the samples in this book:

- Version 1.0 or later of Silverlight, which can be freely downloaded from www.silverlight.net.

- An operating system supported by Silverlight. Version 1.0 supports Windows XP or later (including the non-IA64 server versions) and Mac OS X 10.4.8 or later (either PowerPC or Intel). Future versions of Silverlight will support additional operating systems. (For example, the next version should support Windows 2000.) Note that the .NET features in future versions of Silverlight may only support Intel Macs, but all the features in 1.0 are supported on both architectures.

▷ A web browser supported by Silverlight. Version 1.0 supports Internet Explorer 6 or later, Firefox 1.5 or later, and Safari 2.0.4 or later (on Mac OS X only). Future versions of Silverlight will support additional web browsers.

If you want to run the samples on Linux instead, you can use Moonlight, Novell's open source implementation of Silverlight for Linux. The plan (not yet realized at the time of writing) is for Moonlight to run on all Linux distributions and support the Firefox, Opera, and Konqueror browsers.

Although a lot of Silverlight development can be done with a simple text editor, you can be more productive with the following recommended software:

▷ For developers, Microsoft Visual Studio 2008 or later, which can be a free Express edition downloaded from http://msdn.microsoft.com. (Visual Studio 2005 can be used as well, but the JavaScript editor isn't as rich, and the XAML editor comes with a separate download—the extensions for .NET Framework 3.0 development available from MSDN.)

▷ For designers, Microsoft Expression Studio. Within this suite, Expression Blend is specifically designed for creating XAML-based user interfaces (whether based on Silverlight or WPF), even animated ones. Expression Encoder, covered in Chapter 10, "Audio and Video," makes it easy to produce compelling—even interactive—audio and video content optimized for Silverlight.

Code Examples

The source code for examples in this book can be downloaded via www.informit.com/title/9780672330070 or www.adamnathan.net/silverlight.

How This Book Is Organized

This book is arranged into three parts:

Part I: Fundamentals

▷ Chapter 1: "Getting Started"

▷ Chapter 2: "XAML"

Part II: Creating Static Content

▷ Chapter 3: "Shapes, Lines, and Curves"

▷ Chapter 4: "Text"

▷ Chapter 5: "Brushes and Images"

▷ Chapter 6: "Positioning and Transforming Elements"

Part III: Making Your Content Come to Life

- ▶ Chapter 7: "Responding to Input Events"
- ▶ Chapter 8: "Downloading Content on Demand"
- ▶ Chapter 9: "Animation"
- ▶ Chapter 10: "Audio and Video"

The first two chapters explain the fundamentals. Chapter 1 focuses on ways to get Silverlight content into a web page and your options for how it interacts with HTML. Chapter 2 explores XAML in great depth, giving you the foundation to understand the XAML you'll encounter in the rest of the book and in real life.

Part II covers the variety of static content that Silverlight is capable of rendering. This not only includes text and images, but also sophisticated vector-based content. Chapter 6 ends Part II by showing how to arrange, resize, and even transform multiple pieces of content in rich ways.

The final part of the book explains how you can make your otherwise static content come to life. Chapter 7 is the most important chapter for developers because Silverlight's input events make it possible to create an interactive application. Chapter 8 demonstrates how you can greatly improve the experience with large content by downloading it on-the-fly and showing slick progress indicators. And with animation, audio, and video (covered in Chapters 9 and 10), you can make your content or application quite stunning.

Conventions Used in This Book

Various typefaces in this book identify terms and other special items. These typefaces include the following:

Typeface	Meaning
Italic	Italic is used for new terms or phrases when they are initially defined, and occasionally for emphasis.
Monospace	Monospace is used for screen messages, code listings, and command samples, as well as filenames.
	In code listings, *italic monospace type* is used for placeholder text.
	Code listings are colorized similar to the way they are colorized in Visual Studio. Blue monospace type is used for XML elements and JavaScript keywords, brown monospace type is used for XML element names and JavaScript strings, green monospace type is used for comments, and red monospace type is used for XML attributes.

Throughout this book, you'll find the following sidebar elements:

- ▶ FAQ (Frequently Asked Question) is a sidebar that presents a question readers might have regarding the subject matter in a particular spot in the book—then it provides a concise answer.

- ▶ Digging Deeper sidebars present advanced or more detailed information on a subject than is provided in the surrounding text. Think of Digging Deeper material as stuff you can look into if you're curious, but can ignore if you're not.

- ▶ Tips are bits of information that can help you in real-world situations. They often offer shortcuts or alternative approaches to make a task easier, quicker, or produce better results.

- ▶ Warnings alert you to an action or condition that can lead to an unexpected or unpredictable result, and then tell you how to avoid it.

- ▶ Looking Forward sidebars discuss upcoming functionality planned for future versions of Silverlight.

PART I

Fundamentals

IN THIS PART

Getting Started

Despite all the wonderful things you can say about HTML, CSS, and JavaScript, I think most people doing a lot of web-based development would agree that they form a pretty poor environment for developing modern sites and applications. If you care about your content working on most web browsers (or even just Internet Explorer and Firefox), accommodating their differences can be maddening. Many techniques and JavaScript libraries have been developed and shared over the years that can reduce this frustration, but none of them are silver bullets.

In addition to browser differences, the graphical capabilities of HTML are too limiting for many user experiences that people want to create. Drawing a simple line, incorporating video, and a number of other things are extremely difficult or impossible with HTML alone. It's not that these technologies were poorly designed, but simply that they were designed for hyperlinked documents rather than the extremely rich presentations that most people want to create on the Web these days.

Considering these issues, it's no wonder that Adobe Flash has been so successful. Whether someone wants to create a professionally designed website, an online game (or any number of other applications), or even a simple advertisement, Flash has been a natural choice for escaping the limitations of HTML. If you doubt the pervasiveness of Flash, try this experiment: Think of a brand of food you eat, and then navigate to the brand's website. Chances are you'll find Flash content at your destination. (I just tried pepsi.com, doritos.com, and oscarmayer.com, and all three are using Flash at the time of writing.) The Flash development experience leaves much to be desired, however. Flash (the runtime environment, as well as the tool) suffers from the same basic problem as HTML: Many people are trying to use it for creating rich applications, but it was originally designed for something else (in this case, simple animations).

This is why the introduction of Silverlight is so exciting. A promising alternative to Flash, Silverlight enables the creation of rich web content and applications using a lightweight add-on that is friendly to both designers *and developers*. Yes, the first version of Silverlight is primitive in areas, but it's a true development platform based on concepts and APIs introduced with Windows Presentation Foundation (WPF) in 2006 and in development for many years prior. And, unlike just about any software that has come out of Microsoft, Silverlight is a small download! Version 1.0 is less than 1.5MB, so users who don't have it can get it pretty quickly when browsing to Silverlight content. (By default, Silverlight also automatically updates to later versions when they are available.) Silverlight might just be the silver bullet many designers and developers have been waiting for.

Silverlight 1.0 applications are created with a mixture of XAML (Extensible Application Markup Language), HTML, and JavaScript, so they are easy to integrate into existing web content and compatible with popular Asynchronous JavaScript and XML (AJAX) libraries and techniques. XAML is an XML-based declarative language described in depth in the next chapter. In typical Silverlight applications, a XAML file contains a hierarchy of visual elements that must be rendered on the screen. Silverlight parses the XAML content on initialization, and then renders the content as appropriate.

DIGGING DEEPER

A Note for Those Afraid of JavaScript

A few readers might be excited at the idea of using JavaScript to create Silverlight content or applications. If you're like most developers I know, however, you're disappointed to be "forced" to use it in version 1.0. However, programming in JavaScript isn't the worst thing in the world. JavaScript is a very powerful dynamic language, and you can even use it in an object-oriented way if you follow clever patterns that people have devised over the years. (Note that JavaScript really has nothing to do with Java.)

In addition, now that Asynchronous JavaScript and XML (AJAX) is all the rage, there are a number of useful tools and libraries to help you be productive with JavaScript, and they keep getting better. Visual Studio 2008 boasts a number of improvements for JavaScript development, especially related to debugging and IntelliSense.

The pain of programming in JavaScript (when used as part of a website) is often not because of the language itself but rather differences in the HTML Document Object Model (DOM) provided by various web browsers. Fortunately, writing JavaScript that interacts solely with Silverlight objects doesn't have this issue because the Silverlight object model remains the same regardless of the host browser. Most Silverlight applications still require JavaScript that interacts with the HTML DOM, but your exposure to the DOM can be much more limited. And for those cases, ASP. NET AJAX (or other popular AJAX libraries) is a good fit for hiding browser differences.

Continued

If you're still not convinced, rest assured that the next version of Silverlight (already available in prerelease form) supports procedural code written in C#, Visual Basic, IronRuby, IronPython, and other .NET languages. And for those who love JavaScript, the next version of Silverlight should support compiled (.NET-based) JavaScript, giving performance that is orders of magnitude faster than the interpreted JavaScript running in browsers today. Some of these languages will be part of the core Silverlight download, whereas other languages might require additional on-demand downloads.

FAQ

? What are the differences between Silverlight and Adobe Flash?

"Flash" is the name for both a runtime component and a design tool. "Silverlight" refers to a runtime component only, but there are both design tools (such as Expression Blend) and development tools (such as Visual Studio) for Silverlight.

For years, Flash has been the only viable option for rich web-based content, and now Silverlight is positioned to fill the same need. The two technologies have similar features, but there are naturally pros and cons to each.

The biggest thing Flash (the runtime component) has going for it is ubiquity. A website can use Flash with confidence that the vast majority of viewers already have the necessary player installed. Silverlight, on the other hand, is brand new and will take some time to spread—dependent on the amount of compelling Silverlight content out in the wild. Of course, both Flash and Silverlight are designed to have a quick and painless installation, so sites don't have to inconvenience users *too* much if they don't have the necessary software. But even if Silverlight spreads like wildfire during the first few months, the Flash runtime component can still reach places that Silverlight can't (yet), such as mobile devices.

Flash has a variety of visual features that Silverlight lacks, such as bitmap effects (blurring and glowing) and shape tweening (morphing the shape of an object in an animation). Notable features of Silverlight that Flash lacks are higher quality video (even HD 720p full-screen with reasonable hardware) with VC-1 codecs included, seamless interaction with HTML, support for high-resolution and pressure-sensitive input data from a stylus or touch device, and content that's more discoverable to search engines by default thanks to the use of XML rather than compiled script.

The biggest advantage of Silverlight over Flash is in the design of the platform and its associated tools. This advantage becomes especially apparent if you're building an interactive application rather than a simple piece of content. Flash (the design tool) has a huge learning curve for creating an application with even a small amount of logic, and the resulting code is often quite unnatural (and hard to debug). But most software developers, or even people who dabble with HTML and a little bit of programming, should find the learning curve for Silverlight to be pretty small. And if you happen to already be familiar with WPF, learning Silverlight is a breeze.

FAQ

What are the differences between Silverlight and WPF?

Whereas Silverlight is designed for creating rich web content or applications that can be viewed in multiple browsers and multiple operating systems, WPF is designed for creating rich Windows applications. WPF applications require the .NET Framework 3.0 or later, which is a much larger download than Silverlight, although Windows Vista and later operating systems already have it installed by default.

Silverlight 1.0 is essentially a subset of WPF, although Silverlight also has a few unique pieces related to video, on-demand downloading of any content, and the control that hosts the content inside a web page. Some WPF features missing from Silverlight 1.0 are common user interface controls (such as buttons and scrollbars), layout panels, 3D graphics, data binding, rich document support, performance optimizations from hardware accelerated graphics, and more. In addition, Silverlight 1.0 applications don't have the benefit of the depth and breadth of the .NET Framework APIs, unless you use them from server-side ASP.NET code. The next version of Silverlight will close some of the gap between Silverlight and WPF, but it will undoubtedly always remain a subset of what WPF and the full .NET Framework provide.

Although Silverlight 1.0 coding is done in JavaScript, which is a big departure from the .NET languages used with WPF (and future versions of Silverlight), the two technologies are highly compatible. In some cases, Silverlight code related to user interface—especially XAML content—can be reused in WPF applications with little work, and vice versa. The key to choosing between Silverlight and WPF is whether you want to optimize for reach or for rich functionality. This is really no different than the classic choice of going with a web application or a Windows (or other OS) application. Besides aforementioned features such as 3D graphics, WPF applications are a natural choice if you require offline support or extensive local storage.

WPF doesn't only support Windows applications, but also applications that run inside the browser called XAML Browser Applications (XBAPs). XBAPs can arguably be considered web applications because their content renders seamlessly inside the browser similar to Silverlight content. However, XBAPs require the .NET Framework 3.0 or later, so they only run on Windows (and only then if the .NET Framework is installed) and only work inside Internet Explorer and Firefox. (Furthermore, Firefox support requires the .NET Framework 3.5 or later.) XBAPs support a much larger subset of WPF functionality than Silverlight 1.0, so they can be an appropriate choice for creating very rich applications that are web-like in their deployment. For example, the British Library has an application called "Turning the Pages" (at http://ttpdownload.bl.uk/browserapp.xbap) that takes advantage of WPF 3D graphics inside the browser.

FAQ

What is the relationship between Silverlight 1.0 and the prerelease version of Silverlight?

It's a bit unusual that the next version of Silverlight (currently labeled 1.1) has been available in a prerelease form before Silverlight 1.0 was even finished, but as the version number suggests, it simply is the next version of Silverlight. This next version is a superset of Silverlight 1.0 and is still a subset of WPF and the .NET Framework (but with some unique features of its own). The most notable additions planned for the next version of Silverlight are

▶ .NET support, which not only means additional language support, but also a subset of the .NET Framework's base class libraries

▶ Several features that already exist in WPF: user interface controls, layout, data binding, and more

▶ Potential support for additional browsers and additional operating systems (such as Windows 2000)

Despite all this, everything you learn about Silverlight 1.0 is directly applicable to future versions of Silverlight.

FAQ

What web server is required for serving Silverlight content?

Any web server will do, although be sure to set up the MIME type for .xaml files. Using Windows Server can give additional benefits when it comes to streaming media, such as the Faststream technology in Windows Media Services. Silverlight Streaming by Windows Live (http://streaming.live.com) can also be an attractive option for hosting Silverlight content on someone else's web server. It supports scalable streaming free (if you don't mind advertisements being served with your content) or for a small fee.

FAQ

What are the differences between Silverlight for Windows, Silverlight for Mac OS X, and Silverlight for Linux?

Silverlight supports the same feature set, because it is designed to be completely compatible between all the operating systems and browsers it supports. One advantage Silverlight has on Windows is the ability to get high-resolution and pressure-sensitive input data from a stylus or touch device, although this extra information is given in a way that avoids the need to write Windows-specific code. (See Chapter 7, "Responding to Input Events," for more details.) Silverlight also has different performance characteristics on different browsers and operating systems. For example, windowless controls (described later in the chapter) and elements with transparency are especially slow in Safari on Mac OS X. And of course, Silverlight has bugs that only apply to a specific browser or operating system. Some of these are pointed out in this book.

Embedding the Silverlight Control Manually

Silverlight, just like Adobe Flash, is a web browser add-on. It's a pair of components—one for Internet Explorer (an ActiveX control), and one for all other supported browsers (a Netscape plug-in)—but this is an invisible implementation detail to make things "just work" regardless of the host browser. The standard way for web pages to take advantage of an add-on—whether Silverlight, Flash, or another—is with the OBJECT HTML element.

Listing 1.1 contains a simple web page for a fictional "Great Estates" housing development that embeds a Silverlight logo at the top using the OBJECT element.

LISTING 1.1   A Web Page with Embedded Silverlight Content

```
<html>
  <head>
    <title>Great Estates</title>
  </head>
  <body style="background:blue">
    <!— A Silverlight-based logo: —>
    <object type="application/x-silverlight" id="silverlightControl"
      width="390" height="100">
      <param name="background" value="Yellow" />
      <param name="source" value="Chapter1.xaml" />
    </object>
    <p style="font-family:Tahoma; color:white">
      An idyllic new community located high on a hill and offering captivating
      waterfront views. Tailored to meet both the needs of upsizing and
      downsizing buyers, Great Estates offers custom quality architecture and
      design at an affordable price point.
    </p>
  </body>
</html>
```

The id, width, and height attributes on the OBJECT element work the same way as on elements such as DIV, TABLE, and so on. For example, width and height can be specified in absolute pixel values or as a percentage. The type attribute refers to the MIME type of the add-on content. The Silverlight add-on is invoked by the host browser for any content of type application/x-silverlight.

The Silverlight add-on supports several custom parameters, covered later in the "Understanding Your Hosting Options" section. In this example, the background parameter is set to fill the 390x100 region with the color yellow, and the source parameter is pointing to a separate XAML file containing the content to be rendered on top of the yellow background. This XAML file, Chapter1.xaml, is shown in Listing 1.2.

LISTING 1.2   Chapter1.xaml—A XAML File Containing a Logo

```xml
<Canvas xmlns="http://schemas.microsoft.com/client/2007">
  <MediaElement Name="video" Source="Lake.wmv" Opacity="0" IsMuted="true"/>
  <!-- A circle containing a live video: -->
  <Ellipse Width="100" Height="100">
    <Ellipse.Fill>
      <VideoBrush SourceName="video"/>
    </Ellipse.Fill>
  </Ellipse>
  <!-- Two pieces of text: -->
  <TextBlock FontFamily="Georgia" Foreground="Blue" FontStyle="Italic"
    FontSize="40" Canvas.Left="125" Canvas.Top="20" Text="Great Estates"/>
  <TextBlock Foreground="Blue" Canvas.Left="110" Canvas.Top="70"
    Text="Luxurious Living at an Affordable Price"/>
  <!-- Curves and a line: -->
  <Path Stroke="Red" StrokeThickness="4">
    <Path.Data>
      <PathGeometry>
        <PathFigure StartPoint="0,65">
          <ArcSegment SweepDirection="Clockwise" Size="2,2" Point="25,65"/>
          <ArcSegment SweepDirection="Clockwise" Size="2,2" Point="50,65"/>
          <ArcSegment SweepDirection="Clockwise" Size="2,2" Point="75,65"/>
          <ArcSegment SweepDirection="Clockwise" Size="2,2" Point="100,65"/>
          <LineSegment Point="390,65"/>
        </PathFigure>
      </PathGeometry>
    </Path.Data>
  </Path>
</Canvas>
```

This XAML file defines a logo containing two lines of text, some vector artwork, and even a live video cropped by a circle! Don't worry about the syntax of the XAML file for now. The next chapter covers everything you need to know about XAML syntax, and the various Silverlight elements (Canvas, MediaElement, Ellipse, and so on) are covered throughout the remainder of the book.

Figure 1.1 displays the web page defined by Listings 1.1 and 1.2. Most web pages probably would make the Silverlight

FIGURE 1.1   Silverlight content manually hosted in a web page with the OBJECT element.

content blend in better by giving the OBJECT element a matching background, but for this example, the yellow background helps to highlight the area of the page rendered by Silverlight.

Of course, the Great Estates web page only resembles what's shown in Figure 1.1 if the viewer has the Silverlight add-on installed. Without the add-on, the page looks similar to Figure 1.2 (depending on which browser you use).

Fortunately, there's a relatively easy solution for giving users who don't have the add-on a reasonable experience. If you place content directly inside the OBJECT element, browsers will render that content in the case of failure. Therefore, the OBJECT element in Listing 1.1 could be updated as follows to downgrade the logo to a simple image for viewers without Silverlight:

> **WARNING**
>
> **HTML and CSS fonts, colors, and more are not inherited by Silverlight content!**
>
> The fonts, colors, and other visual aspects of Silverlight content are completely independent from any other settings on the page. If you want to apply different themes to your Silverlight content, you'll need to employ a custom mechanism to make this happen.

FIGURE 1.2   Listing 1.1 doesn't look good when the Silverlight add-on is missing or disabled.

```
<object type="application/x-sil-
verlight" id="silverlightControl"
  width="390" height="100">
  <param name="background"
value="Yellow"/>
  <param name="source"
    value="Chapter1.xaml"/>
  <!-- Alternative content: -->
  <img src="logo.png"/>
</object>
```

The logo in logo.png could look identical to the Silverlight logo shown in Figure 1.1, except that the live video would be a static image instead. If you don't want to create a downgraded version of your Silverlight content, you could always notify the user and help her install the Silverlight add-on:

```
<object type="application/x-silverlight" id="silverlightControl"
  width="390" height="100">
  <param name="background" value="Yellow"/>
  <param name="source" value="Chapter1.xaml"/>
  <!-- Alternative content: -->
  This content requires Silverlight. <a href=
    "http://www.microsoft.com/silverlight/downloads.aspx">Get it here.</a>
</object>
```

Unfortunately, Apple's Safari web browser doesn't currently support the OBJECT element. Instead, you must use an element called EMBED, which also happens to work in Internet Explorer and Firefox. Listing 1.3 contains this update to Listing 1.1 in order to work on Safari as well.

LISTING 1.3   Embedding Silverlight Content Using EMBED Instead of OBJECT

```
<html>
  <head>
    <title>Great Estates</title>
  </head>
  <body style="background:blue">
    <!-- A Silverlight-based logo: -->
    <embed type="application/x-silverlight" id="silverlightControl"
      width="390" height="100" background="Yellow" source="Chapter1.xaml"/>
    <p style="font-family:Tahoma; color:white">
      An idyllic new community located high on a hill and offering captivating
      waterfront views. Tailored to meet both the needs of upsizing and
      downsizing buyers, Great Estates offers custom quality architecture and
      design at an affordable price point.
    </p>
  </body>
</html>
```

Besides the different element name (EMBED versus OBJECT), the only other difference is that the custom parameters are specified as attributes of the EMBED element rather than as child elements. Alternative content (for when the embedding fails) can be specified with a separate NOEMBED element. The result from using EMBED looks the same as Figure 1.1 (at least the Silverlight content), as seen in Figure 1.3.

Using EMBED is the simplest way to get your content rendered in all supported browsers, despite the fact that OBJECT is preferred for Internet Explorer and Firefox.

FIGURE 1.3   Silverlight content manually hosted in a web page with the EMBED element, viewed in Apple's Safari browser on Mac OS X.

Letting Silverlight.js Handle the Dirty Work

Embedding Silverlight content manually with an OBJECT or EMBED element has a number of issues. There's the concern about browser differences (although that can be avoided by always sticking to EMBED). Most importantly, it would be a fair amount of work to properly handle Silverlight detection. For example, although placing a download link as alternative content inside the OBJECT element (or using a NOEMBED element) seems simple enough, it doesn't behave appropriately if somebody has the *wrong version* of Silverlight installed. If a web page contains Silverlight content that uses future features unavailable in 1.0, viewers with 1.0 installed will not see the alternative content. Instead, the Silverlight 1.0 add-on will attempt to render the content and will fail.

Microsoft would be making a huge mistake if they asked everyone to do the appropriate version detection work on their own. The code involved is not straightforward, and version detection logic—for *any* software—is notorious for being done incorrectly. (As silly as it sounds, someone might write logic that behaves properly for version numbers such as 1.0 and 1.1, but would fail years later when version 4.0 appears.) Sure enough, the Silverlight Software Development Kit (Silverlight SDK) provides a JavaScript file called `Silverlight.js` that defines a simple JavaScript function handling everything from injecting an appropriate `OBJECT` or `EMBED` element into an HTML document to checking if the right version of Silverlight is installed, and then directing the viewer to the appropriate place to install it if it isn't. You should always use the functionality in `Silverlight.js` (discussed in this section) rather than directly using `OBJECT` or `EMBED` unless your content must appear in an environment where JavaScript is not allowed.

Silverlight.createObject

The simple function exposed by `Silverlight.js` is `Silverlight.createObject`. Here is how `createObject` could be called in JavaScript to generate an `OBJECT`/`EMBED` element as shown in Listings 1.1 and 1.3:

```
Silverlight.createObject(
  "Chapter1.xaml",                         // source XAML
  document.getElementById("placeholder"), // parent HTML element
  "silverlightControl",                    // id for the control
  // properties:
  { width: "390", height: "100", version: "1.0", background: "Yellow" },
  // events:
  {}
);
```

The first parameter becomes the `source` value for the dynamically generated `OBJECT` or `EMBED` element, and the third parameter becomes its `id`. The second parameter can be an existing HTML element to contain the new `OBJECT` or `EMBED` element. In this example, the standard `document.getElementById` function is used to retrieve an element from the page via its HTML id (placeholder), but you could also pass `document.body` if you want to append the new element directly to the page's body.

The fourth and fifth parameters to `createObject` are associative arrays of properties and events, respectively, supported by the Silverlight add-on. The properties array is a mix of values that

> **TIP**
>
> If you pass `null` for the parent HTML element, `createObject` returns a string containing the `OBJECT` or `EMBED` element that would have otherwise been added to the parent. This gives you some flexibility for morphing the element or otherwise customizing how it is added to your page.

either alter the logic inside `Silverlight.js` (such as version), are applied directly to the OBJECT or EMBED element (such as width and height), or are applied as PARAM element children when the OBJECT element is used (such as background). The various properties (and events) are covered in the upcoming "Understanding Your Hosting Options" section. The only new property shown here is version, which should simply be set to the version of Silverlight you're targeting (1.0).

> **TIP**
>
> The `createObject` function has sixth and seventh (optional) parameters that can both be used to attach custom data to the Silverlight control. For example, if you set the sixth parameter (initParams) to the string "custom", the dynamically generated OBJECT element would have the following additional child:
>
> ```
> <param name="initParams" value="custom"/>
> ```
>
> With this in place, you could write JavaScript that retrieves this value with standard DOM functions for traversing the tree of HTML elements or with a simple Silverlight-specific property called InitParams explained toward the end of this chapter. If you set the seventh parameter (context) to any object, that object will be passed as a parameter to the control's onLoad event handler (covered later in this chapter). This context functionality is specific to `Silverlight.js` and, unlike initParams, cannot be accomplished with a PARAM element in HTML.
>
> The capabilities provided by these two mechanisms are simply additional ways to communicate information between JavaScript files that might be developed as separate components.

Silverlight.createObjectEx

`Silverlight.js` defines a second function for embedding Silverlight content called `Silverlight.createObjectEx`. (The Ex suffix is an old Win32 convention that has mysteriously made its way into this file. It typically denotes a newer or "extra" version of a function.) The only difference between `createObject` and `createObjectEx` is that the latter accepts a single associative array parameter with all the same information. For example, here is the previous call to `createObject` translated into a call to `createObjectEx`:

```
Silverlight.createObjectEx(
  // Just one parameter, an array with 5 elements:
  {
    source: "Chapter1.xaml",
    parentElement: document.getElementById("placeholder"),
    id: "silverlightControl",
    properties:
      { width: "390", height: "100", version: "1.0", background: "Yellow" },
    events: {}
  }
);
```

The nice thing about `createObjectEx` is that calls to it are self-descriptive. You can clearly see what piece of data is the `source`, `parentElement`, and so on without the need for comments. For this reason, examples in this book use `createObjectEx` rather than `createObject`. The syntax for calling `createObjectEx` might look unusual, but it's basically JSON (JavaScript Object Notation), a popular data interchange format based on simple JavaScript constructs.

DIGGING DEEPER

The Implementation of `createObjectEx`

`createObjectEx` is a very simple wrapper over `createObject`, as you can see by looking at its source code inside `Silverlight.js`. It is effectively implemented as follows:

```
Silverlight.createObjectEx = function(params)
{
  return Silverlight.createObject(params.source, params.parentElement, params.id,
    params.properties, params.events, params.initParams, params.context);
}
```

In JavaScript, syntax such as `a.b` is equivalent to `a["b"]`, which is why `params.source` can be used to access the source element of the params array, and so on.

Putting It All Together

The `createObject` or `createObjectEx` function can be called from any JavaScript file or inline `SCRIPT` element, but Microsoft has published the following recommended approach for using these functions:

WARNING

When calling `createObject` or `createObjectEx`, some properties and events can't be omitted!

If you omit the `version` property, you'll get a script error; and if you omit either the `width` or `height`, the resultant element won't be seen. As for `events`, you must at least specify an empty associative array (`{}`); otherwise, you'll get a script error.

1. Create a separate script file called `CreateSilverlight.js` (by convention).

2. Define a parameterless function (called `createSilverlight` by convention) inside `CreateSilverlight.js` that makes the call to `createObject` or `createObjectEx`.

3. Reference both `Silverlight.js` and `CreateSilverlight.js` from `SCRIPT` elements in your HTML document (usually inside the document's `HEAD`).

4. Place an HTML element that you want to contain the Silverlight content, such as a `DIV`, inside the document and choose an `id` (used by your `createSilverlight` function).

5. Call the parameterless function inside inline JavaScript in the HTML document.

Listings 1.4 and 1.5 follow this approach to get the same result pictured in Figures 1.1 and 1.3.

LISTING 1.4   Embedding Silverlight Content Using the Recommended Silverlight.js Approach

```html
<html>
  <head>
    <title>Great Estates</title>
    <script type="text/javascript" src="Silverlight.js"></script>
    <script type="text/javascript" src="CreateSilverlight.js"></script>
  </head>
  <body style="background:blue">
    <!-- A Silverlight-based logo: -->
    <div id="placeholder">
      <script type="text/javascript">createSilverlight();</script>
    </div>
    <p style="font-family:Tahoma; color:white">
      An idyllic new community located high on a hill and offering captivating
      waterfront views. Tailored to meet both the needs of upsizing and
      downsizing buyers, Great Estates offers custom quality architecture and
      design at an affordable price point.
    </p>
  </body>
</html>
```

LISTING 1.5   CreateSilverlight.js—The Recommended Script File with the Parameterless createSilverlight Function

```javascript
function createSilverlight()
{
  Silverlight.createObjectEx(
    {
      source: "Chapter1.xaml",
      parentElement: document.getElementById("placeholder"),
      id: "silverlightControl",
      properties:
        { width: "390", height: "100", version: "1.0", background: "Yellow" },
      events: {}
    }
  );
}
```

DIGGING DEEPER

Avoiding "Click to activate and use this control" in Internet Explorer

Depending on how ActiveX controls are used, current versions of Internet Explorer require viewers of a web page to "activate" it by clicking it (or pressing Enter or the spacebar when it has focus). Once activated, the control can accept keyboard and mouse input. Hovering over such controls shows a border and tooltip, as displayed in Figure 1.4.

This behavior is certainly annoying, but it is especially annoying for content that is supposed to blend seamlessly with HTML. For this example, why would a viewer of this page care about activating a logo? This anti-feature exists because of a recently settled patent case (Eolas v. Microsoft) that had required Microsoft to change Internet Explorer's handling of ActiveX controls.

Fortunately, there are techniques for avoiding the activation behavior, as covered in various articles (such as http://msdn2.microsoft.com/en-us/library/ms537508.aspx). Even better, by following the recommended approach of using Silverlight.js and CreateSilverlight.js, you don't need to do anything further. This is why viewing

FIGURE 1.4   The annoying "Click to activate and use this control" behavior in Internet Explorer.

the pages from Listings 1.1 and 1.3 gives the "Click to activate and use this control" prompt, but the page from Listing 1.4 (and the remaining examples in this book) does not.

DIGGING DEEPER

Silverlight Streaming by Windows Live

Silverlight Streaming by Windows Live is a web service that provides highly scalable hosting and streaming of Silverlight content free (with advertising) or for a small fee. This service has its own procedure to follow for packaging and uploading content, but the consumption of the content is very similar to the normal Silverlight.js approach. Instead of referencing your own copy of Silverlight.js, you can reference a modified Silverlight.js provided by Silverlight Streaming. Then you can call Silverlight.createHostedObjectEx—a special function defined by this service—which embeds an IFRAME into your HTML document rather than an OBJECT or EMBED element directly. The source given to createHostedObjectEx must be a special string containing pieces of information that you must previously register with the Silverlight Streaming service. Alternatively, you can leverage Silverlight Streaming without JavaScript by setting the source of an IFRAME to a special URL specific to your hosted application. For more details, go to http://streaming.live.com.

Understanding Your Hosting Options

Silverlight exposes a number of properties and events that customize the appearance of the Silverlight content and the way it interacts with the HTML document it lives inside. In addition, the source parameter exposed by the Silverlight add-on supports more functionality than previously described. This section examines the extra functionality of source, and then looks at all the properties and events that the add-on directly exposes.

source

Previous listings have demonstrated the most common usage of source setting it to the name (and path, if applicable) of a XAML file on the web server. However, you can alternatively place your XAML inline in the HTML document. There are two steps for doing this:

1. Place your XAML content within a SCRIPT element with type text/xaml somewhere in the document *before* the HTML element that will contain the Silverlight control, and give it a unique id.

2. Use the SCRIPT element's id preceded by a # as the source value given to the Silverlight add-on. The # prefix is what distinguishes an id from a filename.

Listings 1.6 and 1.7 are updates to Listings 1.4 and 1.5 that remove the dependency on the separate Chapter1.xaml file.

LISTING 1.6   Placing Inline XAML Inside HTML

```
<html>
  <head>
    <title>Great Estates</title>
    <script type="text/javascript" src="Silverlight.js"></script>
    <script type="text/javascript" src="CreateSilverlight.js"></script>
  </head>
  <body style="background:blue">
    <!-- A Silverlight-based logo: -->
    <script id="xaml" type="text/xaml">
      <Canvas xmlns="http://schemas.microsoft.com/client/2007">
        <MediaElement Name="video" Source="Lake.wmv" Opacity="0" IsMuted="true"/>
        <!-- A circle containing a live video: -->
        <Ellipse Width="100" Height="100">
          <Ellipse.Fill>
            <VideoBrush SourceName="video"/>
          </Ellipse.Fill>
        </Ellipse>
        <!-- Two pieces of text: -->
        <TextBlock FontFamily="Georgia" Foreground="Blue" FontStyle="Italic"
          FontSize="40" Canvas.Left="125" Canvas.Top="20" Text="Great Estates"/>
```

LISTING 1.6   Continued

```
        <TextBlock Foreground="Blue" Canvas.Left="110" Canvas.Top="70"
          Text="Luxurious Living at an Affordable Price"/>
        <!-- Curves and a line: -->
        <Path Stroke="Red" StrokeThickness="4">
          <Path.Data>
            <PathGeometry>
              <PathFigure StartPoint="0,65">
                <ArcSegment SweepDirection="Clockwise" Size="2,2" Point="25,65"/>
                <ArcSegment SweepDirection="Clockwise" Size="2,2" Point="50,65"/>
                <ArcSegment SweepDirection="Clockwise" Size="2,2" Point="75,65"/>
                <ArcSegment SweepDirection="Clockwise" Size="2,2" Point="100,65"/>
                <LineSegment Point="390,65"/>
              </PathFigure>
            </PathGeometry>
          </Path.Data>
        </Path>
      </Canvas>
    </script>
    <div id="placeholder">
      <script type="text/javascript">createSilverlight();</script>
    </div>
    <p style="font-family:Tahoma; color:white">
      An idyllic new community located high on a hill and offering captivating
      waterfront views. Tailored to meet both the needs of upsizing and
      downsizing buyers, Great Estates offers custom quality architecture and
      design at an affordable price point.
    </p>
  </body>
</html>
```

LISTING 1.7   CreateSilverlight.js—Using Inline XAML as the source

```
function createSilverlight()
{
  Silverlight.createObjectEx(
    {
      source: "#xaml",
      parentElement: document.getElementById("placeholder"),
      id: "silverlightControl",
      properties:
        { width: "390", height: "100", version: "1.0", background: "Yellow" },
      events: {}
    }
  );
}
```

This #id syntax is supported anywhere the `source` might be specified: `createObject`, `createObjectEx`, directly on an `EMBED` element, or as a `PARAM` inside an `OBJECT` element. This functionality is a handy way to combine what would ordinarily be two web requests into one. But in addition to efficiency considerations, removing the dependency on a custom external file enables server-side code (in technologies such as ASP.NET or PHP) to emit Silverlight content in a completely encapsulated way.

Properties

The `width`, `height`, and `version` properties exposed by Silverlight are straightforward, but the `background` property could use a little more explanation. In addition, the Silverlight add-on supports more properties that haven't been discussed yet.

background

The `background` property—which can be set via `createObject`, `createObjectEx`, or directly on an `OBJECT/EMBED` element—is more powerful than a normal HTML color value. Besides named colors—such as `Red` or `Yellow`—and RGB values—such as `#F1F1F1` or `#456`, `background` can be given an alpha channel for creating transparent or translucent background colors. The syntax is `#AARRGGBB` (or `#ARGB`), so a translucent red color would be `#77FF0000` (or `#7F00`). `background` can also be set to the named value `Transparent`, which is the same as any color with an alpha channel value of zero. If you omit `background` altogether, the control will be given a white background.

isWindowless

By default, an instance of the Silverlight control is known as *windowed*, but by setting `isWindowless` to `true` (which can be done via `createObject`, `createObjectEx`, or directly on an `OBJECT/EMBED` element), you can change it to be a *windowless* control. The distinction of windowed versus windowless isn't specific to Silverlight, but rather refers to a low-level implementation detail on Windows (whether the control has its own window handle, or `HWND`).

> **WARNING**
>
> **Inline XAML doesn't work in Firefox unless the DOCTYPE element is removed!**
>
> Putting a DOCTYPE (document type declaration) in your HTML page that specifies which version of HTML or XHTML you're using is a best practice. However, current versions of Firefox have a bug that prevents inline XAML from working on a page with a DOCTYPE. Therefore, if you care about your content rendering on Firefox, you must choose to use only one or the other.

> **WARNING**
>
> **The XAML file used as the source must be served from the same domain as the web page!**
>
> You cannot set the Silverlight control's source to a different domain (or protocol) than the one hosting the HTML document. This limitation is intentional, as a security measure. Although this restriction is unnecessarily strict (in this author's opinion), it is at least consistent with the policy that browsers enforce with their `XmlHttpRequest` object, called the *same origin policy*. (People have come to believe that XML from a different domain is inherently more dangerous than JavaScript from a different domain, because all browsers block the former but allow the latter! I wouldn't be surprised to see browsers change their policy in the next few years.)

TIP

In addition to using literal strings, you can set `background` to the color of any existing HTML element. For example, the following call gives the Silverlight control a background color that matches the host document, if it has one set via the `style` attribute:

```
Silverlight.createObjectEx
  {
    ...
    properties:
      { ... , background: document.body.style.backgroundColor },
    ...
  );
```

This is much preferred to using a background color of `Transparent`, because it works regardless of other Silverlight property settings and it can give dramatically better performance.

The important thing to understand is the two different behaviors of a windowless control:

- A windowless control respects HTML z-indexing, so you can overlay and overlap HTML content on top of Silverlight and vice versa. A windowed control, on the other hand, is always rendered on top.

- A windowless control supports transparency, so it can be given a transparent or translucent background, and content inside it can be transparent or translucent.

Figure 1.5 shows a potential way that the Great Estates website might take advantage of windowless Silverlight content—placing an HTML SELECT element on top of the Silverlight logo.

To create the result in Figure 1.5, Listing 1.8 adds a SELECT element to the page from Listing 1.4 and uses CSS to give it an absolute position and a z-index to ensure that it is placed on top of the Silverlight content.

WARNING

Transparent or translucent background colors only work as expected if `isWindowless` is set to `true`!

Without setting this to `true`, a background set to `Transparent` will appear black, and translucent colors will be blended with black rather than the HTML content behind the Silverlight control.

WARNING

Using a windowless control or a transparent/translucent background can severely degrade performance!

The performance problems with windowless controls and colors with an alpha channel are especially apparent in Safari on Mac OS X. Therefore, unless the behavior enabled by windowless controls and transparent/translucent content is absolutely necessary, you should avoid using these features.

TIP

Despite the performance implications, many rich Internet applications created with Silverlight 1.0 need to set `isWindowless` to `true`. The ability to place HTML-based controls (whether simple controls similar to `INPUT` or `BUTTON` or richer controls such as those found in ASP.NET AJAX) on top of Silverlight content is crucial, due to the lack of such controls natively existing in Silverlight. With a windowless control, you can even overlay Flash on top of Silverlight content! Microsoft Popfly is an example of a rich Internet application that does all these things. If you can confine your Silverlight content and HTML content to regions that don't overlap, however, then you can get away with a windowed control.

FIGURE 1.5   A windowless Silverlight control allows HTML to appear on top of it.

LISTING 1.8   Placing an HTML `SELECT` Element in Front of the Silverlight Control

```html
<html>
  <head>
    <title>Great Estates</title>
    <script type="text/javascript" src="Silverlight.js"></script>
    <script type="text/javascript" src="CreateSilverlight.js"></script>
  </head>
  <body style="background:blue">
    <!-- A Silverlight-based logo: -->
    <div id="placeholder">
      <script type="text/javascript">createSilverlight();</script>
    </div>
    <select style="position:absolute; left:289px; top:18px; z-index:1">
      <option>California</option>
      <option>Pennsylvania</option>
      <option>Washington</option>
    </select>
    <p style="font-family:Tahoma; color:white">
      An idyllic new community located high on a hill and offering captivating
```

LISTING 1.8   Continued

```
      waterfront views. Tailored to meet both the needs of upsizing and
      downsizing buyers, Great Estates offers custom quality architecture and
      design at an affordable price point.
    </p>
  </body>
</html>
```

Listing 1.8 only produces the desired result because the corresponding
CreateSilverlight.js file sets isWindowless to true, as shown in Listing 1.9.

LISTING 1.9   CreateSilverlight.js—Hosting Familiar Silverlight Content in a Windowless
Control

```
function createSilverlight()
{
  Silverlight.createObjectEx(
    {
      source: "Chapter1.xaml",
      parentElement: document.getElementById("placeholder"),
      id: "silverlightControl",
      properties:
        { width: "390", height: "100", version: "1.0", background: "Yellow",
          isWindowless: "true" },
      events: {}
    }
  );
}
```

> **WARNING**
>
> **The Boolean used for isWindowless must be specified as a string!**
>
> The following property setting works in a call to createObject or createObjectEx:
>
> `{ ... , isWindowless: "true", ... }`
>
> But the following setting does not work as expected:
>
> `{ ... , isWindowless: true, ... }`
>
> Any non-string is treated as false, and therefore has no effect!

inplaceInstallPrompt

The inplaceInstallPrompt property, which can only be used with createObject or
createObjectEx, controls the look and behavior of the Silverlight installation graphic
that gets displayed when the viewer doesn't have the appropriate version of Silverlight.

Figure 1.6 shows the appearance of the two options. Setting `inplaceInstallPrompt` to `false` (the default behavior) gives a small graphic that links to the official download page with more information. Setting it to `true` gives additional text, but the link now points directly to the file to download rather than an intermediate page.

`inplaceInstallPrompt=false`

`inplaceInstallPrompt=true`

FIGURE 1.6   The two different install prompts supported by `Silverlight.js`.

WARNING

The Boolean used for `inplaceInstallPrompt` must *not* be specified as a string!

Unlike the case for `isWindowless`, the following property setting works in a call to `createObject` or `createObjectEx`:

`{ ... , inplaceInstallPrompt: false, ... }`

But the following setting does not work as expected:

`{ ... , inplaceInstallPrompt: "false", ... }`

Any string is treated as `true`!

---

maxFramerate

The `maxFramerate` parameter, which can be set via `createObject`, `createObjectEx`, or directly on an `OBJECT/EMBED` element, customizes the maximum frame rate that the Silverlight control renders content, measured in frames per second. (The actual frame rate is dependent on the client computer and its current load.) The default value for `maxFramerate` is 24. If you decide to customize `maxFramerate`, you should select the lowest number possible that gives you the results you need.

The frame rate controls all content inside the Silverlight control—animations and even video—except for audio. You can see this with the Great Estates logo by setting its `maxFramerate` to 1 and changing `IsMuted` to `false` instead of `true` in the XAML file. This causes the video to progress in an extremely choppy fashion, yet the corresponding audio plays smoothly.

WARNING

The number used for `maxFramerate` must be specified as a string!

Similar to `isWindowless`, the following property setting works in a call to `createObject` or `createObjectEx`:

```
{ ... , maxFramerate: "24", ... }
```

But the following setting does not work as most people would expect:

```
{ ... , maxFramerate: 24, ... }
```

Any non-string is treated as zero frames per second!

DIGGING DEEPER

`maxFramerate` Versus `framerate`

You might come across some Silverlight examples that set the `framerate` property instead of `maxFramerate`. Setting `framerate` is exactly the same as setting `maxFramerate`, and it can only be done via `createObject` or `createObjectEx`. The logic in `Silverlight.js` maps both `framerate` and `maxFramerate` to the one true `maxFramerate` property supported by the underlying Silverlight control. It does this simply for compatibility with prerelease versions of Silverlight. For clarity, you should stick to using `maxFramerate` if you feel the need to customize the frame rate.

LOOKING FORWARD

The `enableHtmlAccess` Property

Silverlight also supports a property called `enableHtmlAccess`, but it only applies to versions after 1.0. It controls whether .NET code (such as C#) is capable of accessing the browser's DOM via a special layer designed for .NET. The default value of `enableHtmlAccess` is `true`, but it doesn't apply to JavaScript hosted by the browser because it always has access to the browser's DOM.

Events

The Silverlight control supports two events that can be set directly on the OBJECT or EMBED element: `onLoad` and `onError`. You can assign either event the name of a JavaScript function to be called. For example:

```
<object type="application/x-silverlight" id="silverlightControl"
  width="390" height="100">
  <param name="background" value="Yellow"/>
  <param name="source" value="Chapter1.xaml"/>
  <param name="onLoad" value="myFunction"/>
</object>
```

However, because handling either of these events requires the use of JavaScript, you might as well take advantage of `createObject` or `createObjectEx` rather than attaching these handlers the "raw" way.

onLoad

The `onLoad` event is raised as soon as the XAML content has been loaded. Handling this event is useful for performing custom initialization of Silverlight content, such as initiating animations or dynamic positioning/sizing of the control based on document dimensions. These specific kinds of activities are covered in later chapters, but Listing 1.10 at least demonstrates how to designate a function as a handler for the `onLoad` event.

LISTING 1.10   CreateSilverlight.js—Assigning an onLoad Handler

```
function createSilverlight()
{
  Silverlight.createObjectEx(
    {
      source: "Chapter1.xaml",
      parentElement: document.getElementById("placeholder"),
      id: "silverlightControl",
      properties:
        { width: "390", height: "100", version: "1.0", background: "Yellow" },
      events: { onLoad: myFunction }
    }
  );
}
function myFunction(control, context, rootElement)
{
  // Perform custom initialization
}
```

The purpose of Silverlight's `onLoad` event is similar to the HTML DOM's `onload` event. However, to avoid timing issues, you should stick to the HTML `onload` event for manipulating HTML content and Silverlight's `onLoad` event for manipulating Silverlight content.

Handlers for the `onLoad` event are passed three parameters:

▶ **control**, which is the instance of the Silverlight control. The next section, "Interacting with the Silverlight Control Programmatically," describes some of the things you can do with this object.

▶ **context**, which is simply whatever custom `context` value was given to `createObject` or `createObjectEx` (if one was given).

▶ **rootElement**, which is the instance of the root element in the `source` XAML content. The next chapter explains how you can programmatically interact with Silverlight elements declared in XAML.

> # WARNING
>
> ## The function for onLoad (and onError) must not be specified as a string!
>
> Unlike the strings passed as most property values, the elements in the `events` associative array must contain direct references to the functions you've defined (function pointers), as in Listing 1.10. The following would cause a script error:
>
> `{ onLoad: "myFunction", ... }`

onError

The `onError` event is raised whenever Silverlight throws an exception not already handled by your JavaScript code. (For an exception thrown from a synchronous function call, this means that no corresponding `try/catch` block exists. For an exception thrown from an asynchronous function call, this means that no event handler is attached for that specific failure case.) Exceptions can be raised by Silverlight for XAML parsing errors or for any number of runtime errors.

If you don't specify a handler for `onError` when directly using an `OBJECT` or `EMBED` element, unhandled Silverlight errors are swallowed. But when you use `createObject` or `createObjectEx`, a function called `default_error_handler` is automatically set as the handler for `onError` unless you provide your own. The default handler calls JavaScript's `alert` function to display a simple dialog, such as the one shown in Figure 1.7.

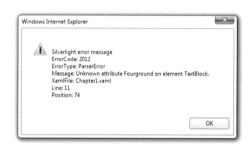

FIGURE 1.7   When good content goes bad.

To understand how to create your own `onError` handler, it is instructive to look at the implementation of `default_error_handler` inside `Silverlight.js`. It is effectively implemented as follows:

```
function default_error_handler(sender, args)
{
  var errMsg = "\nSilverlight error message\n";
  // All errors have a numeric code, a type, and a message
  errMsg += "ErrorCode: " + args.errorCode + "\n";
  errMsg += "ErrorType: " + args.errorType + "\n";
  errMsg += "Message: " + args.errorMessage + "\n";
  if (args.errorType == "ParserError")
  {
    // A parser error gives the location in the XAML content
    errMsg += "XamlFile: " + args.xamlFile + "\n";
    errMsg += "Line: " + args.lineNumber + "\n";
    errMsg += "Position: " + args.charPosition + "\n";
  }
```

```
  else if (args.errorType == "RuntimeError")
  {
    if (args.lineNumber != 0)
    {
      // Display the line number and character, if the information exists
      errMsg += "Line: " + args.lineNumber + "\n";
      errMsg += "Position: " +  args.charPosition + "\n";
    }
    // The name of the function that failed
    errMsg += "MethodName: " + args.methodName + "\n";
  }
  // Display the message in a simple alert box:
  alert(errMsg);
}
```

The sender is the object on which the error occurred, if applicable. For parser errors, such as the one shown in Figure 1.6, sender is null. The args object provides a number of pieces of information that depend on the type of error raised, as seen in the implementation of default_error_handler.

> **TIP**
>
> Despite the presence of an onError handler, it's easy to make a mistake in JavaScript causing an error that doesn't get sent to this function. The behavior of such unhandled JavaScript errors varies from browser to browser. To debug them in Internet Explorer with Visual Studio, be sure to uncheck the **Disable script debugging** settings in the **Advanced** tab of the **Internet Options** pane!

Interacting with the Silverlight Control Programmatically

The OBJECT or EMBED element representing the Silverlight control (whether part of the static HTML document or dynamically injected by Silverlight.js) has an HTML id, so you can write JavaScript to retrieve the element and get or set properties on it just like any other HTML element. For example,

```
// Retrieve the element via a standard HTML DOM function:
var element = document.getElementById("silverlightControl");
// Set properties on the element:
element.width = 500;
element.style.zIndex = 2;
```

Because this element is an instance of the ActiveX object (or Netscape plug-in), it provides a number of useful properties, functions, and events specific to Silverlight. This element returned by document.getElementById is the same object passed as the first parameter to the onLoad event handler. However, you should avoid accessing any Silverlight-specific members on this object before the control has finished loading (and its onLoad event is raised).

The Silverlight control exposes most of its functionality via two properties: Settings and Content.

The Settings Property

Most relevant to this chapter is the control's Settings property, which defines a number of subproperties for getting or setting a number of attributes (many of which could have alternatively been set via createObject, createObjectEx, or directly on the OBJECT/EMBED element):

- **Background**—The same property discussed earlier. However, this makes it easy to change the background color at any time.

- **EnableFramerateCounter**—A Boolean property that toggles the display of the current frame rate in the browser's status bar. (This is potentially useful for debugging purposes.)

- **EnableRedrawRegions**—Another Boolean property meant for debugging, this highlights regions of the screen that are redrawn on each frame, when set to true.

- **EnableHtmlAccess**—The same property discussed earlier.

- **MaxFrameRate**—The same property discussed earlier.

- **Windowless**—The same as the isWindowless property discussed earlier.

For example, the EnableRedrawRegions and Background properties can be set in a Silverlight onLoad event handler as follows:

```
function myFunction(control, context, rootElement)
{
  control.Settings.EnableRedrawRegions = true;
  control.Settings.Background = "Red";
}
```

These properties, and all other members exposed on the control object, are pretty flexible. For example, they are not case sensitive. Many people prefer using lowercase names because it matches JavaScript conventions, as in the following code that produces the same result as the preceding snippet:

```
function myFunction(control, context, rootElement)
{
  control.settings.enableRedrawRegions = true;
  control.settings.background = "Red";
}
```

In addition, the Boolean properties can be set to a true or false string *or* to a true or false Boolean literal, and they work correctly either way.

None of the Settings members are extremely compelling, however, as it's rare you would need to retrieve or change the data after the control has loaded.

The Content Property

The most commonly used member on the Silverlight control is its Content property, which represents the XAML content hosted by the control and exposes some interesting functionality. It has the following subproperties:

- ▷ **ActualWidth and ActualHeight**—Report the dimensions of the Silverlight control. You can discover the same information by using the HTML DOM, although these Silverlight properties give different values than the corresponding HTML properties when the browser zoom level (an Internet Explorer feature) is not 100%. These Silverlight properties always report the real dimensions, whereas the HTML properties report the virtual dimensions (in essence, hiding the zoom level).

- ▷ **Root**—The instance of the root element in the current XAML content. This is the same object passed to onLoad as the rootElement parameter. (This property makes the rootElement parameter unnecessary because the handler can always use control.Content.Root instead.)

- ▷ **FullScreen**—Enables the Silverlight content to fill the entire screen. To prevent hostile Silverlight applications from holding your screen hostage, full-screen mode must be initiated by a user action (such as a mouse click or key press). Therefore, this functionality is covered in Chapter 7, "Responding to Input Events."

- ▷ **Accessibility**—Enables you to customize how the Silverlight control appears to accessibility software. The Accessibility object contains three settable properties: Title, Description, and ActionDescription (see Chapter 7 for more information).

Content exposes three functions explained in Chapter 2, "XAML," and Chapter 8, "Downloading Content on Demand":

- ▷ **CreateFromXaml**—Dynamically creates Silverlight content specified in XAML in a JavaScript string.

- ▷ **CreateFromXamlDownloader**—Dynamically creates Silverlight content specified in a XAML file downloaded on demand.

- ▷ **FindName**—Finds the instance of a Silverlight object defined in XAML based on an assigned name.

Content even exposes two unique events that cannot be consumed any other way. For example, you cannot specify either of these in the events array passed to createObject and createObjectEx. These two events are

- ▷ **OnResize**—Raised whenever the value of Content's ActualWidth or ActualHeight property changes

- ▷ **OnFullScreenChange**—Raised whenever the value of Content's FullScreen property changes

A handler can be attached to either event by assigning a function reference. Listing 1.11 demonstrates this for the OnResize event.

LISTING 1.11   CreateSilverlight.js—Assigning an OnResize Handler

```
function createSilverlight()
{
  Silverlight.createObjectEx(
    {
      source: "Chapter1.xaml",
      parentElement: document.getElementById("placeholder"),
      id: "silverlightControl",
      properties:
        { width: "390", height: "100", version: "1.0", background: "Yellow" },
      events: { onLoad: myFunction }
    }
  );
}
function myFunction(control, context, rootElement)
{
  control.Content.OnResize = function()
  {
    var htmlElement = document.getElementById("silverlightControl");
    alert("Actual Dimensions: " + control.Content.ActualWidth + "x" +
                        control.Content.ActualHeight);
    alert("Virtual Dimensions: " + htmlElement.offsetWidth + "x" +
                        htmlElement.offsetHeight);
  };
}
```

In this example, OnResize is set to a JavaScript closure (a function defined inside another function), which displays the control's dimensions according to Silverlight and according to the HTML DOM. If you try this with any of the examples in this chapter and change Internet Explorer's zoom level to 200%, you'll see that the HTML DOM still reports dimensions of 390x100 but Silverlight reports dimensions of 780x200. Although Internet Explorer doesn't want web pages to know when they are being zoomed (because they could do weird things that interfere with proper zooming), leveraging this information can be critical for Silverlight content because the visual elements inside the control do not get scaled automatically. Chapter 6, "Positioning and Transforming Elements," discusses the resizing of Silverlight content.

Other Members

In addition to the Settings and Content properties, the Silverlight control defines three more properties:

▸ **InitParams**—Gives whatever string was set (if any) for the initParams parameter to createObject or createObjectEx (or directly on the OBJECT/EMBED element). Although InitParams is always exposed to JavaScript as a single string, a comma-delimited list will be split into an array of strings passed to .NET code in future versions of Silverlight.

▸ **IsLoaded**—Reports whether the Silverlight content has been loaded.

▸ **Source**—Gives the control's source URL or #id value. This property can also be set to a new URL or #id value. This causes the control to reload with the new content, and the onLoad event will be raised again.

The control also directly defines two functions:

▸ **CreateObject**—Enables you to create an instance of the downloader object described in Chapter 8.

▸ **IsVersionSupported**—Given an input string containing a version number such as 1.0, this function tells you whether the installed version of Silverlight is compatible with that version. Silverlight.js uses this internally to perform its version checking.

The control also defines a single event—**OnError**—that is the same as the onError event described earlier. By assigning a function reference to the control's OnError member, you can change the default error handler at any time. Note that the control does not have an OnLoad member. You can only assign a handler for the onLoad event using the approaches discussed earlier.

Conclusion

As time passes, more software is targeted for the Web, and more software is expected to deliver high-quality—sometimes *cinematic*—experiences. However, the effort involved in creating such user interfaces has been far too difficult in the past.

If you're a software developer, you might be skeptical about the need for "eye candy" beyond what HTML provides. But like it or not, having an engaging user experience matters, whether you are creating a public consumer-facing site, or a simple intranet application for your manager. You can blame the unrealistic software on movies and on TV, or you can blame real-world software that is starting to catch up to Hollywood's standards! Indeed, modern software has more visual polish than it used to. You can see it in traditional operating systems (such as Mac OS X and, more recently, Windows Vista), in software for devices such as TiVo or Xbox, and of course all over the Web thanks to Adobe Flash. Users have increasing expectations for the experience of using software, and companies are spending a great deal of time and money on user interfaces that differentiate themselves from the competition. Microsoft understands this, and it's apparent in its latest technologies—first on the desktop with WPF, and now on the Web with Silverlight.

Silverlight makes it easier than ever before to create engaging web-based user interfaces, whether you want to create a simple piece of content or an immersive interactive experience worthy of a role in a summer blockbuster! This chapter focused on the HTML and/or JavaScript required for getting any Silverlight content inside a web page, as well as the ways in which the embedding can be customized. The next chapter explores the XAML side of the story in depth, and then the remainder of the book covers all the different types of content and interactivity that can be achieved with Silverlight.

CHAPTER 2

XAML

The preceding chapter touched on the Extensible Application Markup Language known as XAML and its role of defining the visual content to be rendered on the screen. This chapter jumps right into the mechanics of XAML, examining its syntax in depth and explaining how it relates to JavaScript code. Digging into XAML isn't necessarily as fun as learning how to draw lines, perform animations, or play videos, but having this background knowledge before proceeding with the rest of the book will help you understand the examples.

XAML is actually a general-purpose declarative programming language suitable for constructing and initializing just about any objects, rather than a visual language used solely by Silverlight. XAML consists of rules for how parsers/compilers must treat XML and has some keywords, but it doesn't define any interesting elements by itself. So, talking about XAML without a framework such as Silverlight is like talking about a language such as C# without the .NET Framework. That said, Silverlight uses XAML for defining visual elements.

Currently, XAML is used heavily by Silverlight, Windows Presentation Foundation (WPF), and Windows Workflow Foundation (WF). Silverlight includes a runtime parser for XAML that enables the construction and initialization of Silverlight objects. Outside of Silverlight 1.0, the .NET Framework includes a runtime parser *and* a compiler for XAML that enables the construction and initialization of .NET objects. Although the XAML specification defines a lot of functionality that doesn't apply to Silverlight, this chapter focuses on the aspects of XAML that are relevant for Silverlight.

Elements and Attributes

The XAML specification defines rules that map data types, properties, and events into XML elements and attributes. XAML content used by Silverlight, whether in a standalone file or inline in a SCRIPT element, contains a hierarchy of elements representing visual objects known as *user interface elements*, or UI elements for short. UI elements all have a set of common properties and functions, such as Width, Height, Cursor, and Tag properties. (Cursor can be set to values such as Arrow, Hand, IBeam, or Wait; Tag is a place to attach any user-defined data.)

LOOKING FORWARD

UI Elements

In future versions of Silverlight (and in WPF), a .NET class called UIElement serves as the base class for all UI elements. You can define your own UI elements by deriving from this class (or one of its subclasses). In Silverlight 1.0, however, the list of UI elements is not extensible. There are fewer than 20 of them, and they are all covered in this book.

The following simple (but complete) XAML file constructs a Silverlight Ellipse and sets three properties:

```
<Ellipse xmlns="http://schemas.microsoft.com/client/2007"
  Fill="Orange" Width="300" Height="100"/>
```

The result is rendered in Figure 2.1.

Conceptually, declaring an XML element in XAML (known as an *object element*) is equivalent to instantiating the corresponding object via a parameter-

FIGURE 2.1   A simple Silverlight Ellipse declared in a .xaml file.

terless constructor. Setting an attribute on the object element is equivalent to setting a property of the same name (called a *property attribute*) or hooking up an event handler of the same name (called an *event attribute*). All the identifiers for elements (objects) and attributes (properties and events) are case sensitive, and the attributes can be enclosed in single quotes (') or double quotes (").

Here's an update to the Ellipse that not only sets the three properties, but also attaches an event handler to its MouseEnter event:

```
<Ellipse xmlns="http://schemas.microsoft.com/client/2007"
  Fill="Orange" Width="300" Height="100" MouseEnter="onMouseEnter"/>
```

This requires a JavaScript function called onMouseEnter to be defined. Such events are covered in depth in Chapter 7, "Responding to Input Events," but the section called "The Relationship Between XAML and JavaScript" at the end of this chapter has an example implementation of such an event handler.

2

The XML Namespace

The root object element in a XAML file must specify an XML namespace that is used to qualify itself and any child elements. This is set using the xmlns attribute seen in the previous examples. The namespace that defines all the elements you can use in Silverlight 1.0 (such as `Ellipse`) is `http://schemas.microsoft.com/client/2007`. Alternatively, you can use the namespace `http://schemas.microsoft.com/winfx/2006/xaml/presentation`, and things will still work the same way.

DIGGING DEEPER

Continued

http://schemas.microsoft.com/winfx/2006/xaml/presentation, you get WPF IntelliSense (mostly a superset of Silverlight IntelliSense). Getting IntelliSense for the wrong technology can cause a lot of confusion, so samples in this book use the Silverlight-specific http://schemas.microsoft.com/client/2007 namespace.

Silverlight XAML files sometimes use a second namespace with the prefix x (denoted by using xmlns:x instead of just xmlns):

```
xmlns:x="http://schemas.microsoft.com/winfx/2006/xaml"
```

This is the XAML language namespace, which defines some special directives for the XAML parser. Most of the directives in this namespace control how XAML interacts with .NET features. Therefore, this namespace is mostly not applicable for Silverlight 1.0. In fact, it only includes one attribute that's relevant for Silverlight 1.0 called Name, covered in the "The Relationship Between XAML and JavaScript" section at the end of this chapter. However, all relevant Silverlight elements already have their own Name property that means the exact same thing as this "special" Name attribute. Therefore, there is absolutely no need to use this secondary namespace in XAML content for Silverlight 1.0. It's good to be aware of the namespace, however, because it might be used by XAML generated by tools or XAML samples you come across.

Property Elements

Property attribute syntax works great for properties whose value can be represented as a simple string, but not all properties are like this. For example, Ellipse has a RenderTransform property that must be set to an instance of an object such as RotateTransform or ScaleTransform. (The details of the RenderTransform property and associated objects are covered in Chapter 6, "Positioning and Transforming Elements.") An instance of RotateTransform can be declared in XAML as follows:

TIP

The XAML examples in this book explicitly specify their namespace if they are meant to represent complete XAML files because you would get a XAML parser error if no namespace is specified. Many examples, however, simply assume that http://schemas.microsoft.com/client/2007 is declared as the primary namespace and don't bother specifying it (for better readability). If you want to use such content, be sure to add the namespace explicitly.

```
<RotateTransform Angle="45" CenterY="60"/>
```

However, we need some way to assign this element as the value of the Ellipse's RenderTransform property. Trying to jam the RotateTransform XML element into a property attribute string would not work:

```
<Ellipse xmlns="http://schemas.microsoft.com/client/2007"
  Fill="Orange" Width="300" Height="100"
  RenderTransform="<RotateTransform Angle="45" CenterY="60"/>"/>
```

Fortunately, XAML provides an alternative syntax for setting complex property values—*property elements*—which resembles the following:

```
<Ellipse xmlns="http://schemas.microsoft.com/client/2007"
  Fill="Orange" Width="300" Height="100">
  <Ellipse.RenderTransform>
    <RotateTransform Angle="45" CenterY="60"/>
  </Ellipse.RenderTransform>
</Ellipse>
```

The period in `Ellipse.RenderTransform` is what distinguishes property elements from object elements. They always take the form *ElementName.PropertyName*; they are always contained inside a *ElementName* object element; and they can never have attributes of their own.

The result of adding this property element is shown in Figure 2.2.

Note that `RotateTransform` is one of many Silverlight objects that are not considered to be UI elements. Therefore, it can't be used as the root element in a XAML file; it is only valid as the value of a property.

Type Converters

Silverlight objects contain a number of properties that must be set to something more complex than a simple number or string. To enable the use of property attribute syntax for many of these properties, Silverlight contains several *type converters*. Each type converter defines a special shortcut syntax for a specific data type.

For example, `Ellipse`'s `Fill` property is *not* a string property despite the fact that the previous XAML examples set it to the simple string `"Orange"`. The property

FIGURE 2.2   Updating the Silverlight `Ellipse` with a complex property setting.

> **DIGGING DEEPER**
>
> **Property Element Differences Between WPF and Silverlight**
>
> The XAML parser used by WPF allows property element syntax to be used for simple property values as well. Silverlight 1.0 does not allow this, however. String and numeric properties must be set with property attribute syntax.

must be set to a complex object such as `SolidColorBrush`, but a built-in type converter allows for the simple string syntax, whether you set the property in XAML or in JavaScript. (Setting such properties in JavaScript is covered in "The Relationship Between

XAML and JavaScript" later in this chapter.) In this example, Silverlight finds the type converter specific to the expected type, and then asks it to convert the `"Orange"` string into the appropriate object.

Without the type converter, you would have to use property element syntax to set the `Fill`, as follows:

```
<Ellipse xmlns="http://schemas.microsoft.com/client/2007"
  Width="300" Height="100">
  <Ellipse.Fill>
    <SolidColorBrush Color="Orange"/>
  </Ellipse.Fill>
</Ellipse>
```

This more verbose syntax is perfectly valid, and it produces the exact same result as Figure 2.1. It makes sense to leverage type converters when possible, however, because they help readability, make it easier to hand type XAML, and shrink the size of your XAML. In addition, type converters sometimes enable XAML to express functionality that wouldn't otherwise be possible. In other words, sometimes the object hidden behind the type converter cannot be directly declared in XAML the way that `SolidColorBrush` can. (This applies to *value types* such as `Point`, `Rect`, and `Color`, used later in the book. In future versions of Silverlight, these value types can be used much like normal classes. But in version 1.0, they can only be constructed via their type converter string syntax.)

Silverlight contains several type converters for common data types used throughout the remaining chapters. The string format accepted by each type converter is unique to each data type, although it is generally flexible. For example, unlike the XAML language, Silverlight's type converters support case insensitive strings.

Children of Object Elements

A XAML file, like all XML files, must have a single root object element. Therefore, it should come as no surprise that object elements can support child object elements (not just property elements, which aren't true children as far as XAML is concerned). An object element can have two types of children: a value for a content property or items in a collection.

The Content Property

Some Silverlight classes designate a property that should be set to whatever content is inside the XML element. This property is called the *content property*, and it is really just a convenient shortcut to make the XAML representation more natural, and in some cases more compact. For example, Silverlight contains a `TextBlock` element with a `Text` property. `TextBlock` could be used in XAML as follows:

```
<TextBlock Text="I Love XAML"/>
```

However, `TextBlock` supports content property syntax, so the preceding XAML could be rewritten as follows:

```
<TextBlock>I Love XAML</TextBlock>
```

Items in a Collection

XAML enables you to add items to a collection simply by placing multiple elements inside the element representing the collection. For example, an element called LinearGradientBrush has a GradientStops property that can be set to a GradientStopCollection instance. GradientStopCollection can contain one or more GradientStop objects. The following XAML adds two elements to an instance of GradientStopCollection and sets the two-element collection as the value for the GradientStops property:

```
<LinearGradientBrush>
  <LinearGradientBrush.GradientStops>
    <GradientStopCollection>
      <GradientStop Offset="0" Color="Blue"/>
      <GradientStop Offset="1" Color="Red"/>
    </GradientStopCollection>
  </LinearGradientBrush.GradientStops>
</LinearGradientBrush>
```

This assignment of a new collection works because the GradientStopCollection property is read/write. If the property were read-only, you would need to add the two elements directly to the existing property value, which is automatically initialized to an empty collection. This is as simple as omitting the GradientStopCollection element:

```
<LinearGradientBrush>
  <LinearGradientBrush.GradientStops>
    <GradientStop Offset="0" Color="Blue"/>
    <GradientStop Offset="1" Color="Red"/>
  </LinearGradientBrush.GradientStops>
</LinearGradientBrush>
```

The difference between a read/write collection property and a read-only collection property is subtle, because either way you can still add elements to the collection. However, you might as well use the syntax in the preceding snippet no matter what kind of property it is. It not only works for both kinds of collection properties, but the syntax is more compact.

Furthermore, because GradientStops is the content property for LinearGradientBrush, you can shorten the XAML even further, as follows:

```
<LinearGradientBrush>
  <GradientStop Offset="0" Color="Blue"/>
  <GradientStop Offset="1" Color="Red"/>
</LinearGradientBrush>
```

Chapter 5, "Brushes and Images," explains how this and other brush objects can be used.

DIGGING DEEPER

A Subtlety with the Content Property on `Canvas`

Canvas, an important element in both Silverlight and WPF, has a read-only `Children` content property that is a collection of UI elements. Because `Children` is a content property, you almost never see it set explicitly. Instead, it's common to see child elements added directly to the `Canvas` element, such as:

```
<Canvas>
  <Ellipse Fill="Orange" Width="300" Height="100"/>
  <Ellipse Fill="Blue" Width="100" Height="300"/>
</Canvas>
```

Technically, you should be able to use the normal property element syntax to set `Children`, such as:

```
<Canvas>
  <Canvas.Children>
    <Ellipse Fill="Orange" Width="300" Height="100"/>
    <Ellipse Fill="Blue" Width="100" Height="300"/>
  </Canvas.Children>
</Canvas>
```

This works in WPF, but does not work in Silverlight 1.0. This is a bug, but a harmless one because the workaround is trivial: Just remove the `Canvas.Children` element!

Attached Properties

XAML supports a special kind of property, known as an *attached property*, that can be set on any object, not just the one defining the property. This might sound strange at first, but this mechanism has a few important applications in Silverlight. Two commonly used attached properties are the `Left` and `Top` properties on the `Canvas` element.

Canvas's `Left` and `Top` properties are meant to be applied to children of the `Canvas` to position them relative to its top left corner. This can be done as shown in Listing 2.1, which produces the result in Figure 2.3:

LISTING 2.1   Three Ellipses in a Canvas

```
<Canvas xmlns="http://schemas.microsoft.com/client/2007">
  <Ellipse Fill="Purple" Width="80" Height="80"/>
  <Ellipse Canvas.Left="25" Canvas.Top="25" Fill="Red" Width="80" Height="80"/>
  <Ellipse Canvas.Left="50" Canvas.Top="50" Fill="Green" Width="80" Height="80"/>
</Canvas>
```

The syntax for setting an attached property is the same as setting a normal property, except that the property must be prefixed with the name of the element defining the property (Canvas, in this case) and a period. Omitting the prefix to Left and Top in this example would not work because Ellipse doesn't have Left and Top properties of its own.

FIGURE 2.3   Using the Canvas.Left and Canvas.Top attached properties to position Ellipses.

Attached properties are important because they enable common behavior to be applied to arbitrary elements. For example, *any* UI element can be added to a Canvas and participate in the positioning enabled by the Left and Top properties. Future versions of Silverlight will contain other layout elements more sophisticated than Canvas, and these layout elements can define their own attached properties to be applied to children rather than requiring the additional properties to be added to every UI element.

DIGGING DEEPER

Attached Property Differences Between WPF and Silverlight

The XAML parser for WPF allows you to omit the prefix on an attached property if the element type matches the type of the element defining the property. For example, the following XAML with a Canvas inside a Canvas is legal for WPF:

```
<Canvas>
 <Canvas Left="100">
   ...
 </Canvas>
</Canvas>
```

For Silverlight to successfully parse this XAML, you must instead write:

```
<Canvas>
 <Canvas Canvas.Left="100">
   ...
 </Canvas>
</Canvas>
```

The Relationship Between XAML and JavaScript

With XAML alone (and perhaps a small bit of JavaScript to host the XAML), you can create very sophisticated static content, or even dynamic content, with the help of animations and/or video. However, if you want to create an *interactive* application, you need to write some JavaScript that interacts with the elements declared in XAML. This section examines not only how to perform this interaction with existing XAML content, but also how to generate and render XAML on-the-fly in JavaScript.

Interacting with Elements Defined in XAML

Every element defined in XAML represents an object that you can manipulate in JavaScript. After you have an instance of an element defined in XAML, you can easily get and set its property values, attach handlers to its events, or call its functions. (We'll ignore *how* you get the instance for a moment.) For example, the following JavaScript sets an Ellipse's Fill property to the color red and its Width property to 20 pixels:

```
// This assumes that the ellipse variable is set to an
// instance of an Ellipse object defined in XAML:
ellipse.Fill = "Red";
ellipse.Width = 20;
```

And this code sets the Width of one Ellipse to match the Width of another:

```
// This assumes that both variables are set to
// instances of Ellipse objects defined in XAML:
ellipse2.Width = ellipse1.Width;
```

WARNING

Many objects in Silverlight can't be reused!

Just like the setting of one element's Width to the value of another element's Width, you would probably expect the following line of code to work:

```
ellipse2.Fill = ellipse1.Fill;
```

This fails, however, because complex objects such as brushes (used for Fill) cannot be used in more than one place. Simple property values, such as numbers and strings, can be reused in this manner.

This is a case where type converters add confusion because they make complex objects that can't be reused appear to be simple string values that would otherwise be reusable. For example, the following code fails despite the fact that the Fill value appears to be a simple string:

```
ellipse1.Fill = "Red";
ellipse2.Fill = ellipse1.Fill;
```

Yet the following code works:

```
ellipse1.Fill = "Red";
ellipse2.Fill = "Red";
```

Although Fill appears to be set to a string, the property value after the assignment is not a string at all. You can see evidence of this with code such as the following:

```
ellipse1.Fill = "Red";
alert(ellipse1.Fill);
```

The dialog displayed by JavaScript's alert function contains the string SolidColorBrush rather than Red!

The JavaScript language allows you to alternatively express a property access with associative array syntax. For example,

```
ellipse["Fill"] = "Red";
```

This syntax is handy for getting or setting attached property values, which can't be done with the "normal" property syntax because of the period in the name. For example, `Canvas.Left` can be set on an `Ellipse` as follows:

```
ellipse["Canvas.Left"] = 10;
```

DIGGING DEEPER

Getting and Setting Property Values with `GetValue` and `SetValue`

In addition to the "normal" property syntax and the array syntax, all UI elements have a third option for getting and setting property values. UI elements have functions called `GetValue` and `SetValue` that accomplish the same result. They can be used as follows:

```
var fill = ellipse.GetValue("Fill");
```

or,

```
ellipse.SetValue("Fill", "Red");
```

As with the array syntax, the string specifying the property supports attached property syntax (such as `Canvas.Left`). There's no reason to prefer these functions over the more compact syntax, however.

Although you can set properties and attach event handlers purely in XAML, the ability to also do this in JavaScript (covered for events in Chapter 7) gives you a lot of flexibility to change the behavior of your content based on arbitrary logic. Calling functions is unique to JavaScript, however, as XAML has no capability for invoking them. All UI elements contain a handful of useful functions, as you'll see in this chapter and in future ones. (They also contain some not-so-useful functions, such as the `GetValue` and `SetValue` functions described in the preceding sidebar.)

TIP

Unlike inside XAML, a Silverlight element's properties, events, and functions can be referenced in JavaScript in a case insensitive fashion. For example, the following three lines of code all do the same thing:

```
ellipse.Fill = "Red";
ellipse.fill = "Red";
ellipse.FILL = "Red";
```

The "Red" string is also case insensitive thanks to the type converter, but that's true in both JavaScript and XAML.

The only trick to writing JavaScript that interacts with XAML-defined elements, then, is getting a hold of the XAML-defined object in the first place (in other words, how to initialize the `ellipse`, `ellipse1`, and `ellipse2` variables from the previous code snippets). The three basic ways to do this are as follows:

- ► Finding an Element from the Root
- ► Finding an Element from an Event Sender
- ► Finding an Element by Name

Finding an Element from the Root

One way to retrieve the desired object is to start with the `rootElement` parameter (or `control.Content.Root`) passed to the `onLoad` event hander, shown in the preceding chapter. If the element you want to interact with *is* the root element of the XAML file, you're done. If it isn't, you can use properties on the various elements to navigate to the desired one.

For example, imagine that you want to host the XAML from Listing 2.1 in a web page, but you also want the colors of the three `Ellipse`s to change in the evening. The following `onLoad` event handler can do just that:

```
// Silverlight onLoad event handler
function onLoad(control, context, rootElement)
{
  // If the time is 7 PM (19:00) or later, change to an "evening theme"
  if (new Date().getHours() > 18)
  {
    // Get a reference to each of the Ellipse elements
    var ellipse1 = rootElement.Children.GetItem(0);
    var ellipse2 = rootElement.Children.GetItem(1);
    var ellipse3 = rootElement.Children.GetItem(2);
    // Change the values of their Fill properties
    ellipse1.Fill = "Black";
    ellipse2.Fill = "Gray";
    ellipse3.Fill = "DodgerBlue";
  }
}
```

The `rootElement` is a `Canvas`, and its `Children` content property is a collection with the three `Ellipse` objects. The collection defines a `GetItem` function that can be given a zero-based index to retrieve any of its items.

> **TIP**
>
> All UI elements define a `GetParent` function that can be used to navigate "up" the tree of elements in addition to the downward navigation enabled by properties such as `Children`.

The result of adding this `onLoad` handler is shown in Figure 2.4. Note that there is no flicker from changing the `Fill` values; the handler finishes running before the first frame is rendered.

The collections used by Silverlight elements (such as Canvas's Children property used in this example or LinearGradientBrush's GradientStops property) define several functions in addition to GetItem for managing their items. The Add function places a new item at the end of the collection, and

FIGURE 2.4   The Ellipses from Figure 2.3 with an "evening theme" applied in JavaScript.

the Insert function places a new item at a specified zero-based index (shifting later items forward). Clear removes all items from the collection. Remove enables you to remove a single item by passing in that item, for example:

```
rootElement.Children.Remove(ellipse2);
```

RemoveAt enables you to remove an item by passing in its zero-based index, for example:

```
rootElement.Children.RemoveAt(1);
```

When an item is removed from a collection of elements being rendered, it immediately disappears from the scene. Figure 2.5 shows what happens when either of the two preceding lines of code is included in the onLoad event handler to remove the middle Ellipse.

FIGURE 2.5   Removing the middle Ellipse via JavaScript, viewed with the "evening theme" applied.

The code for picking elements out of the Children collection via numeric index is brittle. Minor changes to the XAML content could break the JavaScript code in subtle ways. This approach is the Silverlight analog to finding an HTML element by retrieving the document's body and then navigating down to the specific node, which is just as unpleasant and rarely done in practice.

Fortunately, the other approaches for retrieving instances of elements are much less brittle.

Finding an Element from an Event Sender

If the code you want to write is in response to a user action (such as clicking a specific element), you can take advantage of the fact that the instance raising the event is passed along as the first parameter to the event handler.

For example, if the XAML from Listing 2.1 were updated to attach a MouseEnter event handler,

```
<Canvas xmlns="http://schemas.microsoft.com/client/2007">
  <Ellipse MouseEnter="onMouseEnter" Fill="Purple" Width="80" Height="80"/>
  <Ellipse MouseEnter="onMouseEnter" Canvas.Left="25" Canvas.Top="25"
    Fill="Red" Width="80" Height="80"/>
```

```
<Ellipse MouseEnter="onMouseEnter" Canvas.Left="50" Canvas.Top="50"
    Fill="Green" Width="80" Height="80" />
</Canvas>
```

the corresponding onMouseEnter JavaScript function could be written to change an Ellipse's Fill as soon as you move the mouse pointer over it:

```
function onMouseEnter(sender, eventArgs)
{
    // In this case, sender is set to whichever Ellipse the mouse just hovered over
    sender.Fill = "Black";
}
```

If the sender instance isn't the element you want to interact with, you can always navigate from this element. For example, sender.GetParent() would return the root Canvas element when sender is one of the Ellipses. This approach is analogous to using HTML events and leveraging the fact that this refers to the element raising the event.

TIP

Every UI element has a GetHost function that returns the Silverlight control object discussed in the preceding chapter. This is the same object as the first parameter passed to onLoad, which contains a number of useful properties, functions, and events. For example, you can access the root element from an event handler by using sender.GetHost().Content.Root. It can be helpful to think of the GetHost function as "GetControl," a name that would have been more consistent with the terminology used throughout Silverlight. You can also retrieve this object by calling document.getElementById with the same HTML id passed to Silverlight.createObject or Silverlight.createObjectEx, but GetHost is more flexible because you can call it without having to know the control's id.

Finding an Element by Name

The easiest (and most common) way to find an element is to give it a name, and then call a function called FindName to retrieve a direct reference to the element. This is analogous to the HTML approach of giving an element an id and then retrieving it via document.getElementById.

Giving an element a name is as simple as setting its Name property (or using the x:Name attribute, where x refers to the XAML language namespace). Therefore, Listing 2.1 can be updated as follows:

```
<Canvas xmlns="http://schemas.microsoft.com/client/2007">
  <Ellipse Name="ellipse1" Fill="Purple" Width="80" Height="80" />
  <Ellipse Name="ellipse2" Canvas.Left="25" Canvas.Top="25"
    Fill="Red" Width="80" Height="80" />
  <Ellipse Name="ellipse3" Canvas.Left="50" Canvas.Top="50"
    Fill="Green" Width="80" Height="80" />
</Canvas>
```

Calling FindName is easy because it's not only defined on the Silverlight control's Content property, but also on all UI elements. The FindName function (which would make more sense if called FindElementByName) can find any element in the current content, no matter what object you call it from. (There's one exception to this, which is when namescopes are involved, discussed in the next section.)

Therefore, the code to give the Ellipses an evening theme could be updated as follows:

```
// Silverlight onLoad event handler
function onLoad(control, context, rootElement)
{
  // If the time is 7 PM (19:00) or later, change to an "evening theme"
  if (new Date().getHours() > 18)
  {
    // Get a reference to each of the Ellipse elements
    var ellipse1 = control.Content.FindName("ellipse1");
    var ellipse2 = control.Content.FindName("ellipse2");
    var ellipse3 = control.Content.FindName("ellipse3");
    // Change the values of their Fill properties
    ellipse1.Fill = "Black";
    ellipse2.Fill = "Gray";
    ellipse3.Fill = "DodgerBlue";
  }
}
```

Similarly, the three changed lines of code could be written as

```
var ellipse1 = rootElement.FindName("ellipse1");
var ellipse2 = rootElement.FindName("ellipse2");
var ellipse3 = rootElement.FindName("ellipse3");
```

which is the same as

```
var ellipse1 = control.Content.Root.FindName("ellipse1");
var ellipse2 = control.Content.Root.FindName("ellipse2");
var ellipse3 = control.Content.Root.FindName("ellipse3");
```

Or, if you move the logic to an event handler such as the previous onMouseEnter function, the incoming sender parameter can be used no matter what it points to:

```
var ellipse1 = sender.FindName("ellipse1");
var ellipse2 = sender.FindName("ellipse2");
var ellipse3 = sender.FindName("ellipse3");
```

In all these variations, using FindName is robust in the face of most changes to your XAML content. As long as you keep the same Name on the element, the corresponding JavaScript code can find it.

Generating XAML Dynamically

As with HTML, JavaScript, or any content served by a web server, you can always generate XAML dynamically on the server with ASP.NET or other server-side technologies. But Silverlight contains functionality for parsing, loading, and rendering dynamic XAML all from client-side JavaScript. The key to all this is a function defined on the Silverlight control's Content property called CreateFromXaml. The following code demonstrates how a fourth Ellipse could be dynamically added to the XAML from Listing 2.1:

```
// Silverlight onLoad event handler
function onLoad(control, context, rootElement)
{
  // Parse and load the XAML, and get the root instance
  var ellipse = control.Content.CreateFromXaml(
    "<Ellipse Fill='Magenta' Width='80' Height='80' Canvas.Left='100'/>");
  // Attach it to the existing content, so the new content gets rendered
  rootElement.Children.Add(ellipse);
}
```

CreateFromXaml must be given a string containing XAML. This function parses the XAML, creates the appropriate objects, and returns a reference to the root object. (In this example, it returns the *only* object, which is the magenta Ellipse.)

A step still needs to be taken to get your new content rendered on the screen, however, because the object returned by CreateFromXaml has no automatic relationship to the content already being rendered. You must set it as a property value for some existing element (or add it to the property value if the value is a collection). The preceding code knows that the existing root element is a Canvas, so it adds the new Ellipse to its Children collection. The result of this addition is shown in Figure 2.6.

The object(s) returned by CreateFromXaml are the same as the objects you would get if you retrieved existing XAML-defined elements using any of the approaches in the previous section. Therefore, you can get or set property values, attach event handlers, and call functions. The preceding

FIGURE 2.6   A fourth Ellipse dynamically added to the static XAML content, thanks to CreateFromXaml.

TIP

Although the default XML namespace must be explicitly specified on the XAML content used to initialize the Silverlight control, the XAML content given to CreateFromXaml does *not* need the explicit declaration. (If you choose to use x:Name rather than Name in your content, however, you do need to explicitly specify the XAML language namespace.)

onLoad event handler could be rewritten as follows to accomplish the same effect:

```
// Silverlight onLoad event handler
function onLoad(control, context, rootElement)
{
    // Parse and load the XAML, and get the root instance
    var ellipse = control.Content.CreateFromXaml("<Ellipse/>");

    // Set properties on the root instance
    ellipse.Fill = "Magenta";
    ellipse.Width = 80;
    ellipse.Height = 80;
    ellipse["Canvas.Left"] = 100;

    // Attach it to the existing content, so the new content gets rendered
    rootElement.Children.Add(ellipse);
}
```

Of course, dynamically adding what could easily be static content (such as the magenta Ellipse) in the onLoad event is a bit silly. But the capabilities provided by CreateFromXaml enable a number of interesting scenarios. You can add new pieces of content based on user actions or incoming data; you could add and remove a fancy tooltip; you could persist content as a XAML string (perhaps in a browser cookie), and then later restore that content; and so on. You can even use CreateFromXaml to create a Silverlight-based interactive XAML editor, much like the one provided with this book's source code.

WARNING

UI elements can only have one parent!

If you wanted to add additional magenta Ellipses to the content in Figure 2.6, it might be tempting to call rootElement.Children.Add(ellipse) multiple times. This fails because, as with brushes, UI elements can't be added to more than one place in the hierarchy of rendered objects. (Even if they could, it wouldn't be useful in this case because they would all be rendered in the same spot.) If you want additional elements, you must make additional CreateFromXaml calls (or give CreateFromXaml a string containing a Canvas with as many elements as you'd like as children).

TIP

The Silverlight control must be initialized with at least *some* static XAML, so it's impossible to dynamically generate the entire XAML content in client-side JavaScript. However, you can always initialize the control with an empty Canvas element, and then add all your content as a child of this element.

DIGGING DEEPER

Names and Namescopes

By default, all elements in the current XAML content must have a unique Name (or no Name at all). However, Silverlight supports a way to have duplicate Names by associating a chunk of objects with a context known as a namescope.

CreateFromXaml can be passed a second Boolean parameter (called nameScope). If true, the returned object (and any objects attached to it) is considered to be in an isolated namescope. This enables Name values inside this new content to be duplicates of existing Name values anywhere in the Silverlight control, so you can attach the new content to the live scene without worrying about conflicts. (Names within a single namescope must still be unique.) This scoping mechanism for XAML is much like several scoping mechanisms for procedural programming languages, such as the ability to duplicate local variable names inside separate functions.

For example, imagine that you want to add a new Canvas containing an Ellipse called ellipse1 as a fourth child on the following Canvas (that already has a child named ellipse1):

```
<Canvas xmlns="http://schemas.microsoft.com/client/2007">
 <Ellipse Name="ellipse1" Fill="Purple" Width="80" Height="80"/>
 <Ellipse Name="ellipse2" Canvas.Left="25" Canvas.Top="25"
   Fill="Red" Width="80" Height="80"/>
 <Ellipse Name="ellipse3" Canvas.Left="50" Canvas.Top="50"
   Fill="Green" Width="80" Height="80"/>
</Canvas>
```

You can successfully do this with the following code inside an onLoad event handler:

```
// Parse and load the XAML into a new namescope, and get the root instance
var canvas = control.Content.CreateFromXaml("<Canvas>" +
  "<Ellipse Name='ellipse1' Fill='Magenta' Width='80' Height='80'/></Canvas>",
  true);
// Attach it to the existing content, so the new content gets rendered
rootElement.Children.Add(canvas);
```

Without passing true as the second parameter to CreateFromXaml, the call to rootElement.Children.Add would fail due to the duplicate ellipse1 Name.

Given that namescopes enable a single tree of elements to have duplicate names, you might be wondering how the FindName function is supposed to work in such situations. The answer: FindName searches for the name only inside the namescope of the object it is invoked on. That way, FindName is guaranteed to find at most one object.

In this example, calling FindName("ellipse1") on the canvas variable or its child (which *is* ellipse1) would return the magenta-filled Ellipse. On the other hand, calling FindName("ellipse1") on rootElement, its first three children, or on the Silverlight control's Content property would return the purple-filled Ellipse. Calling FindName("ellipse2") on the canvas variable or its child would return null, but calling FindName("ellipse2") from any other object would return the red-filled Ellipse. The FindName function on the control's Content property always searches the *default namescope*, which is the namescope of the root element (and all other elements if CreateFromXaml is never called with true as a second parameter).

Continued

This namescope functionality is crucial for creating reusable controls. Having an isolated namescope makes it possible for a control to name its own elements without worrying about what names are used by potential parents, or worrying about how to handle multiple instances of itself being used simultaneously. Chapter 7 makes use of this feature when creating a reusable scrollbar control.

Conclusion

You have now seen exactly how XAML works and how it fits in with JavaScript. This foundation is all you need in order to understand the individual Silverlight feature areas described throughout the rest of the book. Unlike XAML's role in other technologies (WPF and WF), you cannot create Silverlight 1.0 content without it. (In contrast, the next version of Silverlight enables .NET code to create new instances of elements such as `Ellipse`, `Canvas`, or `Rectangle` via simple constructors rather than strings containing XAML.)

Although I personally find it enjoyable, you might find typing a lot of XAML by hand to be tedious. That's where tools such as the ones mentioned in this book's introduction come in, however. Some tools help by providing nice shortcuts such as autocompletion, whereas others provide visual designers that can spare you from typing a single angle bracket! The transparent and well-specified nature of XML makes it easy to integrate new tools into a Silverlight-based workflow while at the same time enables easy hand tweaking or troubleshooting.

In some areas of Silverlight, typing XAML by hand isn't practical, such as complicated paths and shapes described in the next chapter. But being familiar with XAML is the best way to learn the technology. It's like understanding how HTML works without relying on a graphical tool.

PART II

Creating Static Content

IN THIS PART

Shapes, Lines, and Curves

Although it might sound simple, drawing shapes, lines, and curves is something that you can't do with HTML (for the most part). Silverlight, however, has features for drawing such items that range from simple to very complex. This support comes in handy for many things, such as creating logos or stylishly separating regions of a page. In addition, because the first version of Silverlight lacks high-level controls like buttons or scrollbars, you must draw them yourself using features in this chapter (or find controls someone else already created this way). With or without Silverlight, you could accomplish similar effects by embedding images. But with the drawing capabilities of Silverlight, you can do all of this with vector drawings that are easy to tweak and scale perfectly to any size.

FAQ

 **Can I create 3D graphics with Silverlight?**

The current version of Silverlight does not support true 3D graphics, but with a little bit of math you can simulate 3D. For example, Telerik's RadControls for Silverlight (from www.telerik.com) contains a RadCube control that does just that to produce a spinning 3D cube with customizable faces.

This chapter starts by showing how to create some basic shapes, and then lines and curves that can form arbitrarily complex shapes. The chapter finishes with discussions about geometries and strokes, which expose the full power of what you can draw with Silverlight.

Basic Shapes

In Silverlight, a shape is a basic 2D drawing with a customizable `Stroke` (the border) and `Fill` (the area inside). Silverlight contains six UI elements that are considered to be shapes. The three covered in this section are

- Rectangle

- Ellipse

- Polygon

Rectangle

A `Rectangle`, like all shapes, has several straightforward properties for customizing its appearance, such as `Width`, `Height`, `Fill`, and `Stroke`. Here are three `Rectangle`s, pictured in Figure 3.1:

A simple square:

```
<Rectangle Width="100" Height="100" Fill="Red"/>
```

A square with a `Fill` and `Stroke`:

```
<Rectangle Width="100" Height="100" Fill="Orange" Stroke="Black"/>
```

Changing the dimensions and adding a `StrokeThickness`:

```
<Rectangle Width="300" Height="100" Fill="Yellow" Stroke="Black"
  StrokeThickness="10"/>
```

If you don't specify a `Stroke`, then you must specify a `Fill`, `Width`, and `Height` for the `Rectangle` (or any other shape) to be visible. If you specify a `Stroke` without a `Width` and `Height`, you'll get a solid square with dimensions equal to `StrokeThickness`.

FIGURE 3.1   Three `Rectangle`s with different property values.

Continued

Note that transforms can be applied to any Silverlight content (covered in Chapter 6, "Positioning and Transforming Elements") that makes a measurement such as `100` actually much larger or smaller than 100 pixels in reality. This is why it can be meaningful to specify measurements with decimal values, such as `10.42`. Although an unscaled shape with `Width` set to `10.42` won't look different compared to a shape with `Width` simply set to `10`, the larger shape would be 42 pixels wider if both were scaled to be 100 times larger.

`Rectangle` even defines `RadiusX` and `RadiusY` properties that enable you to give it rounded corners! Figure 3.2 shows the following three `Rectangles` with various values of RadiusX and RadiusY:

An evenly rounded rectangle:

```
<Rectangle Width="300" Height="100" Fill="Green" Stroke="Black"
  StrokeThickness="10" RadiusX="20" RadiusY="20"/>
```

More rounding on the Y axis:

```
<Rectangle Width="300" Height="100" Fill="Blue" Stroke="Black"
  StrokeThickness="10" RadiusX="20" RadiusY="50"/>
```

Maximum rounding produces an ellipse:

```
<Rectangle Width="300" Height="100" Fill="Purple" Stroke="Black"
  StrokeThickness="10" RadiusX="150" RadiusY="50"/>
```

RadiusX can be at most half the `Width` of the `Rectangle`, and RadiusY can be at most half the `Height`. Setting them any higher makes no difference. You must specify both RadiusX and RadiusY to get any rounding.

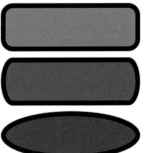

FIGURE 3.2   Three `Rectangles` with different values for RadiusX and RadiusY.

Ellipse

After discovering the flexibility of `Rectangle` and realizing that it can be made to look like an ellipse (or circle), you'd think that a separate `Ellipse` element would be redundant. And you'd be right! All `Ellipse` does is make it easier to get an elliptical shape. Simply set the `Width` and `Height`, and the radii are calculated and applied automatically.

The following `Ellipse` produces the identical result as the last `Rectangle` in Figure 3.2:

```
<Ellipse Width="300" Height="100" Fill="Purple" Stroke="Black"
  StrokeThickness="10"/>
```

Of course, giving an `Ellipse` a matching `Width` and `Height` produces a circle:

```
<Ellipse Width="100" Height="100" Fill="Brown" Stroke="Black"
  StrokeThickness="10"/>
```

Both of these are pictured in Figure 3.3.

FIGURE 3.3   Two simple `Ellipses`.

DIGGING DEEPER

Visibility Versus Opacity

All UI elements (including shapes) have a `Visibility` property that can be set to `Visible` or `Collapsed`. (These two values were chosen for consistency with WPF.) But UI elements also have an `Opacity` property that can be set to any value from `0` to `1`, where `0` is completely transparent and `1` is completely opaque.

So what's the difference between these two properties? The most noticeable difference is that `Opacity` enables a range of transparency rather than an effectively Boolean value. This is handy for animations that fade elements in and out, or for keeping an element in a permanently translucent state.

A more subtle difference between these two properties is that an element with an `Opacity` of `0` still receives input events by default (such as mouse clicks), whereas an element with a `Visibility` of `Collapsed` does not. Therefore, you should use the `Visibility` property rather than the `Opacity` property for normal hiding and showing of elements. Chapter 7, "Responding to Input Events," discusses hit testing in more depth.

DIGGING DEEPER

The `Stretch` Property on Shapes

By default, the content of a shape stretches to fill the area defined by its `Width` and `Height` (except for the `Path` shape, covered later in the chapter). This behavior can be customized, however, by setting its `Stretch` property to a value other than its default value of `Fill`. Setting it to `None` causes the shape to occupy no space (excluding its strokes), and setting it to `Uniform` or `UniformToFill` makes the shape's width equal to its height. The difference between `Uniform` and `UniformToFill` is that the former chooses the smaller of the explicit `Width` and `Height` settings for the actual dimensions of the shape (so it always fits inside the chosen area), whereas the latter chooses the *larger* of the `Width` and `Height` settings (which truncates the shape in one dimension if `Width` and `Height` are not already equal). Figure 3.4 demonstrates these three values of `Stretch` on the purple `Ellipse` from Figure 3.3.

Continued

```
Stretch="None"  Stretch="Uniform"   Stretch="UniformToFill"
```

FIGURE 3.4   Setting Stretch on an Ellipse.

Using any of these nondefault Stretch values on simple shapes is a fairly unusual thing to do. However, the same Stretch property appears on Images and some brushes (covered in Chapter 5, "Brushes and Images"), as well as MediaElements (covered in Chapter 10, "Audio and Video"), and is much more useful on these objects.

3

Polygon

A Polygon enables you to form a shape out of an arbitrary sequence of lines, expressed in its Points property (a collection of Point objects). Because Point doesn't support being instantiated as a XAML element, you must set Points with string syntax supported by a built-in type converter. For example, the following four Polygons are rendered in Figure 3.5:

```
<Polygon Fill="Red" Stroke="Black" StrokeThickness="10" StrokeMiterLimit="0"
  Points="20,20 100,100"/>

<Polygon Fill="Orange" Stroke="Black" StrokeThickness="10"
  Points="20,20 100,100 200,10"/>

<Polygon Fill="Yellow" Stroke="Black" StrokeThickness="10"
  Points="20,20 100,100 200,10 300,100"/>

<Polygon Fill="Green" Stroke="Black" StrokeThickness="10" StrokeMiterLimit="0"
  Points="20,20 100,100 200,10 300,100 100,100"/>
```

The value for Points can be a simple list of alternating x and y values. The commas can help readability, but are optional. You can place a comma between every value or use no commas at all. The StrokeMiterLimit property is set on two of the Polygons to avoid a confusing side effect discussed later in the "Strokes" section of this chapter.

Notice that if you don't add an explicit Point that returns to the origin (as in these four examples), the Polygon automatically adds one. Therefore, it always creates a closed figure.

When you have a complicated Polygon with intersecting points, there can be multiple interpretations of which area is *inside* a shape (and can, therefore, be filled) and which area is *outside* a shape.

FIGURE 3.5   Four Polygons, ranging from two to five points.

Therefore, Polygon has a FillRule property that gives you two choices on how filling is done:

- **EvenOdd** (default)—Fills a region only if you would cross an odd number of segments to travel from that region to the area outside the entire shape.

- **NonZero**—Is a more complicated algorithm that takes into consideration the direction of the segments you would have to cross to get outside the entire shape. For many shapes, it is likely to fill all enclosed areas.

The difference between EvenOdd and NonZero is illustrated in Figure 3.6, created from the following two chunks of XAML:

```
<Polygon Fill="Red" Stroke="Black" StrokeThickness="10"
  Points="50,100 350,100 300,200 250,20 175,200 150,30 100,200 100,200 200,20
  250,200 300,20 350,175" FillRule="EvenOdd"/>
```

```
<Polygon Fill="Red" Stroke="Black" StrokeThickness="10"
  Points="50,100 350,100 300,200 250,20 175,200 150,30 100,200 100,200 200,20
  250,200 300,20 350,175" FillRule="NonZero"/>
```

The shape is the same in both cases, but the `FillRule` setting is different.

EvenOdd   NonZero

FIGURE 3.6   A complex Polygon with different values for `FillRule`.

Lines and Curves

This section examines three elements for drawing lines and curves with Silverlight:

- ▶ Line

- ▶ Polyline

- ▶ Path

These elements are also considered to be shapes by Silverlight (just like `Rectangle`, `Ellipse`, and `Polygon`) so they share the same familiar properties, such as `Fill`, `Stroke`, and `StrokeThickness`.

Line

Line defines four properties to represent a line segment connecting points $(x1,y1)$ and $(x2,y2)$. These properties are called X1, Y1, X2, and Y2. For example, the following three Lines are rendered in Figure 3.7:

A line sloping downward:

```
<Line X1="20" Y1="20" X2="100" Y2="100" Stroke="Black" StrokeThickness="10"/>
```

A horizontal line:

```
<Line X1="20" Y1="20" X2="100" Y2="20" Stroke="Black" StrokeThickness="10"/>
```

A line sloping upward:

```
<Line X1="20" Y1="100" X2="100" Y2="20" Stroke="Black" StrokeThickness="10"/>
```

FIGURE 3.7   Three simple Lines.

Although Line has the same Fill property as all other shapes, it is meaningless because there is never any area to fill.

Polyline

A Polyline represents a sequence of lines, just like a Polygon. In fact, the only difference between the two elements is that Polyline doesn't automatically close the figure. Lines are only drawn between the points you explicitly specify, as demonstrated by the following Polylines pictured in Figure 3.8:

```
<Polyline Stroke="Black" StrokeThickness="10" StrokeMiterLimit="0"
  Points="20,20 100,100"/>
```

```
<Polyline Stroke="Black" StrokeThickness="10"
  Points="20,20 100,100 200,10"/>
```

```
<Polyline Stroke="Black" StrokeThickness="10"
  Points="20,20 100,100 200,10 300,100"/>
```

```
<Polyline Stroke="Black" StrokeThickness="10" StrokeMiterLimit="0"
  Points="20,20 100,100 200,10 300,100 100,100"/>
```

FIGURE 3.8   Four Polylines using the same Points values as the Polygons in Figure 3.5.

You might expect that applying a Fill to a Polyline is meaningless, but Figure 3.9 shows that this actually fills it like a Polygon, pretending that a line segment exists to connect the last point back to the starting point. Figure 3.9 was created simply by taking the Polylines from Figure 3.8 and marking them with Fill="Red", Fill="Orange", Fill="Yellow", and Fill="Green", respectively.

Polyline also has a FillRule property, just like Polygon. Therefore, just as the more powerful Rectangle makes Ellipse redundant, the more powerful Polyline makes Polygon (and Line) redundant.

FIGURE 3.9   The same Polylines from Figure 3.8 but with an explicit Fill.

Path

Path is the ultimate shape, as it can express anything expressible by a Rectangle, Ellipse, Polygon, Line, Polyline, and more. Path is the only element that can represent complex curves in addition to straight lines.

Path has different sizing characteristics than the other shapes. Rather than requiring an explicit Width and Height, Path automatically sizes to fit its content (which has its own explicit measurements) and has a default Stretch value of None. By setting an explicit Width and Height on Path, you can clip, scale, and/or stretch its content (depending on its value of Stretch). You must set both Width and Height of the Path, or neither, otherwise nothing appears!

> **WARNING**
>
> **Try to avoid setting Path's Stretch, Width, and Height!**
>
> The scaling or stretching potentially caused by setting these properties forces Silverlight to do additional work, which can reduce your resulting performance. The impact is usually very slight, but this can often be easily avoided by giving the Path's content the correct size and aspect ratio in the first place.

Path has a Data property that can be set to an instance of an object known as a geometry. The Path element is pretty simple, leaving all the complicated work of specifying the shape to the geometry object. Geometries have a lot of features, and can even be used in more places than inside a Path. Therefore, geometries deserve their own section to examine them in depth.

Geometries

A geometry is the simplest possible abstract representation of a shape or path—even simpler than the Silverlight shape objects already covered in this chapter. The distinguishing characteristic of geometries versus shapes is that geometries don't have visual properties such as Fill, Stroke, StrokeThickness, Opacity, and so on. They're just mathematical descriptions of shapes.

Silverlight defines a number of geometries, including the following four basic ones:

▶ **RectangleGeometry**—Has a Rect property for defining its dimensions and RadiusX and RadiusY properties for defining rounded corners

▶ **EllipseGeometry**—Has RadiusX and RadiusY properties, plus a Center property

▶ **LineGeometry**—Has StartPoint and EndPoint properties to define a line segment

▶ **PathGeometry**—Contains a collection of PathFigure objects in its Figures content property; a general-purpose geometry

At this point, you might be wondering why you would ever use a RectangleGeometry, EllipseGeometry, or LineGeometry when the Rectangle, Ellipse, and Line elements already exist. They're certainly redundant when used inside a Path. For example, the following Path with a RectangleGeometry produces the exact same red square from Figure 3.1:

```
<Path Fill="Red">
  <Path.Data>
    <RectangleGeometry Rect="0,0,100,100"/>
  </Path.Data>
</Path>
```

The Path takes care of visual aspects such as the red Fill, and the RectangleGeometry takes care of describing the shape. The four values inside Rect represent the x and y coordinates for the top-left corner plus the width and height, respectively. But if you use a Path object, you'll likely want to use a PathGeometry object rather than the more limited geometries that are redundant with the basic shapes.

Basic geometries such as RectangleGeometry are quite convenient, however, for another application of geometries: clipping. This section examines using geometries for clipping, using PathGeometry objects inside Paths, and a few convenient options for working with geometries wherever they are used.

Using a Geometry for Clipping

The Clip property on all UI elements can be set to an instance of a geometry to clip the rendering of any such element to an arbitrary shape. The following Ellipse, shown in Figure 3.10, is clipped with a RectangleGeometry:

```
<Ellipse Width="300" Height="100" Fill="Blue" Stroke="Black" StrokeThickness="10">
  <Ellipse.Clip>
    <RectangleGeometry Rect="30,0 240,100"/>
  </Ellipse.Clip>
</Ellipse>
```

The RectangleGeometry cuts off 30 pixels on the left and 30 pixels on the right. It does this with an x coordinate of 30 and a width that's 60 pixels narrower than the Ellipse.

FIGURE 3.10   An Ellipse clipped with a RectangleGeometry.

The following Rectangle, pictured in Figure 3.11, is clipped with an EllipseGeometry:

```
<Rectangle Width="300" Height="300" Fill="Purple" Stroke="Black"
  StrokeThickness="10">
  <Rectangle.Clip>
    <EllipseGeometry RadiusX="100" RadiusY="100"/>
  </Rectangle.Clip>
</Rectangle>
```

Because the EllipseGeometry's Center
property is not set, it defaults to (0,0),
the top-left corner.

FIGURE 3.11   A Rectangle clipped with an
EllipseGeometry.

PathGeometry

The powerful PathGeometry object,
which you'd most likely use in a Path,
provides the most flexibility of all the drawing-related elements. Each PathFigure in a
PathGeometry contains one or more connected path segments in its Segments content
property. A path segment is simply a straight or curvy line segment, represented by one of
seven Silverlight elements:

- **LineSegment**—An element for representing a line segment (of course!)

- **PolyLineSegment**—A shortcut for representing a connected sequence of
  LineSegments

- **ArcSegment**—An element for representing a segment that curves along the circum-
  ference of an imaginary ellipse

- **BezierSegment**—An element for representing a cubic Bézier curve

- **PolyBezierSegment**—A shortcut for representing a connected sequence of
  BezierSegments

- **QuadraticBezierSegment**—An element for representing a quadratic Bézier curve

- **PolyQuadraticBezierSegment**—A shortcut for representing a connected sequence of
  QuadraticBezierSegments

DIGGING DEEPER

Bézier Curves

Bézier curves (named after engineer Pierre Bézier) are commonly used in computer graphics
for representing smooth curves. Bézier curves are even used by fonts to mathematically
describe curves in their glyphs!

The basic idea is that in addition to two endpoints, a Bézier curve has one or more *control
points* that give the line segment its curve. These control points are not visible (and not
necessarily on the curve itself), but rather are used as input to a formula that dictates where
each point on the curve exists. Intuitively, each control point acts like a center of gravity, so
the line segment appears to be "pulled" toward these points.

Continues

DIGGING DEEPER

Continued

Despite the scarier-sounding name, QuadraticBezierSegment is actually simpler than a BezierSegment and computationally cheaper. A quadratic Bézier curve only has one control point, whereas a cubic Bézier curve has two. Therefore, a quadratic Bézier curve can only form a U-like shape (or a straight line), but a cubic Bézier curve can also take the form of an S-like shape.

The following Path contains a PathGeometry with two simple LineSegments that create the "L" shape in Figure 3.12:

```
<Path Stroke="Black" StrokeThickness="10">
  <Path.Data>
    <PathGeometry>
      <PathFigure StartPoint="20,20">
        <LineSegment Point="20,100"/>
        <LineSegment Point="100,100"/>
      </PathFigure>
    </PathGeometry>
  </Path.Data>
</Path>
```

FIGURE 3.12   A PathGeometry that contains a pair of LineSegments.

Notice that the definition for each LineSegment only includes a single Point. That's because it implicitly connects the previous point to the current one. The first LineSegment connects the PathFigure's starting point of (20,20) to (20,100), then the second LineSegment connects (20,100) to (100,100). (The other six path segments act the same way as well.) If you don't specify a custom starting point via the StartPoint property, the default starting point is (0,0).

As with a Polyline, applying a Fill to a Path fills it as if a line segment exists to connect the last point back to the starting point. Figure 3.13 was created by adding the following Fill to the preceding XAML:

```
<Path Stroke="Black" StrokeThickness="10" Fill="Red">
  <Path.Data>
    <PathGeometry>
      <PathFigure StartPoint="20,20">
        <LineSegment Point="20,100"/>
        <LineSegment Point="100,100"/>
      </PathFigure>
    </PathGeometry>
  </Path.Data>
</Path>
```

To turn the imaginary line segment into a real one, you could add a third `LineSegment` to the `PathFigure` explicitly, or you could simply set `PathFigure`'s `IsClosed` property to `true`. The result of doing either is shown in Figure 3.14.

FIGURE 3.13   The `Path` from Figure 3.12 with a red `Fill`.

Because all path segments within a `PathFigure` must be connected, you can place multiple `PathFigures` in a `PathGeometry` if you want disjoint shapes or paths in the same geometry. You could also overlap `PathFigures` to create results that would be complicated to replicate in a single `PathFigure`. For example, the following XAML overlaps the triangle from Figure 3.14 with a triangle that is given a different `StartPoint` but is otherwise identical:

FIGURE 3.14   The `Path` from Figure 3.13, but with `IsClosed = "True"`.

```
<Path Stroke="Black" StrokeThickness="10" Fill="Red">
  <Path.Data>
    <PathGeometry>
      <!-- Triangle #1 -->
      <PathFigure StartPoint="20,20" IsClosed="True">
        <LineSegment Point="20,100"/>
        <LineSegment Point="100,100"/>
      </PathFigure>
      <!-- Triangle #2 -->
      <PathFigure StartPoint="70,20" IsClosed="True">
        <LineSegment Point="20,100"/>
        <LineSegment Point="100,100"/>
      </PathFigure>
    </PathGeometry>
  </Path.Data>
</Path>
```

This dual-`PathFigure` `PathGeometry` is displayed in Figure 3.15.

`PathGeometry` enables you to control this fill behavior with its `FillRule` property, just like `Polygon` and `Polyline`. In this case, changing `FillRule` to `NonZero` would fill all three enclosed regions with red.

FIGURE 3.15   Overlapping triangles created by using two `PathFigures`.

All the segments other than `LineSegment` and `PolyLineSegment` are able to express curves. For example, the following `Path`, shown in Figure 3.16, uses an `ArcSegment` to create a U-like shape.

```
<Path Stroke="Black" StrokeThickness="10">
  <Path.Data>
    <PathGeometry>
      <PathFigure StartPoint="20,20">
        <ArcSegment Size="10,20" Point="100,100"/>
      </PathFigure>
    </PathGeometry>
  </Path.Data>
</Path>
```

The Size of the ArcSegment controls the x-radius and y-radius of the arc. ArcSegment has additional properties for customizing its appearance, such as RotationAngle, SweepDirection (set to Clockwise or Counterclockwise), and IsLargeArc, which ensures that the sweep of the arc is greater than or equal to 180° when set to True.

FIGURE 3.16   A Path containing a single ArcSegment.

To draw a more complicated S-like curve, the following Path uses a BezierSegment, pictured in Figure 3.17:

```
<Path Stroke="Black" StrokeThickness="10">
  <Path.Data>
    <PathGeometry>
      <PathFigure StartPoint="20,20">
        <BezierSegment Point1="150,0" Point2="50,300" Point3="200,200"/>
      </PathFigure>
    </PathGeometry>
  </Path.Data>
</Path>
```

GeometryGroup

GeometryGroup composes one or more geometry instances together. A GeometryGroup is itself a geometry, so it can be used anywhere a simpler geometry can be used. For example, the previously shown XAML for creating the overlapping triangles in Figure 3.15 could be rewritten to use two geometries (each with a single PathFigure) rather than one:

FIGURE 3.17   A Path containing a single BezierSegment.

```
<Path Stroke="Black" StrokeThickness="10" Fill="Red">
  <Path.Data>
    <GeometryGroup>
```

```
    <!-- Triangle #1 -->
    <PathGeometry>
      <PathFigure StartPoint="20,20" IsClosed="True">
        <LineSegment Point="20,100"/>
        <LineSegment Point="100,100"/>
      </PathFigure>
    </PathGeometry>
    <!-- Triangle #2 -->
    <PathGeometry>
      <PathFigure StartPoint="70,20" IsClosed="True">
        <LineSegment Point="20,100"/>
        <LineSegment Point="100,100"/>
      </PathFigure>
    </PathGeometry>
  </GeometryGroup>
 </Path.Data>
</Path>
```

GeometryGroup, like PathGeometry, has a FillRule property set to EvenOdd by default. It takes precedence over any FillRule settings of its children.

This, of course, begs the question, "Why would I create a GeometryGroup when I can just as easily create a single PathGeometry with multiple PathFigures?" One minor advantage is that GeometryGroup enables you to aggregate other geometries such as RectangleGeometry and EllipseGeometry, which can be easier to use. But the major advantage of using GeometryGroup is that you can set various geometry properties independently on each child.

For example, the following GeometryGroup composes two identical triangles, but sets the Transform on one of them to rotate it -15°:

```
<Path Stroke="Black" StrokeThickness="10" Fill="Red">
  <Path.Data>
    <GeometryGroup>
      <!-- Triangle #1 -->
      <PathGeometry>
        <PathFigure StartPoint="20,20" IsClosed="True">
          <LineSegment Point="20,100"/>
          <LineSegment Point="100,100"/>
        </PathFigure>
      </PathGeometry>
      <!-- Triangle #2 -->
      <PathGeometry>
        <PathGeometry.Transform>
          <RotateTransform Angle="-15"/>
        </PathGeometry.Transform>
        <PathFigure StartPoint="20,20" IsClosed="True">
          <LineSegment Point="20,100"/>
          <LineSegment Point="100,100"/>
```

```
      </PathFigure>
    </PathGeometry>
  </GeometryGroup>
 </Path.Data>
</Path>
```

The result of this is shown in Figure 3.18. Creating such a geometry with a single `PathGeometry` and a single `PathFigure` would be difficult. Creating it with a single `PathGeometry` containing two `PathFigures` would be easier, but it would still require manually doing the math to perform the rotation. With `GeometryGroup`, however, creating it is very straightforward. The `RotateTransform` element used here is covered in Chapter 6.

FIGURE 3.18   A `GeometryGroup` with two identical triangles, except that one is rotated.

> **TIP**
>
> Because `Fill` and `Stroke` are specified on a `Path` rather a geometry, `GeometryGroup` doesn't enable you to combine shapes with different fills or outlines. To achieve this, you can use multiple `Paths` inside a `Canvas`.

Representing Geometries as Strings

Representing each segment in a geometry with a separate element is fine for simple shapes and paths, but it can get very verbose for complicated artwork. Although most people use a design tool like Expression Blend to emit XAML-based geometries rather than crafting them by hand, it makes sense to keep the resultant file size as small as reasonably possible. Therefore, Silverlight contains a type converter that supports a flexible syntax for representing just about any `PathGeometry` as a string.

For example, the `PathGeometry` representing the simple triangle displayed back in Figure 3.14:

```
<Path Stroke="Black" StrokeThickness="10" Fill="Red">
  <Path.Data>
    <PathGeometry>
      <PathFigure StartPoint="20,20" IsClosed="True">
        <LineSegment Point="20,100"/>
```

```
        <LineSegment Point="100,100"/>
      </PathFigure>
    </PathGeometry>
  </Path.Data>
</Path>
```

can be represented with the following compact syntax:

```
<Path Stroke="Black" StrokeThickness="10" Fill="Red"
  Data="M 20,20 L 20,100 L 100,100 Z"/>
```

Representing the overlapping triangles from Figure 3.15 requires a slightly longer string:

```
<Path Stroke="Black" StrokeThickness="10" Fill="Red"
  Data="M 20,20 L 20,100 L 100,100 Z M 70,20 L 20,100 L 100,100 Z"/>
```

These strings contain a series of commands that control properties of the PathGeometry and its PathFigures, plus commands that fill one or more PathFigures with path segments. The syntax is pretty simple, but very powerful. Table 3.1 describes all of the available commands.

TABLE 3.1   Geometry String Commands

Command	Meaning
PathGeometry and PathFigure Properties	
F n	Sets FillRule, where 0 means EvenOdd and 1 means NonZero. If you use this, it must be at the beginning of the string.
M x,y	Starts a new PathFigure and sets StartPoint to (x,y). This must be specified before using any other commands (excluding F). The M stands for *move*.
Z	Ends the PathFigure and sets IsClosed to true. You can begin another disjoint PathFigure after this with an M command, or use a different command to start a new PathFigure originating from the current point. If you don't want the PathFigure to be closed, you can emit the Z command entirely.
Path Segments	
L x,y	Creates a LineSegment to (x,y).
A rx,ry d f1 f2 x,y	Creates an ArcSegment to (x,y) based on an ellipse with radii rx and ry, rotated d degrees. The f1 and f2 flags can be 0 (false) or 1 (true) to control two of ArcSegment's properties: IsLargeArc and Clockwise, respectively.
C x1,y1 x2,y2 x,y	Creates a BezierSegment to (x,y) using control points (x1,y1) and (x2,y2). The C stands for *cubic Bézier curve*.
Q x1,y1 x,y	Creates a QuadraticBezierSegment to (x,y) using control point (x1,y1).
Additional Shortcuts	
H x	Creates a LineSegment to (x,y), where y is taken from the current point. The H stands for *horizontal line*.

TABLE 3.1   (Continued)

Command	Meaning
V y	Creates a LineSegment to (x,y), where x is taken from the current point. The V stands for *vertical line*.
S x2,y2 x,y	Creates a BezierSegment to (x,y) using control points (x1,y1) and (x2,y2), where x1 and y1 are automatically calculated to guarantee smoothness. (This point is either the second control point of the previous segment or the current point if the previous segment is not a BezierSegment.) The S stands for *smooth cubic Bézier curve*.
Lowercase commands	Any command can be specified in lowercase to make its relevant parameters be interpreted as *relative* to the current point rather than absolute coordinates. This doesn't change the meaning of the F, M, and Z commands, but it can still be done.

This string syntax can be used wherever a geometry is expected. For example, the Ellipse clipped with a RectangleGeometry from Figure 3.10 could be written much more compactly as follows:

```
<Ellipse Width="300" Height="100" Fill="Blue" Stroke="Black" StrokeThickness="10"
  Clip="M 30,0 l 240,0 l 0,100 L 30,100"/>
```

DIGGING DEEPER

Spaces and Commas in Geometry Strings

The spaces between commands and parameters are optional, and all commas are optional. But you must have at least one space or comma between parameters. Therefore, the string M 20,20 L 20,100 L 100,100 Z is equivalent to the much more confusing M20 20L20 100L100 100Z.

Strokes

The previous shapes and lines have used Stroke and StrokeThickness to customize their borders, but there are seven more Stroke-related properties for achieving a variety of effects:

▸ **StrokeStartLineCap** and **StrokeEndLineCap**—Customizes any open segment endpoints with one of four values: Flat (the default), Square, Round, or Triangle.

▸ **StrokeLineJoin**—Customizes corners (endpoints that join two segments) with one of three values: Miter (the default), Round, or Bevel. A separate **StrokeMiterLimit** property can be used to limit how far a Miter join extends, which can otherwise be very large for small angles. Its default value is 10.

> **StrokeDashArray**—Can make the stroke a nonsolid line composed of dashes. The endpoints of each dash can be customized with **StrokeDashCap**, which works just like StrokeStartLineCap and StrokeEndLineCap. The pattern can be further customized by the **StrokeDashOffset** property.

Line Caps

Figure 3.19 demonstrates the various values of StrokeStartLineCap and StrokeEndLineCap applied to LineSegments.

Line Joins

Figure 3.20 demonstrates each of the StrokeLineJoin values on the corners of a triangle.

For small angles, the Miter line join can extend quite far, and choosing a proper value for StrokeMiterLimit can make a big difference on the end result. Figure 3.21 shows the difference between the following two triangles: one with a StrokeMiterLimit of 0 (which is equivalent to using a Bevel line join instead of Miter) and one with a StrokeMiterLimit of 30 (which is long enough to avoid truncating any of the corners):

```
<Polygon Fill="Red" Stroke="Black"
  StrokeThickness="10"
  StrokeMiterLimit="0"
  Points="50,50 400,50 100,70"/>
```

```
<Polygon Fill="Red" Stroke="Black"
  StrokeThickness="10"
  StrokeMiterLimit="30"
  Points="50,50 400,50 100,70"/>
```

If the angle between two segments is 0°, the Miter line join would extend infinitely if it weren't for the StrokeMiterLimit. Instead, it extends as many pixels as the StrokeMiterLimit value, which is 10 by default. This is why the two of the Polygons back in Figure 3.5 explicitly set StrokeMiterLimit to 0.

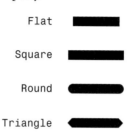

Flat

Square

Round

Triangle

FIGURE 3.19   Each type of line cap on both ends of a LineSegment.

FAQ

? What's the difference between the Flat and Square values used by the various line cap and dash cap properties?

A Flat line cap ends exactly on the endpoint, whereas a Square line cap extends beyond the endpoint. Similar to the Round line cap, you can imagine a square with the same dimensions as the StrokeThickness centered on the endpoint. Therefore, the line ends up extending *half* the length of the StrokeThickness.

Miter   Round   Bevel

FIGURE 3.20   Each type of StrokeLineJoin applied to the familiar triangle.

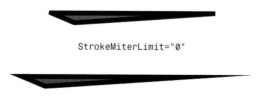

StrokeMiterLimit="0"

StrokeMiterLimit="30"

FIGURE 3.21   Varying the StrokeMiterLimit to achieve different effects.

Otherwise, some corners would have extended 10 pixels past the specified coordinates, leading to a confusing result. Figure 3.22 demonstrates this difference with the two-point Polygon from Figure 3.5:

```
<Polygon Stroke="Black" StrokeThickness="10" StrokeMiterLimit="0"
  Points="50,50 100,100"/>
```

```
<Polygon Stroke="Black" StrokeThickness="10"
  Points="50,50 100,100"/>
```

Because the Polygon implicitly closes the shape with a final point from (100,100) back to (50,50), both endpoints of the resulting line are actually corners. Therefore, with a StrokeMiterLimit of 10, the line becomes 20 pixels longer.

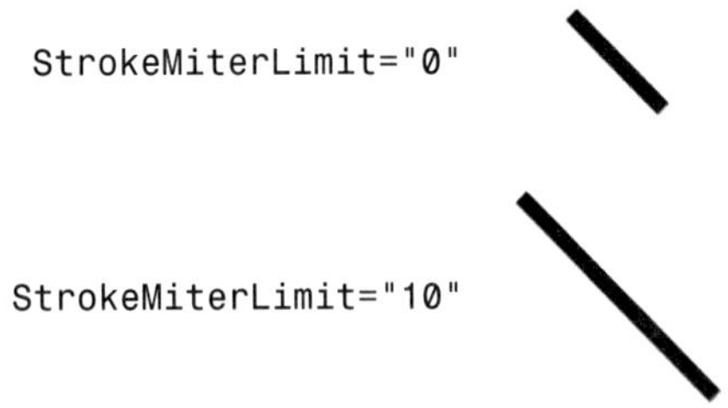

StrokeMiterLimit="0"

StrokeMiterLimit="10"

FIGURE 3.22   Changing the StrokeMiterLimit changes the length of the two-point Polygon.

Dashes

The StrokeDashArray property can contain a list of numbers representing a repeating pattern of dashes and the spaces between them. The values at odd positions in the list represent the widths of dashes (before being scaled by StrokeThickness) and the values at even positions in the list represent the widths of spaces. Whatever pattern you choose is then repeated indefinitely. The value of StrokeDashOffset (0 by default) controls where the pattern begins.

> **TIP**
>
> If you use a StrokeDashCap other than the default Flat, the cap itself adds width to the dash lengths chosen in StrokeDashArray. Therefore, to make a dash nothing but the cap, choose a dash length of 0, as done by the last triangle in Figure 3.23.

Figure 3.23 demonstrates a few common dash values. For example, the first triangle was created as follows:

```
<Path Stroke="Black" StrokeThickness="10" Fill="Red" StrokeDashArray="2,2">
  <Path.Data>
    <PathGeometry>
      <PathFigure StartPoint="20,20" IsClosed="True">
        <LineSegment Point="20,100"/>
        <LineSegment Point="100,100"/>
      </PathFigure>
    </PathGeometry>
  </Path.Data>
</Path>
```

The array of values in StrokeDashArray can be expressed as a comma and/or space-delimited list in XAML.

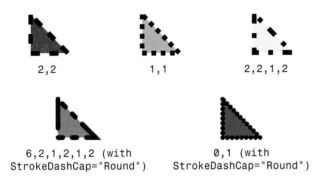

FIGURE 3.23   A few different values for `StrokeDashArray`.

Conclusion

In this chapter, you not only learned the details for drawing just about any shape, line, or curve, but also got a sense for working with a variety of Silverlight elements with XAML. And if you don't want to work with raw XAML, the elements and their properties map very naturally to what you would see in a visual design tool such as Expression Blend. Although you might need to do a lot of drawing of primitive shapes to construct reasonable-looking artwork, you can at least do so without a single line of procedural code. Indeed, this chapter does not have a single line of JavaScript in it!

CHAPTER 4

Text

IN THIS CHAPTER

- Customizing Text Display
- Creating Rich Text Content
- Using Custom Fonts

Silverlight 1.0 contains two elements for displaying text (and no elements for editing text). The element that is almost always used to display text is called `TextBlock`, which has a property called `Text` that can be set to whatever you want to display. (The other element, `Glyphs`, is for advanced scenarios covered later in this chapter.) For example, the following `TextBlock` is rendered in Figure 4.1:

```
<TextBlock Text="Text in a TextBlock"/>
```

Text in a TextBlock

FIGURE 4.1 A `TextBlock` containing simple text.

You could alternatively express the preceding `TextBlock` as follows and get the same result:

```
<TextBlock>Text in a TextBlock</TextBlock>
```

This `TextBlock` element might not seem very exciting, but it contains some hidden power that casual users of Silverlight probably aren't aware of. This chapter first examines several straightforward properties `TextBlock` provides for customizing text display; then it looks at placing richer content inside a `TextBlock`, and it ends by discussing options for using custom fonts.

Customizing Text Display

TextBlock contains a number of simple properties for modifying its appearance or retrieving information about its dimensions (in addition to the standard UI element properties such as Width, Height, Cursor, and more). This section first looks at the properties related to the font, and then at the font-independent properties.

Basic Font Properties

The basic font properties exposed by TextBlock are FontFamily, FontSize, FontStyle, FontWeight, and FontStretch.

FontFamily

As in CSS, FontFamily can be set to a single font family name or a comma-delimited list of names. (In the case of a list, font families further down the list are used as a fallback in case the previous font families could not be used.)

TextBlock's default FontFamily is equivalent to the value Lucida Sans Unicode, Lucida Grande. Lucida Sans Unicode is included with Windows, and Lucida Grande is an almost-identical font included with Mac OS X. If you count these two Lucida families as one, Silverlight supports nine font families, pictured in Figure 4.2.

> **FAQ**
>
> **? How can I provide text input or editing functionality within my Silverlight content?**
>
> If you need a full-featured text box, by far the best thing to do is to use an HTML INPUT element and position it wherever desired over windowless Silverlight content. Although you can construct a simple text box control using the techniques in Chapter 7, "Responding to Input Events," it's impossible to get the full functionality of the HTML INPUT element purely with Silverlight 1.0–based code. However, if you care more about customizing the look of a text box (potentially with animations and transforms) than about its features (even basic things like selecting text with a mouse pointer), you might want to consider simulating a text box with Silverlight.

Arial

Arial Black

Comic Sans MS

Courier New

Georgia

Lucida Sans Unicode, Lucida Grande

Times New Roman

Trebuchet MS

Verdana

FIGURE 4.2   The nine distinct font families supported by Silverlight.

The good news is that text using these font families is guaranteed to render correctly on any platform that Silverlight content can be viewed. The bad news is that *only* these font families can be used (without additional work described in the "Using Custom Fonts" section).

FontSize

The FontSize value, unlike all other measurements in Silverlight, is expressed in terms of points rather than pixels. Points are the standard way to express font sizes, and their size is supposed to be independent of DPI (dots per inch). At 96 DPI, a point equates to 1 ⅓ pixels. The default value of FontSize is 11 points (14 ⅔ pixels at 96 DPI). Silverlight 1.0 is not DPI-aware, however, so a FontSize of 11 points is always rendered as 14 ⅔ pixels regardless of the computer's DPI setting.

> **WARNING**
>
> **Avoid using a font family not shown in Figure 4.2 unless you perform additional work described in the "Using Custom Fonts" section!**
>
> Contrary to most people's intuition, TextBlock does not enable the use of arbitrary fonts on the local computer. Therefore, if you try to give a TextBlock a font family of Calibri, it will be ignored even on Windows Vista and the TextBlock will be rendered with the default Lucida family. It makes no difference that you have the font installed! The motivation behind this behavior is to ensure that Silverlight content gets rendered consistently everywhere. It would be frustrating if the content changed based on subtle characteristics of the client computer.

FontStyle

You can think of FontStyle like a Boolean Italic property because it can only be set to two values: Normal (the default) or Italic. The font family being used must include an italic version of the font; otherwise, this setting is ignored.

FontWeight

Similar to FontStyle, you can think of FontWeight like a Boolean Bold property. Its default value is Normal, and you can set it to Bold. You can actually set it to any one of 10 values (shown in Figure 4.3), but it's rare for a font family to support more than two weights. (The built-in nine font families don't even support it.) Figure 4.3 demonstrates what happens when each of the 10 settings is applied to TextBlocks using the Courier New font family (which has now been "new" for over 50 years, by the way). Silverlight falls back to the closest match.

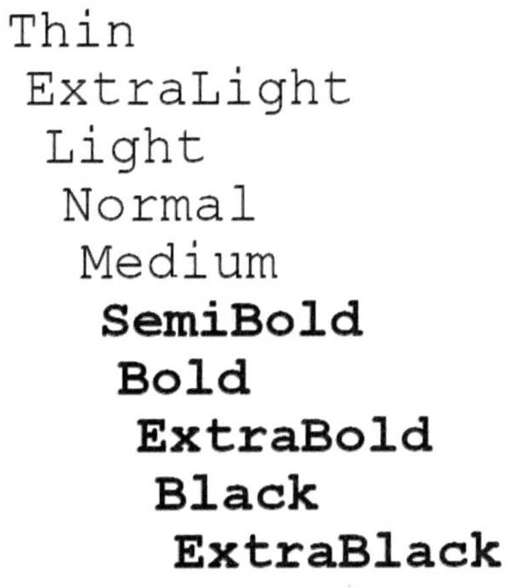

Thin
ExtraLight
Light
Normal
Medium
SemiBold
Bold
ExtraBold
Black
ExtraBlack

FIGURE 4.3   Although there are 10 values for FontWeight, these Courier New TextBlocks fall back to Normal or Bold.

> **WARNING**
>
> **The Lucida Sans Unicode font family does not support bold or italic!**
>
> It's hard to believe, but despite being the default font family for Silverlight text, the Lucida Sans Unicode family does not contain a bold font or an italic font! Therefore, the following three `TextBlocks` render exactly the same way, shown back in Figure 4.1:
>
> ```
> <TextBlock Text="Text in a TextBlock"/>
> ```
>
> ```
> <TextBlock FontWeight="Bold" Text="Text in a TextBlock"/>
> ```
>
> ```
> <TextBlock FontStyle="Italic" Text="Text in a TextBlock"/>
> ```
>
> WPF (and GDI) uses software emulation for supporting bold and italic text on fonts that don't support it natively. The next version of Silverlight might do the same thing in order to remove this surprising behavior.

FontStretch

The `FontStretch` property enables you to control the aspect ratio of a font's glyphs by setting it to one of 10 values. They are, in order from narrow to wide: `UltraCondensed`, `ExtraCondensed`, `Condensed`, `SemiCondensed`, `Normal`, `Medium`, `SemiExpanded`, `Expanded`, `ExtraExpanded`, and `UltraExpanded`.

Like `FontStyle` and `FontWeight`, the values of `FontStretch` depend on the font family supporting these variations. None of the built-in font families support a `FontStretch` other than the default value of `Normal`, so it only makes sense to use this property with custom fonts.

> **WARNING**
>
> **You cannot programmatically detect font fallback behavior!**
>
> Every basic font property other than `FontSize` might be ignored by Silverlight, depending on the characteristics of the requested font. For example, the following `TextBlock` gets rendered with a default `FontFamily` of `Lucida Sans Unicode`, `Lucida Grande` and a default `FontStyle`, `FontWeight`, and `FontStretch` of `Normal` because the font family doesn't exist:
>
> ```
> <TextBlock Text="What font am I?" FontFamily="Non-Existent Font"
>   FontStyle="Italic" FontWeight="Thin" FontStretch="UltraExpanded"/>
> ```
>
> Yet if any code retrieves the values of these properties, it would get the same values that were explicitly set: `Non-Existent Font`, `Italic`, `Thin`, and `UltraExpanded`. It has no way to tell that the fallback occurred.

Additional Customizations

TextBlock has three noteworthy properties for controlling the style and behavior of the text independent of its font: TextDecorations, Foreground, and TextWrapping.

TextDecorations

Just as FontStyle and FontWeight are fancy-sounding properties that specify italic and bold, respectively, TextDecorations is simply a property for underlining text. Its only allowed values are None (the default) and Underline. Unlike the other two properties, however, text in any font can be underlined.

Foreground

As you probably expected, although a TextBlock renders black text by default, it has a property for customizing its color. Unlike the Fill and Stroke properties of a shape, however, TextBlock has a single Foreground property. (There is no built-in way to outline text in a different color.)

TextWrapping

By default, a TextBlock is as long as it needs to be in order to fit all the text in a single line. But if you restrict the width of a TextBlock by setting its Width property, the TextWrapping property enables you to control how to deal with limited space. Unfortunately, the behavior of TextWrapping not only differs from how the same property behaves in WPF, but it has undesirable behaviors and bugs.

The default value for TextWrapping is NoWrap, which truncates the text if the TextBlock Width is too short. The truncation is never done in the middle of a letter, however, or even in the middle of a word. If a word crosses the boundary of the TextBlock, it still renders in its entirety *past* the boundary (but no more words are rendered after it).

TextWrapping can also be set to WrapWithOverflow, which continues to wrap content onto the next line if the text doesn't fit in the allocated Width. Similar to NoWrap, WrapWithOverflow never breaks up a word. If a word crosses the boundary of the TextBlock, it still renders in its entirety past the boundary, but the next word is rendered on the next line. Additional lines are rendered (and the TextBlock grows in height) as many times as it takes to fit all the text. Unlike its Width, you actually can't truncate the height of a TextBlock with an explicit Height setting.

The third TextWrapping setting—Wrap—acts like WrapWithOverflow, except it breaks up words. (If an individual letter crosses the boundary, it still renders in its entirety past the boundary.) The Wrap setting has a bug, however, that causes it to never break up the last word.

The following three TextBlocks, pictured in Figure 4.4, demonstrate these differences between the three values for TextWrapping by restricting their Width to just 10 pixels:

```
<TextBlock Text="This does not wrap."
  Foreground="Red" Width="10" TextWrapping="NoWrap"/>

<TextBlock Text="This does wrap."
  Foreground="Green" Width="10" TextWrapping="WrapWithOverflow"/>
```

```
<TextBlock Text="This does wrap."
   Foreground="Purple" Width="10" TextWrapping="Wrap"/>
```

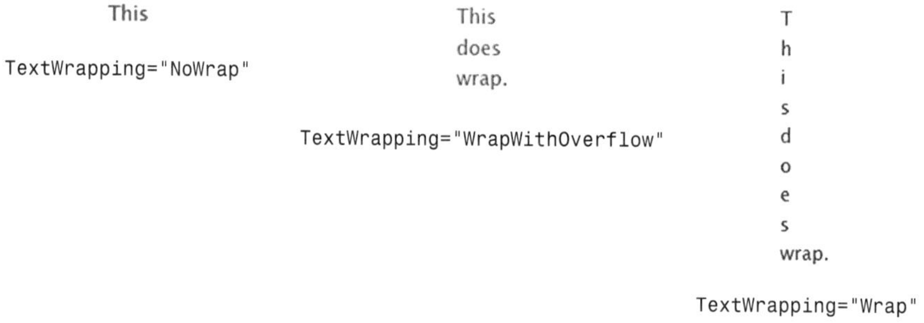

This

TextWrapping="NoWrap"

This
does
wrap.

TextWrapping="WrapWithOverflow"

T
h
i
s
d
o
e
s
wrap.

TextWrapping="Wrap"

FIGURE 4.4   Using TextWrapping to change the behavior of TextBlock.

Retrieving TextBlock Dimensions

Although you can't be certain about characteristics of the rendered font (because of fallback behavior), one thing you *can* discover is the rendered width and height of the TextBlock via its read-only ActualWidth and ActualHeight properties. Even if you explicitly set a Width and Height on the TextBlock, ActualWidth and ActualHeight can differ because they report the actual space occupied by the characters (after any wrapping). For example, short text in a wide TextBlock would report an ActualWidth shorter than Width, and text with a word that bleeds past the TextBlock boundary would report an ActualWidth longer than Width.

> **TIP**
>
> If you want to truncate text to an exact pixel boundary (mid-word or even mid-letter), you must set TextBlock's Clip property to a geometry, as described in Chapter 3, "Shapes, Lines, and Curves." For example, you can clip a TextBlock to a rectangle 100 pixels wide and 20 pixels high with a value such as "M0,0 H100 V20 H0 Z".

ActualWidth and ActualHeight can be useful if you want to position and size other elements based on the space occupied by the TextBlock. For example, although TextBlock doesn't have a property to set a background, you could create one by placing an appropriately sized Rectangle (or other shape) behind the TextBlock. This can be useful for tooltips or other textual displays.

For example, the following XAML:

```
<Canvas>
   <Rectangle Name="rectangle" Fill="Tan" Stroke="Black" RadiusX="15"
      RadiusY="15"/>
   <TextBlock Name="textBlock" Foreground="White" FontSize="40"
      Text="Some simple text."/>
</Canvas>
```

accompanied by the following code:

```
// Silverlight onLoad event handler
function onLoad(control, context, rootElement)
{
  var rectangle = rootElement.FindName("rectangle");
  var textBlock = rootElement.FindName("textBlock");

  rectangle.Width = textBlock.ActualWidth;
  rectangle.Height = textBlock.ActualHeight;
}
```

produces the result in Figure 4.5. You could create some padding by adding a small amount to the Rectangle's Width and positioning it further to the left by setting Canvas.Left.

> Some simple text.

FIGURE 4.5   Using ActualWidth and ActualHeight to give a rounded Rectangle the same size as a TextBlock, no matter what text it contains.

Creating Rich Text Content

The big secret of TextBlock is that its content property is not Text, but rather a collection of objects called Inlines. Therefore, although the following TextBlock (from the beginning of the chapter) gives the same result as setting the Text property, you're really setting a different property:

```
<!-- TextBlock.Inlines is being set here: -->
<TextBlock>Text in a TextBlock</TextBlock>
```

A type converter makes the value resemble a simple string, but it's really a collection with one element called Run. Therefore, the preceding XAML is equivalent to the following:

```
<TextBlock><Run Text="Text in a TextBlock"/></TextBlock>
```

which is also equivalent to the following XAML because Text is Run's content property:

```
<TextBlock><Run>Text in a TextBlock</Run></TextBlock>
```

Silverlight 1.0 has two objects that can be added to the Inlines collection: Run and LineBreak. Both of these can be used to create richer text inside a single TextBlock.

Run

A Run is simply a chunk of text with identical formatting. Using a single explicit Run doesn't add value, but things can start to get interesting when

DIGGING DEEPER

TextBlock and Whitespace

When a TextBlock's content is set via the Text property, any whitespace in the string is preserved. When its content is set via Inlines, however, whitespace is not preserved. Instead, leading and trailing whitespace is ignored, and any contiguous whitespace is coalesced into a single whitespace character (as in HTML).

4

you use multiple Runs in the same TextBlock. For example, the preceding TextBlock could be expressed as follows:

```
<TextBlock>
  <Run>Text</Run>
  <Run> in</Run>
  <Run> a</Run>
  <Run> TextBlock</Run>
</TextBlock>
```

This still doesn't change the rendering behavior; this TextBlock resembles the one from Figure 4.1. Run, however, has several formatting properties that can override the corresponding properties on the parent TextBlock: FontFamily, FontSize, FontStretch, FontStyle, FontWeight, Foreground, and TextDecorations. The following XAML, shown in Figure 4.6, takes advantage of these:

```
<TextBlock>
  <Run FontStyle="Italic" FontFamily="Georgia" Foreground="Red">Rich</Run>
  <Run FontSize="30" FontFamily="Comic Sans MS" Foreground="Blue"> Text </Run>
  <Run FontFamily="Arial Black" Foreground="Orange" FontSize="100">in</Run>
  <Run FontFamily="Courier New" FontWeight="Bold" Foreground="Green"> a </Run>
  <Run FontFamily="Verdana" TextDecorations="Underline">TextBlock</Run>
</TextBlock>
```

Although this is an extreme example, the same technique can be used for something simple like italicizing or underlining a single word in a paragraph. This is much easier than trying to use multiple TextBlocks and worrying about positioning each one correctly. And by using a single TextBlock, you get one consistent clipping and wrapping behavior across the heterogeneous text.

FIGURE 4.6   Several uniquely formatted Runs inside a single TextBlock.

DIGGING DEEPER

Retrieving Text When Inlines Is Set

When you add content to a TextBlock's Inlines property, the (unformatted) content is appended to its Text property. Therefore, it is still valid to programmatically retrieve the value of the Text property when only Inlines is being explicitly set. For example, the value of Text is the expected "Rich Text in a TextBlock" string for the TextBlock in Figure 4.6.

DIGGING DEEPER

Dynamically Adding Runs

You can write JavaScript that dynamically adds a Run to a TextBlock's Inlines collection by calling the collection's Add function. For example,

```
var run = control.Content.CreateFromXaml('<Run FontSize="50" Text="!"/>');
var textBlock = control.Content.FindName("textBlock");
textBlock.Inlines.Add(run);
```

LineBreak

LineBreak functions as a newline (like a <br/> tag in HTML). Simply place an empty LineBreak element between any two Runs, and the second Run will start on the following line.

Adding the following LineBreak to the TextBlock from Figure 4.6 produces the result in Figure 4.7:

```
<TextBlock>
  <Run FontStyle="Italic" FontFamily="Georgia" Foreground="Red">Rich</Run>
  <Run FontSize="30" FontFamily="Comic Sans MS" Foreground="Blue"> Text </Run>
  <Run FontFamily="Arial Black" Foreground="Orange" FontSize="100">in</Run>
  <LineBreak/>
  <Run FontFamily="Courier New" FontWeight="Bold" Foreground="Green"> a </Run>
  <Run FontFamily="Verdana" TextDecorations="Underline">TextBlock</Run>
</TextBlock>
```

FIGURE 4.7   A LineBreak between Runs forces the remaining text onto a new line.

DIGGING DEEPER

Explicit Versus Implicit Runs

Although the following TextBlock,

```
<TextBlock>Text in a TextBlock</TextBlock>
```

is equivalent to

```
<TextBlock><Run>Text in a TextBlock</Run></TextBlock>
```

Continues

DIGGING DEEPER

Continued

the behavior of the type converter is not always straightforward. For example, the following is valid:

```
<TextBlock>Text in<LineBreak/>a TextBlock</TextBlock>
```

whereas the following is not:

```
<TextBlock><Run>Text in<LineBreak/>a TextBlock</Run></TextBlock>
```

The last variation is not valid because Run's content property (Text) is a simple string, and you can't embed a LineBreak element inside a string. The content property of TextBlock (Inlines), however, is converted to one or more Runs via a type converter that specifically handles LineBreak. This type converter makes the following XAML

```
<TextBlock>Text in<LineBreak/>a TextBlock</TextBlock>
```

equivalent to the following TextBlock containing two Runs, one on either side of the LineBreak:

```
<TextBlock><Run>Text in</Run><LineBreak/><Run>a TextBlock</Run></TextBlock>
```

Using Custom Fonts

Silverlight provides two built-in ways to use custom fonts with your text. This section covers these two mechanisms, plus a third option that leverages tools such as Microsoft Expression Blend to get the job done. Custom fonts are not just desirable for achieving a custom look and feel, but they can be essential for international support. Note that although you can display characters from any language with the appropriate font, Silverlight 1.0 is limited to left-to-right text layout.

Downloading Custom Fonts

To use custom fonts with TextBlock, you need to distribute them with your Silverlight content. Fortunately, this is pretty easy. Actually, the hard part is distributing a font without breaking the law!

WARNING

Do not distribute fonts without permission!

Most fonts do not permit free distribution. If you decide to place font files on your web server, be sure that you have the legal rights to do so.

You can download a custom font using the Silverlight downloader covered in Chapter 8, "Downloading Content on Demand." Without going into too much detail here, the following code uses the downloader inside a Silverlight onLoad event handler:

```
// Silverlight onLoad event handler
function onLoad(control, context, rootElement)
{
  var downloader = control.CreateObject("downloader");
  downloader.AddEventListener("Completed", onCompleted);
  downloader.Open("GET", "wingding.ttf");
  downloader.Send();
}

function onCompleted(sender, eventArgs)
{
  var textBlock = sender.FindName("textBlock");

  // Add the downloaded font to the TextBlock's collection of possible fonts.
  // (sender is the downloader object)
  textBlock.SetFontSource(sender);

  // Be sure to use the "friendly name" of the font, not the filename!
  textBlock.FontFamily = "Wingdings";
}
```

If the font file for Wingdings exists in the same directory on the web server, it gets downloaded thanks to the code inside onLoad. The downloader's Open function can be used to retrieve any .ttf file containing a TrueType or OpenType font, or even a .zip file containing one or more .ttf files.

TIP

To reduce the size of downloads, compress your font into a .zip file and point the downloader to that instead of the .ttf file. To reduce the number of downloads, compress multiple fonts into the same .zip file and do a single download of the .zip file rather than separate downloads for each .ttf file. The rest of the code can look identical, no matter which approach you take. (In the case of multiple fonts inside a .zip file, calling SetFontSource automatically adds *every* font to the collection of possible fonts.)

Silverlight also supports .odttf files, font subsets used by the Microsoft XML Paper Specification (XPS) and Microsoft Office. Using such files can significantly reduce the size of otherwise-large font files, whether compressed or not.

When the download finishes, the onCompleted handler retrieves a TextBlock on which to apply the font. This code assumes that a TextBlock exists with the name textBlock, which could be defined as follows in XAML:

```
<TextBlock Name="textBlock" Text="Custom Font"/>
```

The critical part is the call to SetFontSource, which adds the font to the list of valid fonts for the TextBlock. To make this work, simply pass the downloader object as a parameter. SetFontSource can be called as many times as you want, in case you want to initiate multiple downloads.

The final step is to set `FontFamily` to the friendly name of the downloaded font (Wingdings in this case). Figure 4.8 demonstrates what this `TextBlock` looks like before and after the custom font is applied.

Custom Font

Default font   With the Wingdings font

FIGURE 4.8   Downloading and applying a custom font such as Wingdings to turn normal text into a not-so-secret code.

Using the `Glyphs` Element

`Glyphs`, the other element besides `TextBlock` that can display text, is a lower-level mechanism for displaying glyphs (representations of characters in a particular font). `Glyphs` has a number of properties for controlling its display, but the following XAML demonstrates a straightforward use of `Glyphs` to take advantage of custom fonts, displayed in Figure 4.9:

```
<Canvas xmlns="http://schemas.microsoft.com/client/2007">
  <Glyphs FontUri="segoepr.ttf"  Fill="Red"
    FontRenderingEmSize="70" OriginY="70"  UnicodeString="Segoe Print"/>
  <Glyphs FontUri="stencil.ttf"  Fill="Green"
    FontRenderingEmSize="70" OriginY="150" UnicodeString="Stencil"/>
  <Glyphs FontUri="brlnsr.ttf"    Fill="Blue"
    FontRenderingEmSize="70" OriginY="230" UnicodeString="Berlin Sans FB"/>
  <Glyphs FontUri="arialuni.ttf" Fill="Purple"
    FontRenderingEmSize="70" OriginY="310" UnicodeString="도사급 해커"/>
</Canvas>
```

With `Glyphs`, you don't need to explicitly download a `.ttf` file; you simply refer to its path and filename on the web server in the value of the `FontUri` property. As with a shape, `Glyphs` has a `Fill` (but it has no `Stroke`). Rather than a `FontSize` property, `Glyphs` has a `FontRenderingEmSize` property, but it acts the same way.

The `Glyphs` element can be positioned with its `OriginX` and `OriginY` properties; however, note that these refer to the

Segoe Print

STENCIL

Berlin Sans FB

도사급 해커

FIGURE 4.9   Using `Glyphs` to display text with custom fonts.

bottom-left corner of the first glyph. Although the easiest way to set the text rendered by `Glyphs` is by setting its `UnicodeString` property, you can use its numeric `Indices` property instead to represent characters beyond the Unicode Basic Multilingual Plane.

DIGGING DEEPER

FontRenderingEmSize

Because `Glyphs` is meant to be an advanced low-level element, its member names tend to be more specific (and verbose) than the members on other elements. A great example of this is the property named `FontRenderingEmSize`, contrasted with `TextBlock`'s `FontSize`.

There are good reasons for this specificity, however. In the future, `Glyphs` might also implement a `FontHintingEmSize` property that enables fonts to adjust their shape based on the size the font appears to the human eye. (For example, a font could thicken some of its strokes at small sizes or even add more strokes at large sizes.) This size can differ from the normal pixel-based size (`FontRenderingEmSize`) due to factors such as the current screen resolution.

DIGGING DEEPER

Glyphs and Locally Installed Fonts

Unlike the use of the downloader with `TextBlock`, the URI specified as the `Glyphs` element's `FontUri` property can refer to the local file system *if the HTML document is also sitting on the local computer* (as with this book's sample code if you download it locally). For example, Silverlight content sitting in the file system can leverage a locally installed "Stencil" font by specifying a `FontUri` as follows:

```
<Glyphs FontUri="file://c:/Windows/Fonts/stencil.ttf" Fill="Green"
 FontRenderingEmSize="70" OriginY="150" UnicodeString="Stencil"/>
```

or,

```
<Glyphs FontUri="/Windows/Fonts/stencil.ttf" Fill="Green"
 FontRenderingEmSize="70" OriginY="150" UnicodeString="Stencil"/>
```

(URIs in Silverlight must always use forward slashes rather than backslashes. Also, relative URIs are always relative to the host HTML document no matter where the XAML file resides.)

You should avoid `FontUris` such as these, however, because they refer to a path or file that is not under your control. `Glyphs` does not use any fallback behavior; if the specified font file does not exist, an error is raised. The preceding `Glyphs` examples would therefore fail on all non-Windows computers and any Windows computers that don't have the font (or have fonts installed on a different drive).

4

Converting Text into a Path

If all else fails, you can use a tool such as Expression Blend to turn any text into a Path. You can embed the resultant Path in your user interface and get an equivalent-looking result. By doing so, you lose the ability to easily change the text, but you remove the requirement of needing the font file. This is much like taking a screenshot of text and embedding it as an image, except that it's kept in vector form for flawless scaling.

> **WARNING**
>
> **Glyphs elements are invisible by default!**
>
> Unlike a TextBlock, whose default color is black, the default Fill for Glyphs is null! You must explicitly set the Fill for it to be visible.

To convert text to a single Path in Expression Blend, simply select a TextBlock and then select the **Object, Path, Convert to Path** menu item. This is shown in Figure 4.10.

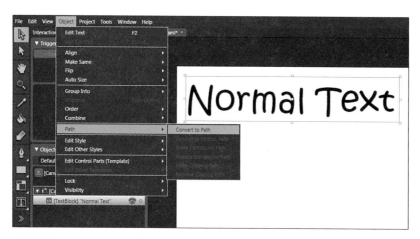

FIGURE 4.10   Converting a TextBlock to a Path in Microsoft Expression Blend.

To convert the Path into multiple Paths (one or more per character), select the **Object, Path, Release Compound Path** menu item.

Conclusion

TextBlock's properties enable you to tweak the display of text in ways that you'd expect any decent word processor to support (color, size, bold, italic, underline, and so on). In addition to these properties, the Run and LineBreak elements are a convenient way to add a bit more richness to a TextBlock's content. And because of Silverlight's refusal to use locally installed fonts in a TextBlock (which is often frustrating but appropriate for cross-platform consistency), the three techniques for using custom fonts often come in handy for constructing professional-looking content.

Silverlight's text support can feel a bit limiting, but it covers just about all the basics for displaying simple labels in your user interface. The lack of built-in scrolling makes the display of long documents unnatural; the lack of built-in editing capabilities makes the act of collecting text input a burden; and the restriction to left-to-right text layout makes the handling of certain languages extremely difficult. Fortunately, as with other Silverlight features, you can avoid such limitations by using HTML elements instead, positioned seamlessly on top of windowless Silverlight content as shown in Chapter 1, "Getting Started."

4

CHAPTER 5

Brushes and Images

Throughout the previous chapters, properties such as Foreground, Fill, and Stroke have been set to names of colors (Red, Orange, and so on). You probably guessed that they can also be set to colors with raw RGB values (such as #F1C2D9). However, these properties can be set to much more than just colors. They can be set to any instance of a brush object, which is a surprisingly powerful feature. It's so powerful that an entire chapter of this book is devoted almost exclusively to the topic of Silverlight brushes.

The fact that the Foreground, Fill, and Stroke properties can (and must) be set to an instance of a brush is often overlooked because of the simple syntax often seen for setting these properties to a solid color:

```
<Ellipse Width="300" Height="100" Fill="Red"/>
```

As explained in Chapter 2, "XAML," this shortcut syntax is enabled by a type converter, hiding what is really going on:

```
<Ellipse Width="300" Height="100">
  <Ellipse.Fill>
    <SolidColorBrush Color="Red"/>
  </Ellipse.Fill>
</Ellipse>
```

With this more explicit syntax, you can see the brush object and imagine how alternate brushes can be swapped in.

Silverlight contains three *color brushes*:

- SolidColorBrush

- LinearGradientBrush

- RadialGradientBrush

and two *media brushes*:

▷ ImageBrush

▷ VideoBrush

As these names indicate, anything that you can fill or outline with a solid color, you can fill or outline with a gradient, image, or live video! This chapter digs into the details of each of these five brushes, and then shows another interesting use for brushes—opacity masks. It also looks at Silverlight's Image element, which behaves much like ImageBrush but is a UI element, so it can be used in a standalone fashion.

SolidColorBrush

SolidColorBrush, used implicitly throughout this book, fills the target area with a single color. It has a simple Color property that accepts values like Blue or #FFFFFF. Its default value is Transparent.

Although it is the most basic brush in Silverlight, even the humble SolidColorBrush supports more functionality than you might expect. It natively supports two color spaces:

▷ **sRGB**—The standard RGB color space designed for CRT monitors and familiar to most programmers and web designers. The values for red, green, and blue are each represented as a byte, so there are only 256 possible values for each (ignoring the alpha channel for varying opacity). Of course, the combination of 256 reds, greens, and blues gives over 16 million possible colors.

▷ **scRGB**—An enhanced RGB color space that represents red, green, and blue as floating-point values. This enables a much wider gamut (a subset of colors that can be accurately represented). Red, green, and blue values of 0.0 represent black, whereas three values of 1.0 represent white. However, scRGB allows for values outside this range, so information isn't lost if you apply transformations to Colors that temporarily push any channel outside its normal range.

You can set the Color property via several different string representations:

▷ A name, like Red, Khaki, Olive, or DodgerBlue. Silverlight supports 141 predefined color names, matching the same names used by the .NET Framework.

▷ The sRGB representation *#AARRGGBB* or *#ARGB*, where *A*, *R*, *G*, and *B* are hexadecimal values for the alpha, red, green, and blue channels, respectively. For example, opaque Red is #FFFF0000 or more simply #FF0000 (because the alpha channel is assumed to be the maximum 255, by default). In the 3 or 4 digit syntax, each hexadecimal value is duplicated to get the color value. Therefore, #1234 is the same as #112233344, and #FF00 and #F00 are both valid representations for opaque Red.

▷ The scRGB representation *sc#A R G B*, where *A*, *R*, *G*, and *B* are *decimal* values for the four channels. In this representation, opaque Red is sc#1.0 1.0 0.0 0.0 or more simply sc#1.0 0.0 0.0. Commas are also allowed between each value.

In addition to the flexibility you have with specifying the underlying Color, SolidColorBrush also has an Opacity property that enables you to vary the transparency of the chosen color. This is technically unnecessary thanks to the color's alpha channel, but Opacity is a common property defined on every brush. Therefore, all brushes in Silverlight support custom Opacity values.

LinearGradientBrush

LinearGradientBrush fills an area with a gradient defined by colors at specific points along an imaginary line segment, with linear interpolation between those points.

LinearGradientBrush contains a collection of GradientStop objects in its GradientStops content property, each of which contains a Color and an Offset. The offset is a numeric value relative to the bounding box of the area being filled, where 0 is the beginning and 1 is the end. Therefore, the following LinearGradientBrush can be applied as the Foreground of a TextBlock to create the result in Figure 5.1:

> **TIP**
>
> The background color for the Silverlight control itself, passed to Silverlight.createObject or Silverlight.createObjectEx, supports all the same string representations that SolidColorBrush supports for its Color property. It does not support any of the other Silverlight brushes, however, so you're limited to a solid color. To get a more complex background, you could give your content a root Canvas element whose Background property is set to any complex brush you'd like. (Or you could use a Rectangle with its Fill set to a complex brush.) The "Brushes as Opacity Masks" section at the end of this chapter shows an example of this.

```
<TextBlock FontWeight="Bold" FontSize="100" FontFamily="Arial" Text="Silverlight">
  <TextBlock.Foreground>
    <LinearGradientBrush>
      <GradientStop Offset="0" Color="Blue"/>
      <GradientStop Offset="1" Color="Red"/>
    </LinearGradientBrush>
  </TextBlock.Foreground>
</TextBlock>
```

By default, the gradient starts at the top-left corner of the area's bounding box and ends at the bottom-right corner. You can customize these points, however, with LinearGradientBrush's StartPoint and EndPoint properties. The values of these points are relative to the bounding box, just like the Offset in each GradientStop. Therefore, the default values for StartPoint and EndPoint are (0,0) and (1,1), respectively.

Silverlight

FIGURE 5.1   A simple blue-to-red LinearGradientBrush applied to a TextBlock.

If you want to use absolute units instead of relative ones, set LinearGradientBrush's MappingMode property to Absolute (rather than the default RelativeToBoundingBox). Note that this only applies to StartPoint and EndPoint; the Offset values in each GradientStop are always relative.

Figure 5.2 shows a few different settings of StartPoint and EndPoint on the LinearGradientBrush used in Figure 5.1 (with the default relative MappingMode). For example, the first variation was created as follows:

```
<TextBlock FontWeight="Bold" FontSize="100" FontFamily="Arial" Text="Silverlight">
  <TextBlock.Foreground>
    <LinearGradientBrush StartPoint="0,0" EndPoint="0,1">
      <GradientStop Offset="0" Color="Blue"/>
      <GradientStop Offset="1" Color="Red"/>
    </LinearGradientBrush>
  </TextBlock.Foreground>
</TextBlock>
```

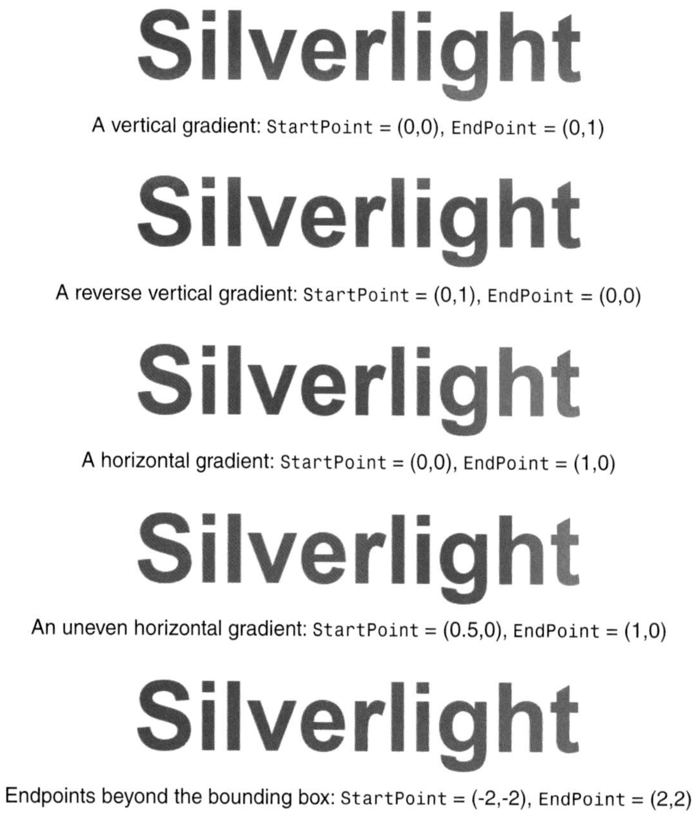

Silverlight

A vertical gradient: StartPoint = (0,0), EndPoint = (0,1)

Silverlight

A reverse vertical gradient: StartPoint = (0,1), EndPoint = (0,0)

Silverlight

A horizontal gradient: StartPoint = (0,0), EndPoint = (1,0)

Silverlight

An uneven horizontal gradient: StartPoint = (0.5,0), EndPoint = (1,0)

Silverlight

Endpoints beyond the bounding box: StartPoint = (-2,-2), EndPoint = (2,2)

FIGURE 5.2   Various settings of StartPoint and EndPoint.

Notice that the relative values are not limited to a range of 0 to 1. You can specify smaller or larger numbers to make the gradient logically extend *past* the bounding box. (This applies to GradientStop Offset values as well.)

The default interpolation of colors is done using the sRGB color space, but you can set ColorInterpolationMode to ScRgbLinearInterpolation to use the scRGB color space instead:

```
<TextBlock FontWeight="Bold" FontSize="100" FontFamily="Arial" Text="Silverlight">
  <TextBlock.Foreground>
    <LinearGradientBrush ColorInterpolationMode="ScRgbLinearInterpolation">
      <GradientStop Offset="0" Color="Blue"/>
      <GradientStop Offset="1" Color="Red"/>
    </LinearGradientBrush>
  </TextBlock.Foreground>
</TextBlock>
```

The result is a much smoother gradient, as shown in Figure 5.3.

The final property for controlling LinearGradientBrush is SpreadMethod, which determines how any leftover area not covered by the gradient should be filled. This only makes sense when the LinearGradientBrush is explicitly set to *not* cover the entire bounding box. The default value is Pad, meaning that the remaining space should be filled with the color at the endpoint. You could alternatively set it to Repeat or Reflect. Both of these values repeat the gradient in a never ending pattern, but Reflect reverses every other gradient to maintain a smooth transition. Figure 5.4 demonstrates each of these SpreadMethod values on the following LinearGradientBrush that forces the gradient to cover only the middle 2% of the bounding box:

SRgbLinearInterpolation

ScRgbLinearInterpolation

FIGURE 5.3   The ColorInterpolationMode affects the appearance of the gradient.

```
<TextBlock FontWeight="Bold" FontSize="100" FontFamily="Arial" Text="Silverlight">
  <TextBlock.Foreground>
    <LinearGradientBrush StartPoint=".49,.49" EndPoint=".51,.51"
      SpreadMethod="XXX">
      <GradientStop Offset="0" Color="Blue"/>
      <GradientStop Offset="1" Color="Red"/>
    </LinearGradientBrush>
  </TextBlock.Foreground>
</TextBlock>
```

And don't forget; because brushes can be used in many places, you can do exotic things such as outline a shape with a complicated gradient. Figure 5.5 shows the following `Ellipse` with both its `Fill` *and* `Stroke` set to a `LinearGradientBrush`:

Pad

Repeat

Reflect

FIGURE 5.4   Different values of `Spread-Method` can create vastly different effects.

```
<Ellipse Width="300" Height="100"
  StrokeThickness="10">
  <Ellipse.Fill>
    <LinearGradientBrush>
      <GradientStop Offset="0"
        Color="White"/>
      <GradientStop Offset="1"
        Color="Black"/>
    </LinearGradientBrush>
  </Ellipse.Fill>
  <Ellipse.Stroke>
    <LinearGradientBrush>
      <GradientStop Offset="0" Color="Red"/>
      <GradientStop Offset="0.2" Color="Orange"/>
      <GradientStop Offset="0.4" Color="Yellow"/>
      <GradientStop Offset="0.6" Color="Green"/>
      <GradientStop Offset="0.8" Color="Blue"/>
      <GradientStop Offset="1" Color="Purple"/>
    </LinearGradientBrush>
  </Ellipse.Stroke>
</Ellipse>
```

Notice that the second `LinearGradientBrush` uses six `GradientStops` spaced equally along the gradient path, rather than just two.

FIGURE 5.5   Outlining an `Ellipse` using a `LinearGradientBrush`.

TIP

To get crisp lines inside a gradient brush, you can simply add two `GradientStops` at the same `Offset` with different `Colors`. The following `LinearGradientBrush`, shown in Figure 5.6, does this at `Offsets` 0.4 *and* 0.6 to get two distinct lines defining the `DarkBlue` region:

```
<Ellipse Width="300" Height="300">
 <Ellipse.Fill>
   <LinearGradientBrush EndPoint="0,1">
```

Continued

```
    <GradientStop Offset="0" Color="Aqua"/>
    <GradientStop Offset="0.4" Color="Blue"/>
    <GradientStop Offset="0.4" Color="DarkBlue"/>
    <GradientStop Offset="0.6" Color="DarkBlue"/>
    <GradientStop Offset="0.6" Color="Blue"/>
    <GradientStop Offset="1" Color="Aqua"/>
  </LinearGradientBrush>
 </Ellipse.Fill>
</Ellipse>
```

FIGURE 5.6   Two crisp lines inside the gradient, enabled by duplicate `Offsets`.

RadialGradientBrush

RadialGradientBrush works like LinearGradientBrush, except that it has a single starting point with each GradientStop emanating from it in the shape of an ellipse. RadialGradientBrush has the same GradientStops, SpreadMethod, ColorInterpolationMode, and MappingMode properties that we already examined on LinearGradientBrush.

Figure 5.7 shows the following simple RadialGradientBrush applied to a Rectangle:

```
<Rectangle Width="300" Height="300">
  <Rectangle.Fill>
    <RadialGradientBrush>
      <GradientStop Offset="0" Color="Blue"/>
      <GradientStop Offset="1" Color="Red"/>
    </RadialGradientBrush>
  </Rectangle.Fill>
</Rectangle>
```

By default, the imaginary ellipse controlling the gradient is centered in the bounding box, with a width and height matching the width and height of the bounding box. This can clearly be seen on the preceding example by setting SpreadMethod to Repeat, as shown in Figure 5.8.

FIGURE 5.7 A simple blue-to-red RadialGradientBrush.

To customize the size and position of the imaginary ellipse, RadialGradientBrush defines Center, RadiusX, and RadiusY properties. These have default values of (0.5,0.5), 0.5, and 0.5, respectively, because they're expressed as coordinates relative to the bounding box. Because the default size of the ellipse often doesn't cover the corner of the area being filled (as in Figure 5.8), increasing the radii is a simple way to cover the area without relying on SpreadMethod.

RadialGradientBrush also has a GradientOrigin property that specifies where the gradient should originate independently of the defining ellipse. To

FIGURE 5.8 Setting SpreadMethod to Repeat clearly reveals the bounds of the ellipse.

avoid getting strange results, it should be set to a point within the defining ellipse. Its default value is (0.5,0.5), the center of the default ellipse, but Figure 5.9 shows what happens when set to a different value, such as (0,0):

```
<Rectangle Width="300" Height="300">
  <Rectangle.Fill>
    <RadialGradientBrush GradientOrigin="0,0" SpreadMethod="Repeat">
      <GradientStop Offset="0" Color="Blue"/>
      <GradientStop Offset="1" Color="Red"/>
    </RadialGradientBrush>
  </Rectangle.Fill>
</Rectangle>
```

If you set MappingMode to Absolute, the values for all four of these RadialGradientBrush-specific properties (Center, RadiusX, RadiusY, and GradientOrigin) are treated as absolute coordinates instead of relative to the bounding box.

FIGURE 5.9 Shifting the gradient's origin within the ellipse with the GradientOrigin property.

Because all `Colors` have an alpha channel, you can incorporate transparency and translucency into any gradient by changing the alpha channel on any `GradientStop`'s `Color`. The following `RadialGradientBrush` uses two blue colors with different alpha values:

```
<Rectangle Width="300" Height="300">
  <Rectangle.Fill>
    <RadialGradientBrush RadiusX="0.7" RadiusY="0.7">
      <GradientStop Offset="0" Color="#FF0000FF"/>
      <GradientStop Offset="1" Color="#220000FF"/>
    </RadialGradientBrush>
  </Rectangle.Fill>
</Rectangle>
```

Figure 5.10 shows the result of placing this Silverlight content on top of some HTML (so the transparency is apparent).

FIGURE 5.10   A `Rectangle` with translucency, accomplished by using a color with a nonopaque alpha channel.

> **TIP**
>
> If you want to see non-Silverlight content underneath transparent or translucent Silverlight content (such as the background of the HTML page), you must initialize the control with an `isWindowless` value of `true` *and* a background value of `Transparent` (or a value with an alpha channel less than 255). In addition, to make the Silverlight control float on top of other content (as in Figure 5.10), you can place the control in an HTML `DIV` element with a CSS style containing `position: absolute`.

ImageBrush and Image

With `ImageBrush`, you can paint any area with the content of an image file. Simply set its `ImageSource` property to the URL of an image. Here is how it can be applied as the `Foreground` brush for a `TextBlock`:

```
<TextBlock FontWeight="Bold" FontSize="100" FontFamily="Arial" Text="Silverlight">
  <TextBlock.Foreground>
    <ImageBrush ImageSource="Waterfall.jpg"/>
  </TextBlock.Foreground>
</TextBlock>
```

Figure 5.11 shows the `TextBlock` along with the entire image, for reference.

The `TextBlock`

The original image

FIGURE 5.11   A `TextBlock` with an `ImageBrush` `Foreground`.

By default, the image stretches or shrinks in both dimensions to fill the bounding box of the element being painted. You can control this behavior, however, with `ImageBrush`'s `Stretch` property. `Stretch` can be set to one of the following values:

▶ **None**—The image is left at its original size.

▶ **Fill** (the default value)—The image's dimensions are set to match the element's dimensions. Therefore, the image's aspect ratio is not necessarily preserved.

▶ **Uniform**—The image is scaled as large as it can be while still fitting entirely within the element's bounding box and preserving its aspect ratio. Therefore, there will be extra space in one dimension if its aspect ratio doesn't match.

▶ **UniformToFill**—The image is scaled to entirely fill the element's bounding box while preserving its aspect ratio. Therefore, the content will be cropped in one dimension if its aspect ratio doesn't match.

Figure 5.12 demonstrates the four `Stretch` values on an `ImageBrush` applied as a `Fill` to a `Rectangle` rather than a `TextBlock` (so it's easier to see the behavior).

When `Stretch` is set to a value other than `Fill`, the image is centered both horizontally and vertically if it is smaller than the bounding box. But this behavior can also be customized by setting `AlignmentX` to `Left`, `Center`, or `Right` and `AlignmentY` to `Top`, `Center`, or `Bottom`.

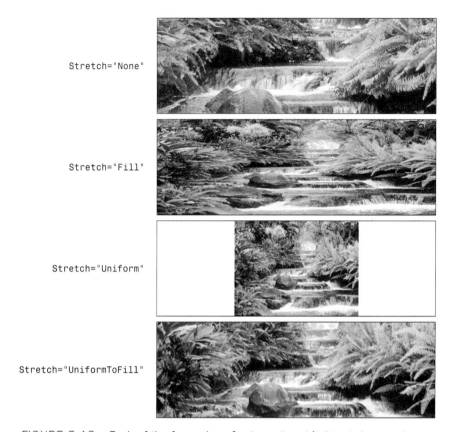

Stretch="None"

Stretch="Fill"

Stretch="Uniform"

Stretch="UniformToFill"

FIGURE 5.12   Each of the four values for ImageBrush's Stretch property.

To display an image in a simple rectangular fashion, you could fill a Rectangle with an ImageBrush. But there's an easier option, which is to use UI element called Image. Image is analogous to an HTML IMG element. In addition to the normal UI element properties such as Width, Height, Opacity, Clip, and more, Image contains a Source property that works just like ImageBrush's ImageSource. You can construct an Image in XAML as follows:

```
<Image Source="Waterfall.jpg"/>
```

This renders the entire rectangular photo, as seen in Figure 5.11, in its original size.

Image also has a Stretch property that works just like the one on ImageBrush. Whereas the default ImageBrush Stretch is Fill, the default Image Stretch is Uniform. The different values for Stretch are only relevant on Image if you explicitly set its Width and/or Height to a value other than its natural size.

> **TIP**
>
> With the existence of both `Image` and `ImageBrush`, there are multiple ways to achieve the same effect. For example, if you want to display a photo cropped as a circle, you could create an `Ellipse` and set its `Fill` to an `ImageBrush`, or you could create an `Image` and set its `Clip` property to an `EllipseGeometry`.

> **WARNING**
>
> **Silverlight 1.0 does not support GIF or BMP file formats!**
>
> It comes as a surprise to many, but you can't set the `Source` of a Silverlight `Image` (or the `ImageSource` of an `ImageBrush`) to a GIF or BMP file. You must convert them to one of the two supported formats: PNG and JPEG. Furthermore, Silverlight doesn't support every type of file that is possible to create with these formats. For example, 64bpp (bits per pixel) images are not supported.
>
> Fortunately, PNG is a great replacement for GIF. (In fact, it was *designed* to be a replacement for GIF.) It uses lossless data compression and supports a full alpha channel for achieving both transparency and translucency. The only advantage GIF has over PNG is its support for animation. JPEG, with its lossy compression and lack of transparency, is the best choice for photos. (Chances are that any photos you'd work with are already in the JPEG format. JPEG has a number of advantages for photos, such as supporting Exif data from digital cameras.)
>
> If you were hoping to use an animated GIF, no automatic approach exists for displaying it via Silverlight. The easiest solution would be to use an HTML `IMG` element positioned appropriately over windowless Silverlight content.

When an `Image` element (or an element with an `ImageBrush` applied) is rendered, the content specified by the URL is fetched asynchronously. Depending on network conditions, file size, and more, there may be a noticeable wait before the actual content is seen or a failure is reported. Similarly, you can't set the `Source` (or `ImageSource`) property in JavaScript and expect a surrounding `try/catch` block to capture an error such as a missing file or invalid file format. Instead, such errors get reported to the Silverlight control's `onError` handler.

To give you flexibility in handling these asynchronous conditions, `Image` and `ImageBrush` define two interesting events: `ImageFailed` and `DownloadProgressChanged`. `ImageFailed` can be used to handle image-specific failures in a custom fashion. `DownloadProgressChanged` can tell you when the asynchronous file download is complete. (`Image`, like all UI elements, also has a `Loaded` event, but this tells you when the XAML element has loaded rather than when its content has loaded.)

For example, when an attempt to retrieve or render an image file fails, you might want to dynamically swap the `Image` `Source` with your own error image file. The following function does just that:

```
function onImageFailed(sender, errorEventArgs)
{
  // sender is the Image instance, so you can check sender.Source to see the
  // offending URL.
  // errorEvent contains ErrorCode, ErrorMessage, and ErrorType properties,
  // as seen in Chapter 1.

  // Attempt to change the source to "error.png" unless we've already done that
  if (sender.Source != "error.png")
    sender.Source = "error.png";
}
```

This handler can be attached to an Image as follows:

```
<Image Source="Waterfall.jpg" ImageFailed="onImageFailed"/>
```

Note that the Silverlight control's default onError handler still shows its alert dialog despite the custom handler for ImageFailed. If you want to suppress the alert, you can add your own onError handler that ignores errors with an ErrorType of DownloadError (for files not found) and/or ImageError (for unsupported file formats). Of course, if you do that, you might as well perform the Source-swapping logic inside the onError handler and not even bother with ImageFailed.

The DownloadProgressChanged event provides updates as the image retrieval progresses, so you can know exactly when it has finished and is therefore ready to be rendered. This is useful if you want to wait to show other elements (perhaps a background picture frame) until the content is rendered, or for slick special effects such as fading an Image in once it is ready to appear. The handler can be implemented as follows:

```
function onProgressChanged(sender, eventArgs)
{
  // sender.DownloadProgress starts at 0 and reaches 1 when complete
  if (sender.DownloadProgress == 1)
  {
    // The content is ready!  Do something custom here.
  }
}
```

This can be attached to an Image as follows:

```
<Image Source="Waterfall.jpg" DownloadProgressChanged="onProgressChanged"/>
```

For more details about working with such events, see Chapter 7, "Responding to Input Events," and Chapter 8, "Downloading Content on Demand."

TIP

Although Image does not have ActualWidth and ActualHeight properties, its Width and Height properties are automatically set to the natural dimensions of the file if you don't set them yourself. This doesn't happen until the content has rendered, however. Therefore, to programmatically discover the dimensions of an image file, you can set an Image's Source to that file and attach a handler such as the following to its DownloadProgressChanged event:

```
function onProgressChanged(sender, eventArgs)
{
  if (sender.DownloadProgress == 1)
  {
    actualWidth = sender.FindName("MyImage").Width;
    actualHeight = sender.FindName("MyImage").Height;
  }
}
```

VideoBrush

VideoBrush works much like ImageBrush, but it enables you to paint any area with live video. Using a VideoBrush is a two-step process. You must first create a MediaElement that points to the video source (such as a .wmv file) and give it a name. (MediaElement is covered in Chapter 10, "Audio and Video.") Then you can set VideoBrush's SourceName property to the name of the MediaElement. This approach was taken in the "Great Estates" logo from Chapter 1, "Getting Started." The following XAML also demonstrates this technique, producing the result in Figure 5.13:

```
<Canvas xmlns="http://schemas.microsoft.com/client/2007">
  <MediaElement Name="video" Source="Lake.wmv" Opacity="0" IsMuted="true"/>
  <TextBlock FontWeight="Bold" FontSize="100" FontFamily="Arial"
    Text="Silverlight">
    <TextBlock.Foreground>
      <VideoBrush SourceName="video"/>
    </TextBlock.Foreground>
  </TextBlock>
</Canvas>
```

FIGURE 5.13   A TextBlock with a VideoBrush Foreground.

(You'll have to imagine that the content is live video, or simply run the example in the source code accompanying this book.)

Because this example involves two elements, they must be placed in a Canvas. MediaElement can render the video on its own, but we don't want the MediaElement to be seen in this case. Instead, we only want the video to appear within the characters in the TextBlock. Therefore, the Opacity of the MediaElement is set to 0. Figure 5.14 shows what happens if you omit the Opacity setting, leaving it at its default value of 1.

FIGURE 5.14   A TextBlock with a VideoBrush Foreground in front of a visible MediaElement containing the video.

Although setting Visibility to Collapsed is generally preferred over setting Opacity to 0, Visibility does not accomplish the desired effect in this case. If the MediaElement's Visibility is set to Collapsed, it still doesn't render in the background, but it also doesn't render inside the VideoBrush!

The relationship between VideoBrush and MediaElement is similar to the relationship between ImageBrush and Image. The first element of each pair is a brush, and the second element of each pair is a UI element. In both cases, filling a shape with the brush could also be accomplished by clipping the UI element with a corresponding geometry. The main difference between the relationships is

DIGGING DEEPER

URLs Used With ImageBrush, Image, and VideoBrush

As with the Glyphs element from the preceding chapter, the URL used with elements in this chapter can point to a local file (via explicit use of the file:// protocol or via a relative path), but only if the host HTML document is also loaded from the local file system. And whether the URL points to the local file system or a web server, only forward slashes can be used. It's also important to remember that no matter whether a URL is specified in XAML or JavaScript, relative URLs are always treated as relative to the host HTML document. Note that Silverlight allows URLs for image and media files to point to any domain, not just the domain serving the host HTML document.

simply that both `ImageBrush` and `Image` can be given the URL directly, whereas `VideoBrush` cannot accept a URL. Because it is linked to a `MediaElement`, the video inside `VideoBrush` can be paused, stopped, and more via members on `MediaElement` covered in Chapter 10. Note that multiple `VideoBrushes` can be linked to the same `MediaElement`.

`VideoBrush` supports the `Stretch`, `AlignmentX`, and `AlignmentY` properties like `ImageBrush`.

Brushes as Opacity Masks

All UI elements have an `Opacity` property that affects the entire object evenly, but they also have an `OpacityMask` that can be used to apply custom opacity effects. `OpacityMask` can be set to any brush, and that brush's alpha channel is used to determine which parts of the object should be opaque, which parts should be transparent, and which parts should be somewhere in-between.

The alpha channel used by `OpacityMask` can come from the colors in a color brush or from images in an `ImageBrush` (PNG transparency). The following example uses three `LinearGradientBrushes`—one as the `Canvas` Background, one as the `TextBlock` Foreground, and then another as an `OpacityMask` for the `TextBlock`:

```
<Canvas xmlns="http://schemas.microsoft.com/client/2007" Width="490" Height="130">

  <Canvas.Background>
    <LinearGradientBrush StartPoint="0,0" EndPoint="0,1">
      <GradientStop Offset="0" Color="Yellow"/>
      <GradientStop Offset="1" Color="Orange"/>
    </LinearGradientBrush>
  </Canvas.Background>

  <TextBlock FontWeight="Bold" FontSize="100" FontFamily="Arial"
    Text="Silverlight">

    <TextBlock.Foreground>
      <LinearGradientBrush StartPoint="0,0" EndPoint="0,1">
        <GradientStop Offset="0" Color="Black"/>
        <GradientStop Offset="1" Color="Red"/>
      </LinearGradientBrush>
    </TextBlock.Foreground>

    <TextBlock.OpacityMask>
      <LinearGradientBrush StartPoint=".49,.49" EndPoint=".51,.51"
        SpreadMethod="Reflect">
        <GradientStop Offset="0" Color="Blue"/>
        <GradientStop Offset="1" Color="Transparent"/>
      </LinearGradientBrush>
    </TextBlock.OpacityMask>

  </TextBlock>
</Canvas>
```

The result is shown in Figure 5.15.

The `LinearGradientBrush` used for the
`OpacityMask` defines a repetitive gradient between blue and transparent, but
the blue color is immaterial. All that
matters is that it's a gradient that repeatedly varies between a completely opaque
color and a completely transparent
color.

FIGURE 5.15   A `TextBlock` with a striped
`OpacityMask`, courtesy of a
`LinearGradientBrush`.

Conclusion

You've now seen how to unlock the hidden power in Silverlight brushes and inject slick
designs or rich media into places where solid colors just won't do. This chapter contains a
number of effects that are pretty garish simply to demonstrate the functionality. But a
graphic designer (or a developer with taste) can find a number of subtle ways these
features can be used to enhance (rather than detract from) a user interface.

With shapes, lines, curves, text, brushes, and images under your belt, there are only two
topics left to master in order to know everything about arranging static user interfaces.
These topics are positioning elements and transforming elements, the subject of the next
chapter.

CHAPTER 6

Positioning and Transforming Elements

Any useful Silverlight content or application is bound to need more than a single UI element. Canvas is the only UI element in Silverlight 1.0 that can contain child UI elements (other than the special-purpose InkPresenter described in Chapter 7, "Responding to Input Events"), so it is almost always used as the root element. Canvas not only contains UI element children, but also enables you to position them. Canvas has already been used a few times in this book (whenever an example needs more than one UI element), but this chapter examines everything you can do with it.

The bulk of this chapter, however, focuses on a much more exotic set of features for transforming elements. Transforms (such as rotation or scaling) are not only useful for static user interfaces, but also are a common target for animations (covered in Chapter 9, "Animation"). Transforms make it easy to accomplish effects that are simply impossible with plain HTML and CSS.

All About Canvas

If you're used to a system with sophisticated layout panels (such as WPF or Windows Forms), Canvas will seem very primitive. It *is* primitive, but it provides enough core functionality to accomplish just about anything with a little bit of work. This section examines Canvas in depth, demonstrating how to do the following:

▶ Position elements

▶ Place elements behind or in front of others

▶ Control Canvas size and clipping

▶ Work with multiple Canvas elements

Positioning Elements

The `Canvas` element can contain any number of other elements in its content property called `Children`. You can position the child elements in a `Canvas` using its `Canvas.Left` and `Canvas.Top` attached properties. For example, the following XAML produces the result in Figure 6.1:

```
<Canvas xmlns="http://schemas.microsoft.com/client/2007">
  <Rectangle Canvas.Left="0" Canvas.Top="0" Fill="Red" Width="100" Height="100"/>
  <Rectangle Canvas.Left="20" Canvas.Top="20" Fill="Orange" Width="100"
    Height="100"/>
  <Rectangle Canvas.Left="40" Canvas.Top="40" Fill="Yellow" Width="100"
    Height="100"/>
  <Rectangle Canvas.Left="60" Canvas.Top="60" Fill="Green" Width="100"
    Height="100"/>
</Canvas>
```

Omitting `Canvas.Left` or `Canvas.Top` on an element is equivalent to setting it to 0. Therefore, elements appear in the top-left corner of their parent `Canvas` by default.

FIGURE 6.1   Four overlapping `Rectangles` in a Canvas.

TIP

The `Canvas.Left` and `Canvas.Top` properties aren't just for the children of a Canvas; you can even set these properties on the root element (whether or not the root is even a Canvas). This gives the root element an offset relative to the host Silverlight control.

TIP

An easy way to achieve a drop shadow on text (or any other element) is to duplicate the element with a different color. One copy of the element represents the "real thing," whereas the other represents the shadow. For this to work, you can position the shadow element at an offset with `Canvas.Left` and `Canvas.Top`. The following XAML, rendered in Figure 6.2, performs this trick with some simple text:

```
<Canvas xmlns="http://schemas.microsoft.com/client/2007">
  <!-- The shadow element: -->
  <TextBlock Canvas.Left="2" Canvas.Top="2" Foreground="Black" FontSize="50"
    FontWeight="Bold" Text="Drop Shadow!"/>
  <!-- The main element: -->
  <TextBlock Foreground="Orange" FontSize="50" FontWeight="Bold"
```

Continued

```
    Text="Drop Shadow!"/>
</Canvas>
```

Drop Shadow!

FIGURE 6.2   A drop shadow effect created by placing a shadow element at an offset.

TIP

To center an element in Silverlight 1.0, you must programmatically update the values of `Canvas.Left` and `Canvas.Top` when the containing region is resized. Figure 6.3 demonstrates simple content in a `Canvas` that remains centered in its host document.

 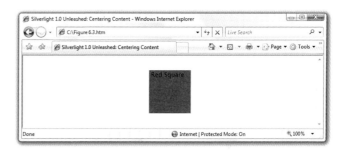

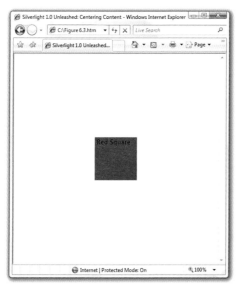

FIGURE 6.3   Content that stays centered as the web browser window resizes.

Continues

TIP

Continued

The XAML for this example is nothing special:

```
<Canvas xmlns="http://schemas.microsoft.com/client/2007" Width="100" Height="100">
  <Rectangle Canvas.Left="0" Canvas.Top="0" Fill="Red"
    Width="100" Height="100"/>
 <TextBlock Canvas.Left="5" Text="Red Square"/>
</Canvas>
```

The HTML that hosts the content includes the necessary script files and sets the body's margin to 0px so that it doesn't interfere with the centering effect:

```
<html>
  <head>
    <title>Silverlight 1.0 Unleashed: Centering Content</title>
    <script type="text/javascript" src="Silverlight.js"></script>
    <script type="text/javascript" src="CreateSilverlight.6.3.js"></script>
    <style type="text/css">body { margin: 0px }</style>
  </head>
  <body>
    <script type="text/javascript">createSilverlight();</script>
  </body>
</html>
```

The "magic" is in the `CreateSilverlight.6.3.js` file, shown in Listing 6.1.

LISTING 6.1   CreateSilverlight.6.3.js—JavaScript Code Enabling the Centering in
            Figure 6.3

```
function createSilverlight()
{
  Silverlight.createObjectEx(
    {
      source: "Figure 6.3.xaml",
      parentElement: document.body,
      id: "silverlightControl",
      properties:
        { width: "100%", height: "100%", version: "1.0" },
      events: { onLoad: onLoad }
    }
  );
}
// Silverlight onLoad event handler
function onLoad(control, context, rootElement)
{
 control.Content.OnResize = onResize;
 // Force the resize call to ensure the content starts out centered
```

Continued

```
 onResize(rootElement);
}
// Silverlight OnResize event handler
function onResize(sender)
{
  var content = sender.GetHost().Content;
  content.Root["Canvas.Left"] = (content.ActualWidth - content.Root.Width) / 2;
  content.Root["Canvas.Top"] = (content.ActualHeight - content.Root.Height) / 2;
}
```

The Silverlight control is given a width and height of 100% so that the content is not only centered within the control's bounds, but centered in the page as well. An onLoad event handler is used to attach an event handler to OnResize and force a one-time resize so that the initial position is correct. Inside onResize, the values for Canvas.Left and Canvas.Top are calculated and set on the root Canvas instance using the JavaScript syntax for setting attached properties.

Placing Elements Behind or in Front of Others

The default Z order (defining which elements are "on top of" other elements) is determined by the order in which the children are added to the Canvas. Elements added later are placed on top of elements added earlier. This is why the green Rectangle is on top of the stack in Figure 6.1, and also why the shadow element is listed *first* to get the result in Figure 6.2.

You can customize the Z order of any child element by marking it with the Canvas.ZIndex attached property. Canvas.ZIndex is an integer with a default value of 0 that you can set to any number (positive or negative). Elements with larger values are rendered on top of elements with smaller values, so the element with the smallest value is in the back and the element with the largest value is in the front. The following example, pictured in Figure 6.4, reverses the Z order on the Rectangles from Figure 6.1:

```
<Canvas xmlns="http://schemas.microsoft.com/client/2007">
  <Rectangle Canvas.ZIndex="3" Canvas.Left="0" Canvas.Top="0" Fill="Red"
    Width="100" Height="100"/>
  <Rectangle Canvas.ZIndex="2" Canvas.Left="20" Canvas.Top="20" Fill="Orange"
    Width="100" Height="100"/>
  <Rectangle Canvas.ZIndex="1" Canvas.Left="40" Canvas.Top="40" Fill="Yellow"
    Width="100" Height="100"/>
  <Rectangle Canvas.ZIndex="0"
    Canvas.Left="60" Canvas.Top="60"
    Fill="Green"
    Width="100" Height="100"/>
</Canvas>
```

FIGURE 6.4   Four overlapping Rectangles in a Canvas with custom Canvas.ZIndex values.

If multiple children have the same ZIndex value, the order is determined by their order in the Children collection, as in the default case.

Therefore, programmatically manipulating Z order is as simple as adjusting the Canvas.ZIndex attached property value. The source code accompanying this book includes an example that updates the preceding XAML file as follows:

```
<Canvas xmlns="http://schemas.microsoft.com/client/2007">
  <Rectangle Canvas.ZIndex="3" Canvas.Left="0" Canvas.Top="0" Fill="Red"
    Width="100" Height="100" MouseLeftButtonDown="onClick"/>
  <Rectangle Canvas.ZIndex="2" Canvas.Left="20" Canvas.Top="20" Fill="Orange"
    Width="100" Height="100" MouseLeftButtonDown="onClick"/>
  <Rectangle Canvas.ZIndex="1" Canvas.Left="40" Canvas.Top="40" Fill="Yellow"
    Width="100" Height="100" MouseLeftButtonDown="onClick"/>
  <Rectangle Canvas.ZIndex="0" Canvas.Left="60" Canvas.Top="60" Fill="Green"
    Width="100" Height="100" MouseLeftButtonDown="onClick"/>
</Canvas>
```

and defines the following event handler in an included JavaScript file:

```
var topMostZIndex = 3;
function onClick(sender, eventArgs)
{
  topMostZIndex++;
  sender["Canvas.ZIndex"] = topMostZIndex;
}
```

This change makes each Rectangle jump to the front when you click on it. (Event handlers such as this are examined in depth in the next chapter.) Note that the maximum valid value for Canvas.ZIndex is exactly one million. Setting it to any higher value (even 1,000,001) raises an error stating that the value is out of range.

TIP

Although it has the same meaning, Canvas.ZIndex is completely independent from the CSS z-index property that can be applied to HTML elements (including the host Silverlight control). Canvas.ZIndex only controls the Z order for the elements contained by the Canvas. Therefore, to sandwich an HTML element between two Silverlight elements in terms of Z order, you would need two independent Silverlight controls and you'd need to use the CSS z-index property.

Controlling Size and Clipping

Canvas has Width and Height properties, but they usually have no relevance because the contents inside a Canvas still get rendered beyond its bounds. This can be seen by the following XAML, rendered in Figure 6.5:

```
<Canvas xmlns="http://schemas.microsoft.com/client/2007"
  Width="50" Height="50" Background="Blue">
  <Ellipse Width="200" Height="200" Fill="Red" Stroke="Black"
    StrokeThickness="5"/>
</Canvas>
```

The explicit blue Background (Canvas's property that behaves like a shape's Fill) demonstrates that the Ellipse is rendered the same way regardless of the size of its parent Canvas.

FIGURE 6.5   A large red Ellipse extends beyond the bounds of its containing blue Canvas.

WARNING

A Canvas Background won't be seen by default!

Canvas actually has a default Width and Height of 0, so be sure to set an explicit size if you set its Background property because the Background only renders within the bounds of the Canvas.

FAQ

When do the Width and Height properties on Canvas have relevance?

The three main scenarios in which the size of a Canvas matters are as follows:

 When the Canvas has a visible Background brush (as explained by the preceding warning).

When mouse event handlers are attached to the Canvas, because mouse events from the Canvas itself are only raised within its bounds. (Children outside its bounds still raise mouse events, which bubble up to the parent Canvas, as explained in Chapter 7.

When JavaScript uses the values of Width and Height for custom behavior (such as the centering code in a previous tip).

If you want to prevent the content in a Canvas from extending past its bounds, you can set its Clip property to a geometry (as seen in Chapter 3, "Shapes, Lines, and Curves"). The natural choice is a RectangleGeometry with a position of (0,0) and a Width and Height matching the Width and Height of the Canvas. Here is how to apply it to the preceding example, producing the result in Figure 6.6:

```
<Canvas xmlns="http://schemas.microsoft.com/client/2007"
  Width="50" Height="50" Background="Blue">
  <Canvas.Clip>
    <RectangleGeometry Rect="0,0,50,50"/>
```

```
    </Canvas.Clip>
    <Ellipse Width="200" Height="200" Fill="Red" Stroke="Black"
      StrokeThickness="5"/>
</Canvas>
```

Of course, you can choose a Clip that has nothing to do with the Width and Height of the Canvas. The following Canvas, shown in Figure 6.7, clips its content to twice the size of its own bounds:

FIGURE 6.6   The large red Ellipse from Figure 6.5 is now clipped by its containing blue Canvas.

```
<Canvas xmlns="http://schemas.microsoft.com/client/2007"
  Width="50" Height="50" Background="Blue">
  <Canvas.Clip>
    <RectangleGeometry Rect="0,0,100,100"/>
  </Canvas.Clip>
  <Ellipse Width="200" Height="200" Fill="Red" Stroke="Black"
    StrokeThickness="5"/>
</Canvas>
```

Previous chapters discuss clipping shapes, text, and images, but performing clipping on a Canvas is powerful because it applies to all of its children simultaneously. The following Canvas contains three children and clips itself to an EllipseGeometry:

FIGURE 6.7   The large red Ellipse from Figure 6.5 is clipped by a geometry that's larger than the containing blue Canvas.

```
<Canvas xmlns="http://schemas.microsoft.com/client/2007">
  <Canvas.Clip>
    <EllipseGeometry Center="245,145" RadiusX="240" RadiusY="145"/>
  </Canvas.Clip>
  <Image Source="TeamPhoto.jpg"/>
  <Rectangle Canvas.Top="145" Width="500" Height="200" Fill="#AAFFDDDD"
    Stroke="Black"/>
  <TextBlock Text="//////" Foreground="#99000000" FontSize="180"/>
</Canvas>
```

Figure 6.8 shows the Canvas with and without its Clip set.

Creating Maintainable User Interfaces with Multiple Canvas Elements

A Canvas can be a child of another Canvas, so you can use it not only to arrange all your elements, but also to divide elements into any number of groups. This grouping into multiple Canvas elements can be useful for a number of reasons. Because every Canvas has its own Background, Clip, Visibility, Opacity, and OpacityMask properties, you can do things such as show/hide entire chunks of user interface, give each group a distinct background, and so on. Transforms (covered in the next section) can also be applied to each Canvas and uniformly affect all of its children.

Perhaps the most important aspect of using more than one Canvas is that all Canvas.Left and Canvas.Top settings (and coordinates on shapes) are relative to the immediate parent Canvas only. Therefore, you can encapsulate little pieces of user interface (or "controls") into each Canvas and move them to different places without having to recalculate all the positions of their children.

The following Canvas contains three child Canvas elements—one at the default (0,0), one at (150,50), and one at (300,100):

The unclipped content

Clipped to an EllipseGeometry

FIGURE 6.8   Clipping a Canvas with an Image, Rectangle, and TextBlock to an EllipseGeometry makes it resemble an American football.

```
<Canvas xmlns="http://schemas.microsoft.com/client/2007">

  <Canvas>
    <Rectangle Width="120" Height="330" RadiusX="20" RadiusY="20" Fill="#FAAA"/>
    <Ellipse Canvas.Left="10" Canvas.Top="10" Width="100" Height="100"
      Fill="Red"/>
    <Ellipse Canvas.Left="10" Canvas.Top="115" Width="100" Height="100"
      Fill="Yellow"/>
    <Ellipse Canvas.Left="10" Canvas.Top="220" Width="100" Height="100"
      Fill="Green"/>
  </Canvas>

  <Canvas Canvas.Left="150" Canvas.Top="50">
    <Rectangle Width="120" Height="330" RadiusX="20" RadiusY="20" Fill="#FAAA"/>
    <Ellipse Canvas.Left="10" Canvas.Top="10" Width="100" Height="100"
      Fill="Red"/>
    <Ellipse Canvas.Left="10" Canvas.Top="115" Width="100" Height="100"
      Fill="Yellow"/>
    <Ellipse Canvas.Left="10" Canvas.Top="220" Width="100" Height="100"
      Fill="Green"/>
  </Canvas>
```

```
  <Canvas Canvas.Left="300" Canvas.Top="100">
    <Rectangle Width="120" Height="330" RadiusX="20" RadiusY="20" Fill="#FAAA"/>
    <Ellipse Canvas.Left="10" Canvas.Top="10" Width="100" Height="100"
      Fill="Red"/>
    <Ellipse Canvas.Left="10" Canvas.Top="115" Width="100" Height="100"
      Fill="Yellow"/>
    <Ellipse Canvas.Left="10" Canvas.Top="220" Width="100" Height="100"
      Fill="Green"/>
  </Canvas>

</Canvas>
```

Each child `Canvas` contains identical content—a traffic light composed of four shapes. The result is shown in Figure 6.9.

This book's source code contains a variation of this example that starts with an empty `Canvas`:

```
<Canvas xmlns="http://schemas.microsoft.com/client/2007">
</Canvas>
```

and uses a bit of JavaScript to dynamically add a traffic light every second at a random position:

```
// Silverlight onLoad event handler
function onLoad(control, context,
  rootElement)
{
  // Call addChild every second
  setInterval(addChild, 1000);
}
function addChild()
{
  var control = document.
  getElementById
  ("silverlightControl");
  // Construct the Canvas XAML with a
  // random Left and Top
  var xaml = '<Canvas Canvas.Left="' + Math.random() *
   control.Content.ActualWidth
    + '" Canvas.Top="' + Math.random() * control.Content.ActualHeight + '">'
    + '<Rectangle Width="120" Height="330" RadiusX="20" RadiusY="20"'
    + ' Fill="#FFAAAAAA"/>'
    + '<Ellipse Canvas.Left="10" Canvas.Top="10" Width="100" Height="100"'
    + ' Fill="Red"/>'
    + '<Ellipse Canvas.Left="10" Canvas.Top="115" Width="100" Height="100"'
    + ' Fill="Yellow"/>'
```

FIGURE 6.9   A "traffic light control" appearing three times on the parent Canvas.

```
    + '<Ellipse Canvas.Left="10" Canvas.Top="220" Width="100" Height="100"'
    + ' Fill="Green"/>'
    + '</Canvas>';

  // Create the Canvas instance and add it to the root Children collection
  var child = control.Content.CreateFromXaml(xaml);
  control.Content.Root.Children.Add(child);
}
```

Figure 6.10 shows the result of letting this code run for awhile.

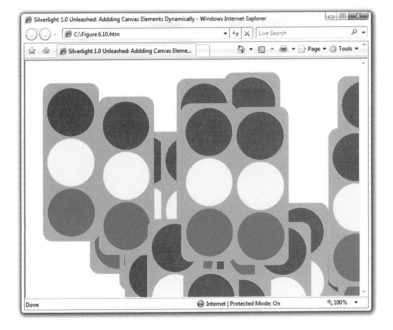

FIGURE 6.10   Adding randomly positioned children to a Canvas.

Applying Transforms

Silverlight contains a handful of 2D transform elements that enable you to change the size and position of elements independently from their Canvas.Left, Canvas.Top, Width, and Height settings. Some also enable you to alter elements in more unusual ways, such as rotating or skewing them.

All UI elements have a property called RenderTransform that can be set to an instance of any transform element. For example, you could apply a transform called RotateTransform to a Rectangle as follows:

```
<Canvas xmlns="http://schemas.microsoft.com/client/2007"
  Width="200" Height="100" Background="Yellow">
  <Rectangle Width="200" Height="100" Fill="Red">
```

```
    <Rectangle.RenderTransform>
      <RotateTransform Angle="45"/>
    </Rectangle.RenderTransform>
  </Rectangle>
</Canvas>
```

The result of this property assignment is shown in Figure 6.11. The parent Canvas has a yellow Background to make it clear where the red Rectangle would normally appear without the transform.

FIGURE 6.11   Setting a red Rectangle's RenderTransform property to an instance of RotateTransform.

The rotated Rectangle is cut off on the left side because it is being rotated beyond the bounds of the host Silverlight control.

This section looks at all five 2D transforms:

▶ RotateTransform

▶ ScaleTransform

▶ SkewTransform

▶ TranslateTransform

▶ MatrixTransform

RotateTransform

RotateTransform, demonstrated in Figure 6.11, rotates an element according to the values of three properties:

▶ **Angle**—Angle of rotation, specified in degrees (default value = 0)

▶ **CenterX**—Horizontal center of rotation (default value = 0)

▶ **CenterY**—Vertical center of rotation (default value = 0)

The default (CenterX,CenterY) point of (0,0) represents the top-left corner.

Every element that has a RenderTransform property also has a handy RenderTransformOrigin property that represents the center point of the transform (the point that remains stationary). For the RotateTransform used in Figure 6.11, the origin is the Rectangle's top-left corner, which the rest of the Rectangle pivots around.

RenderTransformOrigin can be set to any point, with (0,0) being the default value. This represents the top-left corner, as shown in Figure 6.11. An origin of (0,1) represents the bottom-left corner, (1,0) is the top-right corner, and (1,1) is the bottom-right corner. You can use negative numbers or numbers greater than 1 to set the origin to a point outside the bounds of an element, and you can use fractional values. Therefore, (0.5,0.5) represents the middle of the object. Figure 6.12 demonstrates the five most common origins used with the RenderTransform from Figure 6.11.

For example, the Rectangle rotated around its center from the final image in Figure 6.12 can be created as follows:

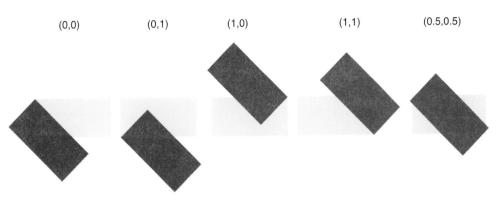

FIGURE 6.12   Five common `RenderTransformOrigins` used on the rotated `Rectangle` from Figure 6.11.

```
<Canvas xmlns="http://schemas.microsoft.com/client/2007"
  Width="200" Height="100" Canvas.Left="80" Canvas.Top="150" Background="Yellow">
  <Rectangle Width="200" Height="100" Fill="Red" RenderTransformOrigin="0.5,0.5">
    <Rectangle.RenderTransform>
      <RotateTransform Angle="45"/>
    </Rectangle.RenderTransform>
  </Rectangle>
</Canvas>
```

The root `Canvas` is given an explicit position so the rotated `Rectangle` can be completely seen even as it extends to the left and top.

FAQ

❓ Why do transforms such as `RotateTransform` have `CenterX` and `CenterY` properties when elements already have a `RenderTransformOrigin` property?

The `CenterX` and `CenterY` properties do appear to be redundant with `RenderTransformOrigin` at first. However, `CenterX` and `CenterY` are specified in pixels rather than the normalized values used by `RenderTransformOrigin`. Therefore, the top-right corner of an element with a `Width` of 20 would be specified with `CenterX` set to 0 and `CenterY` set to 20 rather than the point (0,1). Also, when multiple `RenderTransforms` are applied to the same element (described later in the chapter), `RenderTransformOrigin` applies to all of them, whereas `CenterX` and `CenterY` on individual transforms enables more fine-grained control.

That said, `RenderTransformOrigin` is generally more useful than `CenterX` and `CenterY`. For the common case of transforming an element around its middle, the relative (0.5,0.5) `RenderTransformOrigin` is easy to specify in XAML, whereas accomplishing the same thing with `CenterX` and `CenterY` would require JavaScript for elements that are dynamically sized (such as a `TextBlock`).

Note that you can use `RenderTransformOrigin` on an element simultaneously with using `CenterX` and `CenterY` on its transform. In this case, the two X values and two Y values are added together to calculate the final origin point.

ScaleTransform

ScaleTransform enlarges or shrinks an element horizontally, vertically, or in both directions. This transform has four straightforward properties:

▸ **ScaleX**—Multiplier for the element's width (default value = 1)

▸ **ScaleY**—Multiplier for the element's height (default value = 1)

▸ **CenterX**—Origin for horizontal scaling (default value = 0)

▸ **CenterY**—Origin for vertical scaling (default value = 0)

A ScaleX value of 0.5 shrinks an element's rendered width in half, whereas a ScaleX value of 2 doubles the width. The values for ScaleX and ScaleY can even be negative. Negative values flip the content in addition to potentially scaling it.

The following XAML applies ScaleTransform to a TextBlock to make it stretch three times as wide as its ActualWidth:

```
<TextBlock FontSize="20" Text="Simple Text">
  <TextBlock.RenderTransform>
    <ScaleTransform ScaleX="3"/>
  </TextBlock.RenderTransform>
</TextBlock>
```

Simple Text

Simple Text

FIGURE 6.13   A TextBlock with and without a ScaleTransform.

The result is shown in Figure 6.13.

CenterX and CenterY work the same way as with RotateTransform. The (CenterX,CenterY) point is the spot that remains stationary while the element is scaled. Figure 6.14 demonstrates how the origin point (whether specified with these properties or with RenderTransformOrigin) impacts scaling.

Note that CenterX is only relevant when ScaleX is a value other than 1, and CenterY is only relevant when ScaleY is a value other than 1.

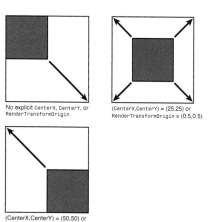

No explicit CenterX, CenterY, or
RenderTransformOrigin

(CenterX,CenterY) = (25,25) or
RenderTransformOrigin = (0.5,0.5)

(CenterX,CenterY) = (50,50) or
RenderTransformOrigin = (1,1)

FIGURE 6.14   Choosing different scaling origins when doubling the size of a 50x50 Rectangle.

FAQ

 How do transforms such as `ScaleTransform` affect properties such as `Width`, `Height`, `ActualWidth`, and `ActualHeight`?

Applying a transform to an element never changes the values of these properties. Therefore, because of transforms, these properties can "lie" about the actual size of an element on the screen. For example, the two `TextBlocks` in Figure 6.13 have the identical `ActualHeight` *and* `ActualWidth`.

Such "lies" might surprise you, but it's for the best. First, it's debatable how such values should even be expressed for some transforms. More important, the point of transforms is to alter an element's appearance without the element's knowledge. Giving elements the illusion that they are being rendered normally enables arbitrary elements to be transformed the same way without special handling.

TIP

`ScaleTransform` provides an easy way to create a user interface that resizes along with the host document. This is a nice enhancement to the technique to center content described in an earlier tip. To do this with the content from Figure 6.3, simply add a named `ScaleTransform` to the root element (with the default `ScaleX` and `ScaleY` values of 1 and 1):

```
<Canvas xmlns="http://schemas.microsoft.com/client/2007" Width="100"
  Height="100">
  <Canvas.RenderTransform>
    <ScaleTransform Name="rootScale"/>
  </Canvas.RenderTransform>
  <Rectangle Canvas.Left="0" Canvas.Top="0" Fill="Red"
    Width="100" Height="100"/>
  <TextBlock Canvas.Left="5" Text="Red Square"/>
</Canvas>
```

Then change the `OnResize` event handler to retrieve the `ScaleTransform` element, dynamically set its `ScaleX` and `ScaleY` values, and adjust the centering code to account for the scaling:

```
// Silverlight OnResize event handler
function onResize(sender)
{
  var content = sender.GetHost().Content;
  var transform = content.FindName("rootScale");

  // Maximize the scale to fit everything yet maintain the aspect ratio:
  var scale = Math.min(content.ActualWidth / content.Root.Width,
                       content.ActualHeight / content.Root.Height);
  transform.ScaleX = scale;
  transform.ScaleY = scale;
  content.Root["Canvas.Left"] =
```

Continues

6

TIP

Continued

```
    (content.ActualWidth - content.Root.Width * scale) / 2;
  content.Root["Canvas.Top"] =
    (content.ActualHeight - content.Root.Height * scale) / 2;
}
```

The result is shown in Figure 6.15. In this case, the resizing code maintains the aspect ratio and keeps all the content in bounds (like a Stretch of UniformToFill), but you could tweak the code to provide a stretching effect like Uniform or Fill instead. You can get rid of the unnecessary scrollbar in Internet Explorer by placing a CSS style containing overflow: auto directly on the HTML element.

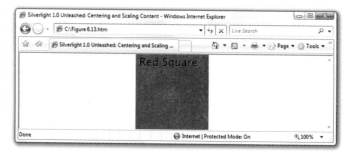
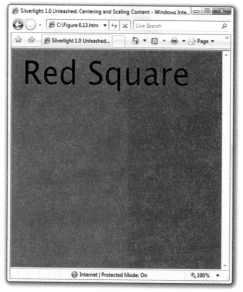

FIGURE 6.15   Content that scales and stays centered as the web browser window resizes.

TIP

`ScaleTransform` can be used to provide a "reflection" effect. The trick is to create a duplicate copy of the content, position it correctly, and then apply a `ScaleTransform` to the copy with a negative value for `ScaleY`. The following XAML, rendered in Figure 6.16, shows a very basic reflection effect:

```
<Canvas xmlns="http://schemas.microsoft.com/client/2007">
  <!-- The main image -->
  <Image Source="TeamPhoto.jpg"/>
  <!-- The reflection -->
  <Image Source="TeamPhoto.jpg"Canvas.Top="507">
    <Image.RenderTransform>
      <ScaleTransform ScaleY="-0.75"/>
    </Image.RenderTransform>
  </Image>
</Canvas>
```

The second `Image` is flipped upside down, but a value of `-0.75` is used for `ScaleY` rather than `-1` to give the reflection a little bit of perspective.

This effect isn't quite satisfactory, however, because the reflection is too crisp and clear. If you simply set `Opacity` to `0.25` on the second `Image`, the effect improves dramatically, as shown in Figure 6.17.

Better yet, you can give the second `Image` an `OpacityMask` set to a `LinearGradientBrush` that decreases the opacity as you get further away from the `Image`. The following XAML does this, and is shown in Figure 6.18:

FIGURE 6.16   A simple reflection effect.

```
<Canvas
xmlns="http://schemas.microsoft.com/client/2007">
  <!-- The main image -->
  <Image Source="TeamPhoto.jpg"/>
  <!-- The reflection -->
  <Image Source="TeamPhoto.jpg" Canvas.Top="507">
    <Image.RenderTransform>
      <ScaleTransform ScaleY="-0.75"/>
    </Image.RenderTransform>
    <Image.OpacityMask>
      <LinearGradientBrush StartPoint="0,0" EndPoint="0,1">
        <GradientStop Offset="0" Color="Transparent"/>
        <GradientStop Offset="1" Color="#44FFFFFF"/>
```

Continues

TIP

Continued

```
        </LinearGradientBrush>
      </Image.OpacityMask>
    </Image>
  </Canvas>
```

FIGURE 6.17   A more sophisticated reflection effect.

FIGURE 6.18   The final reflection effect.

SkewTransform

SkewTransform slants an element according to the values of four properties:

- ▶ **AngleX**—Amount of horizontal skew (default value = 0)

- ▶ **AngleY**—Amount of vertical skew (default value = 0)

▶ **CenterX**—Origin for horizontal skew (default value = 0)

▶ **CenterY**—Origin for vertical skew (default value = 0)

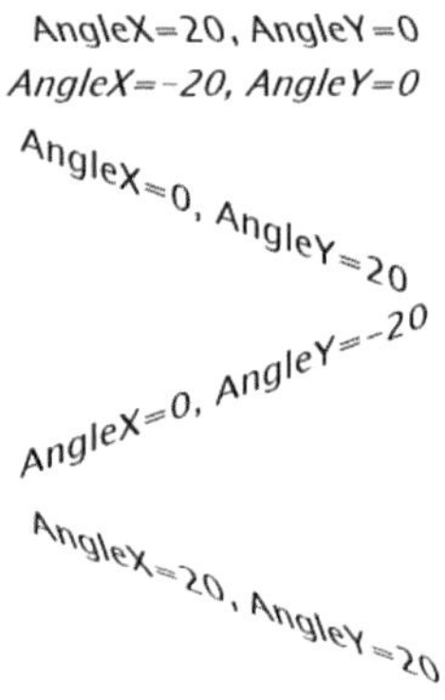

These properties behave much like the properties of the previous transforms. Figure 6.19 demonstrates SkewTransform applied to TextBlocks with a few different values of AngleX and AngleY and the default center of the top-left corner.

By using different SkewTransforms on over-laid TextBlocks, you can achieve interesting text effects with otherwise-boring fonts. For example, the following XAML is rendered in Figure 6.20:

FIGURE 6.19   SkewTransform applied to several TextBlocks.

```
<Canvas xmlns="http://schemas.microsoft.com/client/2007">
  <!-- TextBlock #1 -->
  <TextBlock FontSize="60" Text="Funky Text">
    <TextBlock.RenderTransform>
      <SkewTransform AngleX="3"/>
    </TextBlock.RenderTransform>
  </TextBlock>
  <!-- TextBlock #2 -->
  <TextBlock FontSize="60" Text="Funky Text">
    <TextBlock.RenderTransform>
      <SkewTransform AngleX="-3"/>
    </TextBlock.RenderTransform>
  </TextBlock>
</Canvas>
```

TranslateTransform

TranslateTransform simply moves an element according to two properties:

▶ **X**—Amount to move horizontally (default value = 0)

▶ **Y**—Amount to move vertically (default value = 0)

Funky Text

FIGURE 6.20   Two different SkewTransforms convert simple text into something more interesting.

TranslateTransform is an easy way to "nudge" elements one way or another. Most likely, you'd do this dynamically based on user actions (and perhaps in an animation). But this transform doesn't provide any visual effect that you can't already accomplish with Canvas.Left and Canvas.Top.

MatrixTransform

`MatrixTransform` is a low-level mechanism that can be used to create custom 2D transforms. `MatrixTransform` has a single `Matrix` property representing a 3x3 affine transformation matrix. In case you're not a linear algebra buff, this basically means that all the previous transforms (or any combination of them) can also be expressed using `MatrixTransform`.

The 3x3 matrix has the following values:

The final column's values are fixed, but the other six values can be set as properties of the `Matrix` type (with the same names as shown). Using the most explicit XAML syntax, applying a `MatrixTransform` could look as follows:

```
<Rectangle>
  <Rectangle.RenderTransform>
    <MatrixTransform>
      <MatrixTransform.Matrix>
        <Matrix OffsetX="20"/>
      </MatrixTransform.Matrix>
    </MatrixTransform>
  </Rectangle.RenderTransform>
</Rectangle>
```

DIGGING DEEPER

MatrixTransform's Shortcut Syntax

`MatrixTransform` is the only transform that can be applied as a simple string in XAML (thanks to a type converter). For example, you can translate a `Rectangle` 10 units to the right and 20 units down with the following syntax:

```
<Rectangle RenderTransform="1,0,0,1,10,20" />
```

The comma-delimited list represents the M11, M12, M21, M22, OffsetX, and OffsetY values, respectively. Values of 1,0,0,1,0,0 give you the identity matrix (meaning that no transform is done), so making `MatrixTransform` act like `TranslateTransform` is as simple as starting with the identity matrix then using OffsetX and OffsetY as `TranslateTransform`'s X and Y values. Scaling can be done by treating the first and fourth values (the 1s in the identity matrix) as ScaleX and ScaleY, respectively. Rotation and skewing are more complicated as they involve sin, cos, and angles specified in radians.

But if you're comfortable with the matrix notation, representing transforms with this concise (and less-readable) syntax can be a time-saver when writing XAML by hand.

Combining Transforms

A few different options exist for combining multiple transforms, such as rotating an element while simultaneously scaling it. You could figure out the correct `MatrixTransform` representation to get the combined effect. Most likely, however, you would take advantage of the `TransformGroup` element.

`TransformGroup` is itself a transform, so it can be used wherever the previous elements are used. Its purpose is to combine child transform objects added to its `Children` content property. From XAML, you could use it as follows:

```
<TextBlock FontSize="20" Canvas.Left="70" Text="Help!">
  <TextBlock.RenderTransform>
    <TransformGroup>
      <RotateTransform Angle="45"/>
      <ScaleTransform ScaleX="5" ScaleY="1"/>
      <SkewTransform AngleX="30"/>
    </TransformGroup>
  </TextBlock.RenderTransform>
</TextBlock>
```

The result of all three transforms being applied to the `TextBlock` is shown in Figure 6.21. Note that the order of the child transforms does not matter; the rendered result is always the same.

For maximum performance, Silverlight calculates a combined transform out of a `TransformGroup`'s children and applies it as a single transform (as if you had used `MatrixTransform`). Note that you can apply multiple instances of the same transform to a `TransformGroup`. For example, applying two separate 45° `RotateTransforms` would result in a 90° rotation.

FIGURE 6.21   A `TextBlock` that has been thoroughly tortured by being rotated, scaled, and skewed.

DIGGING DEEPER

Other Places to Use Transforms

`RenderTransform` on a UI element isn't the only property that can be set to an instance of a transform; all geometries have a `Transform` property, and all brushes have both `Transform` and `RelativeTransform` properties.

Here's an example that applies a transform to a `RectangleGeometry`:

```
<Image Source="TeamPhoto.jpg">
  <Image.Clip>
    <RectangleGeometry Rect="0,0,380,290">
      <RectangleGeometry.Transform>
        <SkewTransform AngleX="20"/>
```

Continues

DIGGING DEEPER

Continued

```
      </RectangleGeometry.Transform>
    </RectangleGeometry>
  </Image.Clip>
</Image>
```

Rather than skewing the Image itself, this skews the imaginary rectangle used to clip the Image, as shown in Figure 6.22.

The Transform property on a brush works the same way. The following XAML rotates what would have been a vertical linear gradient:

FIGURE 6.22   Applying a SkewTransform to a RectangleGeometry used to clip an Image with no transforms of its own.

```
<Rectangle Width="200" Height="100">
  <Rectangle.Fill>
    <LinearGradientBrush StartPoint="0,0" EndPoint="0,1">
      <LinearGradientBrush.Transform>
        <RotateTransform Angle="45"/>
      </LinearGradientBrush.Transform>
      <GradientStop Offset="0" Color="Blue"/>
      <GradientStop Offset="1" Color="Red"/>
    </LinearGradientBrush>
  </Rectangle.Fill>
</Rectangle>
```

Figure 6.23 demonstrates that applying this RotateTransform to a LinearGradientBrush does not produce the same effect as tweaking its StartPoint and EndPoint values. It also demonstrates the behavior change from setting a brush's RelativeTransform property instead of its Transform property. RelativeTransform scales the result to the bounding box, whereas Transform does not.

No transform

Setting Transform to the RotateTransform

Setting RelativeTransform to the RotateTransform instead

FIGURE 6.23   Applying a RotateTransform to a LinearGradientBrush applied to a Rectangle.

Continued

The extra red area appears because of the brush's default `SpreadMethod` of `Pad`. Changing it to `Repeat` or `Reflect` fills the area differently, as seen in the preceding chapter.

Conclusion

The layout features provided by `Canvas` are much more primitive than what can be done with layout in HTML, but this chapter demonstrates how to leverage these basic features to get your job done. Transforms, on the other hand, are much richer than anything you can do in plain HTML. Whether you're scaling, rotating, skewing, or more, Silverlight provides a simple, consistent approach for transforming any content.

PART III

Making Your Content Come to Life

IN THIS PART

Responding to Input Events

Silverlight's input events are the key to creating not just fancy content, but true interactive applications. The input events inform you about various actions the user has initiated with the mouse, keyboard, or other input devices such as a stylus. Overall, the amount of information Silverlight gives you in version 1.0 isn't as feature-rich as what you can get with HTML, but it's still enough to build sophisticated applications or reusable controls.

This chapter first takes a look at patterns used by almost all Silverlight events, and then examines mouse events (which includes stylus support), keyboard events (which includes limited focus support), and Silverlight's special full-screen mode. In examining these features, you'll also see how to build reusable controls in JavaScript, such as a Silverlight-based scrollbar.

About Silverlight Events

Table 7.1 lists all the events supported by Silverlight 1.0 associated with the objects they are defined on, including the input events that are the focus of this chapter.

TABLE 7.1   Silverlight 1.0 Events

Object	Relevant Chapter(s)	Events	
Silverlight Control	1	onLoad	
		onError	
Control's Content Property	1, 6, and 7	OnResize	
		OnFullScreenChange	
Image and ImageBrush	4	DownloadProgressChanged	
		ImageFailed	
All UI Elements	7	MouseMove	
		MouseEnter	
		MouseLeave	Mouse
		MouseLeftButtonDown	
		MouseLeftButtonUp	
		KeyDown	Keyboard
		KeyUp	
		GotFocus	Focus
		LostFocus	
		Loaded	
Accessibility	7	PerformAction	
Downloader	8	DownloadProgressChanged	
		Completed	
		DownloadFailed	
Storyboard	9	Completed	
MediaElement	10	BufferingProgressChanged	
		DownloadProgressChanged	
		MediaOpened	
		MediaEnded	
		MediaFailed	
		CurrentStateChanged	
		MarkerReached	

All UI elements have a Loaded event, but you can alternatively use the Silverlight control's onLoad event discussed in Chapter 1, "Getting Started." The control's onLoad event is raised after all UI elements have raised their Loaded event. (I personally recommend using onLoad rather than Loaded. In some obscure situations it can avoid a subtle bug in the current version of Firefox.)

Event Handlers

With the exception of the two events defined directly on the Silverlight control, the event handler functions that get called when each event is raised follow the same pattern. They are sent one or two parameters. The first one—sender—is always the instance of the object that raised the event. The second one—typically named args or eventArgs—provides additional data about the event, if applicable. For example, a handler for the `MouseEnter` event can be defined as follows:

```
function onMouseEnter(sender, eventArgs)
{
  // sender is the element that the mouse pointer just entered
  // eventArgs contains more about the current state of the mouse pointer,
  // such as its position
}
```

Although the convention is to include both parameters, it is perfectly legal in JavaScript to omit the second parameter or both parameters if you have no use for them inside the function.

The `sender` parameter is useful for distinguishing the event source when you attach the same event handler to multiple elements. One easy way to distinguish between (named) elements is to compare the `sender`'s `Name` property with an expected value, for example:

```
if (sender.Name == "element1") { … }
else if (sender.Name == "element2") { … }
else { … }
```

If you want to distinguish between elements that differ by type, you can leverage the fact that every Silverlight element implements a `ToString` function that returns its type name. For example:

```
if (sender.ToString() == "Canvas") { … }
else if (sender.ToString() == "Rectangle") { … }
else { … }
```

Because the JavaScript engine implicitly calls `toString` on objects when used in a string context (with a lowercase t, but it's still the same as Silverlight's `ToString` thanks to case insensitivity), you can often omit the explicit call. The previous code can be rewritten as the following more subtle code:

```
if (sender == "Canvas") { … }
else if (sender == "Rectangle") { … }
else { … }
```

Attaching Event Handlers to Events

As explained in Chapter 2, "XAML," you can attach an event handler to an event on an object defined in XAML using attribute syntax, such as

```
<Ellipse Fill="Orange" Width="300" Height="100" MouseEnter="onMouseEnter"/>
```

This, of course, doesn't apply to objects that can't be defined in XAML—the Silverlight control, its `Content` property, the downloader, and the `Accessibility` object. All event handlers can be alternatively attached in JavaScript, however. Chapter 1 demonstrates how to attach handlers to events on the Silverlight control, which is a bit different. All other objects with events define a function called `AddEventListener` that can be used to attach one or more handlers to any of its events.

`AddEventListener` takes two parameters—the name of the event and the handler. This handler can be identified via a string (as in the XAML attribute syntax):

```
element.AddEventListener("MouseEnter", "onMouseEnter");
```

or as a direct function reference, such as

```
element.AddEventListener("MouseEnter", onMouseEnter);
```

or

```
element.AddEventListener("MouseEnter", function(sender, eventArgs) { … });
```

Multiple handlers can be attached to the same function by calling `AddEventListener` multiple times. For example,

```
element.AddEventListener("MouseEnter", handler1);
element.AddEventListener("MouseEnter", handler2);
element.AddEventListener("MouseEnter", handler3);
```

If you attach *the same handler* to the same event multiple times, the handler will be called as many times every time the event is raised.

TIP

If you want to define an event handler as an instance function rather than a global function, a simple trick can help you avoid a common pitfall. Inside an event handler (whether you use Silverlight or not), `this` is set to the element raising the event (or sometimes just the containing `window`) rather than the instance of the object defining the event handler function. Therefore, the following line of code will not work as most people would expect if the implementation of `onMouseEnter` tries to access other instance members via the `this` variable:

```
// onMouseEnter won't see the same "this" when called!
element.AddEventListener("MouseEnter", this.onMouseEnter);
```

Instead, you can define a function as follows that "corrects" the `this` variable seen by the handler by using the `apply` function defined on all JavaScript functions:

```
function delegate(target, callback)
{
  return function() { callback.apply(target, arguments); };
}
```

Continued

(A "delegate," in .NET terminology, is a function reference associated with an object instance.) This helper function can then be used as follows:

```
// onMouseEnter now sees the same "this"
element.AddEventListener("MouseEnter", delegate(this, this.onMouseEnter));
```

You can also *remove* an event handler at any time, if you want it to stop receiving events. This can be done with the RemoveEventListener function, defined on all objects that define AddEventListener. If you added a handler in XAML or by passing a string as the second parameter to AddEventListener, you can call RemoveEventListener with the name of the event and the name of the handler function:

```
element.RemoveEventListener("MouseEnter", "onMouseEnter");
```

If you pass a function reference as the second parameter to AddEventListener, you must pass a special token as the second parameter to RemoveEventListener instead. This token is always returned (but usually ignored) by AddEventListener, so the procedure to add and remove a handler can look as follows:

```
token = element.AddEventListener("MouseEnter", onMouseEnter);
…
element.RemoveEventListener("MouseEnter", token);
```

DIGGING DEEPER

Silverlight and Accessibility

The accessibility functionality built into Silverlight 1.0 is basically no more than the opportunity for the control author to provide some alternative human-readable text and respond to the notion of a default action. This is similar to setting an ALT attribute on HTML elements such as IMG, but with a bit more richness. The alternative text can be set via three subproperties on the control's Content.Accessibility property:

- ▹ **Title**—The main description of the Silverlight content. (Its default value is simply "Silverlight Content".)
- ▹ **Description**—Additional details that describe the visual appearance of the content.
- ▹ **ActionDescription**—A description of the default action (if any) that the user can perform on the content. This is meant to be a short verb phrase. For example, a Silverlight advertisement might use an ActionDescription of "Click for more information".

These three pieces of text are reported to accessibility software based on Microsoft Active Accessibility (MSAA), which can do any number of things with the information. Examples of MSAA-based programs are screen readers (such as the Narrator program that ships with Windows) and programs that display captions. MSAA-based programs receive this information via the IAccessible COM interface. (These programs can retrieve Title via IAccessible.get_accName, Description via IAccessible.get_accDescription, and

Continues

DIGGING DEEPER

Continued

ActionDescription via IAccessible.get_accDefaultAction.) Because you can retrieve the hierarchy of Silverlight elements with a little bit of custom JavaScript, you could write some code to report additional dynamic information via MSAA if desired.

One additional piece of built-in accessibility functionality is Content.Accessibility's PerformAction event. This is raised by an MSAA-based program (via IAccessible.accDoDefaultAction) when the user wants to perform the action described by the ActionDescription property. Therefore, a Silverlight advertisement with the ActionDescription of "Click for more information" should attach a handler to PerformAction that navigates to the appropriate URL (which is presumably already done in another event handler to handle normal clicks). For example:

```
// Silverlight onLoad event handler
function onLoad(control, context, rootElement)
{
  rootElement.addEventListener("MouseLeftButtonDown", onRootClick);

  control.Content.Accessibility.Title = "Advertisement for Great Estates";
  control.Content.Accessibility.ActionDescription = "Click for more information";
  control.Content.Accessibility.addEventListener("PerformAction", onRootClick);

}

// Navigate to the target URL on click or Accessibility default action
function onRootClick()
{
  document.location = "http://ad.doubleclick.net/ … ";
}
```

Note that Mac OS X does not currently support accessibility for Safari or Firefox add-ons. Because MSAA is specific to Windows, Silverlight's accessibility support (just like Flash's accessibility support) is also limited to Windows. (It is unclear at the time of writing whether version 1.0 of Moonlight, the Silverlight implementation for Linux, will support these accessibility features.) One accessibility feature you can accomplish on any platform is closed captioning on video content. Chapter 10, "Audio and Video," explains how this can be done, and how Expression Encoder makes it easy.

Mouse Events

The five mouse events supported by all UI elements are MouseMove, MouseEnter, MouseLeave, MouseLeftButtonDown, and MouseLeftButtonUp. With these five events, you can implement a wide range of behaviors: rollover (mouse hover) effects, drag-and-drop, and decent versions of just about any common control missing from Silverlight 1.0 (buttons, check boxes, scrollbars, and more).

Note that Silverlight has no Click event, but MouseLeftButtonDown (or MouseLeftButtonUp) can serve the same purpose. Also, there are no events corresponding to the right mouse button. Right-clicking on the Silverlight control gives the standard context menu for configuring the add-on, and that behavior can't be customized in version 1.0.

Listing 7.1 contains JavaScript that loads the following XAML, attaches handlers for all five mouse events on both `Ellipses`, and reports when each event occurs:

```
<Canvas xmlns="http://schemas.microsoft.com/client/2007">
  <Ellipse Name="one" Width="200" Height="200" Fill="Red"/>
  <Ellipse Name="two" Width="200" Height="200" Canvas.Left="100" Canvas.Top="100"
    Fill="Red"/>
  <TextBlock Name="eventInfo" Canvas.Top="250"/>
</Canvas>
```

The result looks like Figure 7.1.

LISTING 7.1   Demonstrating Every
                Mouse Event

```
function createSilverlight()
{
  Silverlight.createObjectEx(
    {
      source: "Figure 7.1.xaml",
      parentElement: document.body,
      id: "silverlightControl",
      properties:
      { width: "100%", height:
        "100%", version: "1.0" },
      events: { onLoad: onLoad }
    }
  );
}
```

MouseMove: Ellipse named two

FIGURE 7.1   Tracking mouse events on two Ellipses.

```
// Silverlight onLoad event handler
function onLoad(control, context, rootElement)
{
  for (var i = 0; i < rootElement.Children.Count; i++)
  {
    var element = rootElement.Children.GetItem(i);

    // Add the same five handlers to both Ellipses
    if (element.ToString() == "Ellipse")
    {
      element.AddEventListener("MouseMove", onMouseMove);
      element.AddEventListener("MouseEnter", onMouseEnter);
      element.AddEventListener("MouseLeave", onMouseLeave);
      element.AddEventListener("MouseLeftButtonDown", onMouseLeftButtonDown);
      element.AddEventListener("MouseLeftButtonUp", onMouseLeftButtonUp);
    }
  }
}
```

LISTING 7.1   Continued

```
  // Save the eventInfo instance in a global variable used by the handlers
  eventInfo = rootElement.FindName("eventInfo");
}

function onMouseMove(sender, mouseEventArgs)
{
  sender.Fill = "Orange";
  eventInfo.Text = "MouseMove: " + sender + " named " + sender.Name;
}

function onMouseEnter(sender, mouseEventArgs)
{
  sender.Fill = "Yellow";
  eventInfo.Text = "MouseEnter: " + sender + " named " + sender.Name;
}

function onMouseLeave(sender, mouseEventArgs)
{
  sender.Fill = "Green";
  eventInfo.Text = "MouseLeave: " + sender + " named " + sender.Name;
}

function onMouseLeftButtonDown(sender, mouseEventArgs)
{
  sender.Fill = "Blue";
  eventInfo.Text = "MouseLeftButtonDown: " + sender + " named " + sender.Name;
}

function onMouseLeftButtonUp(sender, mouseEventArgs)
{
  sender.Fill = "Purple";
  eventInfo.Text = "MouseLeftButtonUp: " + sender + " named " + sender.Name;
}
```

Rather than retrieving each Ellipse individually by name and assigning the event handlers to each one separately, the onLoad event handler loops through all the root Canvas's children to assign the handlers with the same five lines of code. The eventInfo TextBlock is saved in a global variable, so the handlers can directly set its Text property. Each handler could have alternatively called sender.FindName("eventInfo") to retrieve this instance, but it's more efficient to only call FindName once during load rather than during every mouse event.

The code inside onLoad leverages the ToString function defined on all Silverlight elements to determine whether the current element is an Ellipse. (This generic code helps to keep everything working as expected even if the XAML file is changed.) It's vital that the handlers do not get attached to mouse events raised by the TextBlock because each handler assumes that the sender has a Fill property. Because TextBlock doesn't have this property (but rather a Foreground property instead), an attempt to set it would raise an error.

TIP

Creating a "rollover effect" (such as making an element glow when the mouse pointer hovers over it) is as simple as changing its appearance in a `MouseEnter` event handler then restoring it in a `MouseLeave` handler. For example, the following gray `Rectangle` (that could serve as the background for a button) is set up for such an effect:

```
<Rectangle MouseEnter="onMouseEnter" MouseLeave="onMouseLeave"
  Canvas.Top="10" Width="300" Height="100" Fill="Gray"/>
```

The following handlers accomplish a simple rollover effect that makes the `Rectangle` aqua when the mouse pointer hovers over it:

```
function onMouseEnter(sender, mouseEventArgs)
{
   sender.Fill = "Aqua"; // This assumes sender has a Fill!
}

function onMouseLeave(sender, mouseEventArgs)
{
   sender.Fill = "Gray"; // This assumes sender has a Fill!
}
```

DIGGING DEEPER

Simulating a Double-Click Event

Silverlight 1.0 does not expose a double-click event, but you can simulate one without much code. The idea is to record the time when a click (`MouseLeftButtonDown`) occurs, and then treat a subsequent click as the double-click if it happens within a small enough window of time. For example, the following function treats two clicks on the same element within 300 milliseconds as a double-click:

```
function onMouseLeftButtonDown(sender, mouseEventArgs)
{
   var now = new Date();
   if (timeOfLastClick && now - timeOfLastClick < 300)
   {
      // This is a double-click!
   }
   else
   {
      timeOfLastClick = now;
   }
}
```

This technique is not ideal, because users can customize the speed of double-clicking on their own computer, and you can't discover this setting from normal JavaScript running in a web browser. But this is about as close as you can get to a true double-click.

Bounds and Hit Testing

If you run the code from Listing 7.1 and interact with the content, you'll notice some interesting characteristics about the bounds of objects. As you'd probably expect, shapes such as Ellipse only raise a mouse event when the mouse pointer is (or was, in the case of MouseLeave) directly inside their elliptical bounds. However, a TextBlock's bounds are considered to be the bounding rectangle containing the text rather than the precise shapes formed by the glyphs. This means that mouse events are raised from a TextBlock when the mouse pointer comes *near* its glyphs in addition to being directly over them. Although Listing 7.1 doesn't listen for any TextBlock events, this behavior is relevant because the rectangular bounds of the TextBlock *prevent* mouse events from being raised by the Ellipse underneath. When the pointer moves from the second Ellipse toward the TextBlock, the Ellipse's MouseLeave event is raised as soon as the TextBlock's invisible boundary is entered. (TextBlock's MouseEnter and subsequent mouse events are raised as well, but they get ignored by Listing 7.1.) You can see the exact rectangular boundary of a TextBlock if you place a Rectangle in the same spot and give it a Width and Height equal to the TextBlock's ActualWidth and ActualHeight, as demonstrated in Chapter 4, "Text."

> **TIP**
>
> If you don't want a UI element to raise any mouse events (or block mouse events underneath), you can set its IsHitTestVisible property to false. For example, this is appropriate to do on the TextBlock from Figure 7.1 to prevent it from interfering with the Ellipses.

> **WARNING**
>
> **Transparent regions raise mouse events, but null regions do not!**
>
> Although you can count on IsHitTestVisible suppressing mouse events when set to false, the conditions for raising mouse events in the first place is a bit subtle. As mentioned in Chapter 3, "Shapes, Lines, and Curves," setting an element's Visibility to Collapsed suppresses its mouse events, whereas setting an element's Opacity to 0 does not affect its event-related behavior. One more subtlety is that the default Background for a Canvas, the default Fill and Stroke for a shape, and so on, produce areas that don't raise mouse events. However, explicitly setting the Background, Fill, or Stroke to Transparent (or any other color) produces areas that *do* raise mouse events. This happens because the default Background, Fill, and Stroke are actually null rather than Transparent. (A null brush looks like a Transparent brush, but differs in its hit-testability.)

More About the Mouse Pointer

The eventArgs parameter passed to mouse event handlers (named mouseEventArgs by convention) has a few members:

▷ A **GetPosition** function that returns a Point with X and Y properties, revealing the exact coordinates of the mouse pointer

▶ A Boolean **Shift** property that is true if either Shift button on the keyboard is currently pressed

▶ A Boolean **Ctrl** property that is true if either Ctrl button on the keyboard is currently pressed

▶ **GetStylusInfo** and **GetStylusPoints** functions, described later in the "Using Silverlight's Stylus Support" section

GetPosition is a function rather than a simple property because it enables you to get the mouse pointer position in more than one way. You can get the position relative to the top-left corner of the Silverlight control, or you can get the position relative to the top-left corner of any rendered UI element. To get the control-relative position, you can pass null as the single parameter to GetPosition. To get an element-relative position, pass the desired element as the parameter.

Therefore, the MouseMove event handler from Listing 7.1 could be updated as follows to display all the information to be gleaned from mouseEventArgs:

```
function onMouseMove(sender, mouseEventArgs)
{
  sender.Fill = "Orange";
  var pt1 = mouseEventArgs.GetPosition(null);
  var pt2 = mouseEventArgs.GetPosition(sender.GetHost().Content.Root);
  var pt3 = mouseEventArgs.GetPosition(sender);
  var pt4 = mouseEventArgs.GetPosition(sender.FindName("one"));
  var pt5 = mouseEventArgs.GetPosition(sender.FindName("two"));
  var pt6 = mouseEventArgs.GetPosition(eventInfo);

  eventInfo.Text = "MouseMove: " + sender + " named " + sender.Name
    + ". Shift: " + mouseEventArgs.Shift + ", Ctrl: " + mouseEventArgs.Ctrl
    + ", Position Relative To Control: " + pt1.X + "," + pt1.Y
    + ", Position Relative To Root: " + pt2.X + "," + pt2.Y
    + ", Position Relative To Sender: " + pt3.X + "," + pt3.Y
    + ", Position Relative To one: " + pt4.X + "," + pt4.Y
    + ", Position Relative To two: " + pt5.X + "," + pt5.Y
    + ", Position Relative To eventInfo: " + pt6.X + "," + pt6.Y;
}
```

When you get the position relative to the top-left corner of an element, you're really getting the position relative to the top-left corner *of an element's bounding rectangle*. For example, this onMouseMove function can never see the mouse at a point of (0,0) relative to one because no mouse events are being captured at location. Moving the mouse to the center of one gives a point of (100,100) relative to the control, the root element, sender, and one (which is the same as the sender in this case), and (0,0) relative to two.

Note that the X and Y values can easily be negative when you want the position relative to anything but the control. Also, the relative offsets can indeed be different between the

control and the root element, if the root has been given an offset already with
`Canvas.Left` and/or `Canvas.Top` settings. If you want to retrieve the mouse pointer
position more globally (such as relative to the top-left corner of the HTML document),
you need to leverage the HTML DOM to get more information.

Event Bubbling

Silverlight's mouse events support the
concept of *bubbling*, which means that
when an event is raised, it is also raised
on all of its ancestor elements. The
event "bubbles" from the original
element to its parent, and then its
parent's parent, and so on until the root
is reached. This makes it possible to treat
an arbitrary hierarchy of elements as a
single entity. Chapter 6, "Positioning
and Transforming Elements,"
demonstrated that you can move and

> ### WARNING
>
> **The `mouseEventArgs` parameter is always `null` for handlers of the `MouseLeave` event!**
>
> If you need to get the position of the mouse pointer (or information about the Shift and Ctrl keys) right after it has left an element, you must use a different event. For example, you could use `MouseMove` or perhaps `MouseEnter` on a different element.

transform multiple elements by moving/transforming its root, so event bubbling helps
to round out this important aspect of Silverlight. For example, you could create a complicated vector-based logo yet receive clicks on it as if it's a single blob.

The effects of event bubbling can be seen by changing Listing 7.1 to attach the five mouse
event handlers to the root `Canvas` rather than both `Ellipses`. This is done in Listing 7.2.

LISTING 7.2   Letting Mouse Events Bubble Up to the Root Canvas

```
function createSilverlight()
{
  Silverlight.createObjectEx(
    {
      source: "Figure 7.1.xaml",
      parentElement: document.body,
      id: "silverlightControl",
      properties:
      { width: "100%", height: "100%", version: "1.0" },
      events: { onLoad: onLoad }
    }
  );
}
// Silverlight onLoad event handler
function onLoad(control, context, rootElement)
{
  // Add the five handlers to the root Canvas
  rootElement.AddEventListener("MouseMove", onMouseMove);
  rootElement.AddEventListener("MouseEnter", onMouseEnter);
  rootElement.AddEventListener("MouseLeave", onMouseLeave);
```

LISTING 7.2   Continued

```
rootElement.AddEventListener("MouseLeftButtonDown", onMouseLeftButtonDown);
rootElement.AddEventListener("MouseLeftButtonUp", onMouseLeftButtonUp);
// Save the eventInfo instance in a global variable used by the handlers
eventInfo = rootElement.FindName("eventInfo");
}
function onMouseMove(sender, mouseEventArgs)
{
  eventInfo.Text = "MouseMove: " + sender + " named " + sender.Name;
}
function onMouseEnter(sender, mouseEventArgs)
{
  eventInfo.Text = "MouseEnter: " + sender + " named " + sender.Name;
}
function onMouseLeave(sender, mouseEventArgs)
{
  eventInfo.Text = "MouseLeave: " + sender + " named " + sender.Name;
}
function onMouseLeftButtonDown(sender, mouseEventArgs)
{
  eventInfo.Text = "MouseLeftButtonDown: " + sender + " named " + sender.Name;
}
function onMouseLeftButtonUp(sender, mouseEventArgs)
{
  eventInfo.Text = "MouseLeftButtonUp: " + sender + " named " + sender.Name;
}
```

Note that the assignments to sender.Fill have been removed from the five handlers because the sender is now the root Canvas, which doesn't have a Fill property. The events are raised when the mouse pointer interacts with either Ellipse or the TextBlock—all three children of the Canvas. No mouse events are raised directly by the Canvas in this case because of its default Width and Height of 0 and null Background. The sender in this example is always the Canvas, however. Information about which event originally raised the event is lost unless you also attach the relevant handler to the relevant element. (The next version of Silverlight should include an OriginalSource property on the mouseEventArgs object that reveals this information.)

> **WARNING**
>
> **Canvas only raises its own mouse events within the area defined by its Width and Height!**
>
> It's easy to forget that Canvas has a Width and Height of 0 by default because its children get rendered outside the Canvas's bounds. But mouse events for the Canvas itself (ignoring events bubbled up from any children) only get raised within the bounding box defined by its Width and Height (and only then when it has a non-null Background). Therefore, by default, Canvas-level mouse events are only raised for its children.

Capturing the Mouse

It's easy to imagine using the `MouseLeftButtonDown`, `MouseMove`, and `MouseLeftButtonUp` events to implement drag-and-drop. You could start a drag action by setting a Boolean variable inside an element's `MouseLeftButtonDown` handler, move the element to remain under the mouse pointer if the Boolean is `true` inside its `MouseMove` handler, and then clear the Boolean inside its `MouseLeftButtonUp` event to end the dragging. It turns out that this simple scheme isn't quite good enough, however, because it's easy to move the mouse too fast or under another element, causing the mouse pointer to separate from the element you're trying to drag.

Fortunately, Silverlight enables any UI element to *capture* and *release* the mouse at any time. When an element captures the mouse, it receives all mouse events even if the mouse pointer is not within its bounds. When an element releases the mouse, the event behavior returns to normal. Capture and release can be done with two functions defined on UI elements—`CaptureMouse` and `ReleaseMouseCapture`.

For a drag-and-drop implementation, you should capture the mouse inside `MouseLeftButtonDown` and release it inside `MouseLeftButtonUp`. Listing 7.3 contains a function that can be used to turn any UI element into something that can be dragged and dropped.

LISTING 7.3   `DragDrop.js`—How to Enable Drag-and-Drop on Any UI Element

```
function dragDropEnable(element)
{
  // Attach three "private" event handlers contained inside this function
  element.AddEventListener("MouseLeftButtonDown", onMouseLeftButtonDown);
  element.AddEventListener("MouseMove", onMouseMove);
  element.AddEventListener("MouseLeftButtonUp", onMouseLeftButtonUp);

  var dragging = false;
  var lastPoint = null;

  function onMouseLeftButtonDown(sender, mouseEventArgs)
  {
    // Start the drag
    sender.CaptureMouse();
    lastPoint = mouseEventArgs.GetPosition(null);
    dragging = true;
  }

  function onMouseMove(sender, mouseEventArgs)
  {
    if (dragging)
    {
      // Move the element and remember this position for next time
      var point = mouseEventArgs.GetPosition(null);
      sender["Canvas.Left"] += point.X - lastPoint.X;
      sender["Canvas.Top"] += point.Y - lastPoint.Y;
      lastPoint = point;
```

LISTING 7.3   Continued

```
    }
  }

  function onMouseLeftButtonUp(sender, mouseEventArgs)
  {
    // Here is the "drop" part of drag-and-drop
    sender.ReleaseMouseCapture();
    dragging = false;
  }
}
```

The `dragDropEnable` function defines the three relevant event handlers as inner functions that operate on local variables. (There is no function to ask if an element already has captured the mouse, which is why the `dragging` Boolean variable is still necessary.) The result is a nice little script that can be dropped into just about any project without fear of conflicts with existing functions or global variables. The only thing exposed to consumers is the `dragDropEnable` function, which can be called with any UI element.

With Listing 7.3 included, the following emphasized line of code could be added to Listing 7.1 to enable the individual dragging and dropping of both `Ellipses` from Figure 7.1:

```
if (element.ToString() == "Ellipse")
{
  dragDropEnable(element);
  element.AddEventListener("MouseMove", onMouseMove);
  element.AddEventListener("MouseEnter", onMouseEnter);
  element.AddEventListener("MouseLeave", onMouseLeave);
  element.AddEventListener("MouseLeftButtonDown", onMouseLeftButtonDown);
  element.AddEventListener("MouseLeftButtonUp", onMouseLeftButtonUp);
}
```

To drag and drop both `Ellipses` as a single intact shape, simply pass their parent `Canvas` to the `dragDropEnable` function instead.

WARNING

Mouse capture is automatically released when the mouse pointer escapes the Silverlight control!

Despite the use of `CaptureMouse`, it is still easy to lose mouse capture if you move the mouse pointer past the edge of the Silverlight control, or even over HTML content floating on top of the Silverlight control. This is problematic for drag-and-drop implementations such as Listing 7.3. You can easily end up in an inconsistent state, where `dragging` is still `true` yet the element has no longer captured the mouse and might never receive the expected `MouseLeftButtonUp` event. This inconsistent state can result in bizarre behavior, such as the element following the mouse pointer even when no mouse buttons are pressed.

Continues

WARNING

Continued

The easiest way to prevent the inconsistent state is to attach a handler to the root element's MouseLeave event that sets dragging to false. The following code could be added inside dragDropEnable in Listing 7.3:

```
element.GetHost().Content.Root.AddEventListener("MouseLeave", onMouseLeave);

function onMouseLeave(sender, mouseEventArgs)
{
  dragging = false;
}
```

This technique only works, however, if the area where drag-and-drop is valid has a non-null Fill or Background. For the two-Ellipse example, this means giving the root Canvas an explicit Width and Height as well as a Background of Transparent (or any color). If you don't set all three properties, MouseLeave events from the Ellipses get bubbled up to the root Canvas and interfere.

TIP

You could use the drag-and-drop scheme to simulate a custom cursor over Silverlight content. Simply set the root UI element's Cursor property to None, and then drag (but never drop) arbitrary content along with the invisible mouse pointer!

Putting It All Together: Building a Scrollbar

The functionality described so far can be used to put together a sophisticated control, such as a scrollbar. Although Silverlight 1.0 doesn't support creating your own custom UI elements (or anything else usable from XAML other than event handlers), this section shows how you can encapsulate control-like functionality in a JavaScript class and make it reusable.

This section creates a ScrollingCanvas class that enables you to apply automatic vertical scrolling to any UI element. Take, for example, the following XAML whose root has three children:

```
<Canvas xmlns="http://schemas.microsoft.com/client/2007">
  <!-- one -->
  <Ellipse Name="one" Width="100" Height="5000" Fill="Blue"/>

  <!-- two -->
  <TextBlock Name="two" Canvas.Left="150" Canvas.Top="50" Width="200"
    Height="500" TextWrapping="Wrap">
    The functionality described so far …
  </TextBlock>
  <!-- three -->
  <Canvas Name="three" Canvas.Left="400" Canvas.Top="100" Background="Tan"
    Width="200" Height="400">
```

```
  <Rectangle Canvas.Left="10" Canvas.Top="10" Width="100" Height="100"
    Fill="Yellow"/>
  <Line Stroke="Green" StrokeThickness="5" X1="20" Y1="20" X2="200" Y2="200"/>
  </Canvas>
</Canvas>
```

With the custom ScrollingCanvas, you can remove each of the children, wrap them in a ScrollingCanvas instance (which makes each one a child of a new dynamically generated Canvas), and then add each of these new Canvas instances back to the root:

```
// Silverlight onLoad event handler
function onLoad(control, context, rootElement)
{
  var one = rootElement.FindName("one");
  var two = rootElement.FindName("two");
  var three = rootElement.FindName("three");

  // Remove the children then add them back, each wrapped in a Scrolling Canvas
  rootElement.Children.Clear();

  var c1 = new ScrollingCanvas(one);
  var c2 = new ScrollingCanvas(two);
  var c3 = new ScrollingCanvas(three);

  rootElement.Children.Add(c1.canvas);
  rootElement.Children.Add(c2.canvas);
  rootElement.Children.Add(c3.canvas);

  // Set the height of each ScrollingCanvas independent of its content height
  c1.resize(400);
  c2.resize(200);
  c3.resize(100);
}
```

Note that the ScrollingCanvas class about to be defined is not a Canvas itself. We don't have the ability to derive from or otherwise augment UI elements in Silverlight 1.0. Instead, ScrollingCanvas *contains* a Canvas and exposes it as a canvas property. That's why c1, c2, and c3 can't be directly added to the root's Children collection, but rather their canvas property. Similarly, ScrollingCanvas doesn't have the normal members you'd expect a UI element to have, such as Width and Height. You could try setting these directly on the Canvas exposed by its canvas property, but that would interfere with assumptions made by the ScrollingCanvas implementation. Instead, you're supposed to call ScrollingCanvas's resize function whenever you want to adjust its height (or the Width or Height of the scrolled content changes). It's not a seamless experience, but it's about as close as you can get given the lack of support for custom elements in Silverlight 1.0.

Figure 7.2 reveals how the preceding content appears when each of the three children are wrapped in a ScrollingCanvas. The custom scrollbar used by ScrollingCanvas supports a draggable "thumb" that resizes based on the ratio of content height to scrollbar height and up/down arrows that can be held down to repeatedly scroll the content in small increments. The scrollbar lacks several bells and whistles (such as the ability to make the thumb jump to a specific location on the scrollbar, mouse wheel support, horizontal scrolling, hover effects, and so on), but it provides a foundation for adding additional features without much effort. Listing 7.4 contains the entire source code for ScrollingCanvas.

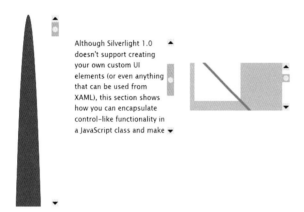

FIGURE 7.2   Applying the custom ScrollingCanvas to an Ellipse, a TextBlock, and a Canvas containing multiple shapes.

LISTING 7.4   ScrollingCanvas.js—Attaching a Simple Scrollbar to Any UI Element

```
// Constructor for ScrollingCanvas
function ScrollingCanvas(content)
{
  // Used for scrollbar Width, upArrow/downArrow Width and Height, and the
  // delta for position and time when perfoming continuous scrolling:
  this.SMALLVALUE = 16;

  // Build up the XAML for the ScrollingCanvas, including the scrollbar
  var xaml = '<Canvas>';
  xaml += '  <Canvas.Clip><RectangleGeometry Name="clip"/></Canvas.Clip>';
  xaml += '  <Canvas Name="scrollBar" Width="' + this.SMALLVALUE
          + '" Background="WhiteSmoke">';
  xaml += '    <Canvas Name="upArrow" Width="' + this.SMALLVALUE
          + '" Height="' + this.SMALLVALUE + '" Background="LightGray">';
  xaml += '      <Line X1="8" X2="8" Y1="11" Y2="11.1" Stroke="Black"'
          + '        StrokeThickness="12" StrokeStartLineCap="Triangle"/>';
  xaml += '    </Canvas>';
  xaml += '    <Canvas Name="downArrow" Width="' + this.SMALLVALUE + '" Height="'
          + this.SMALLVALUE + '" Background="LightGray">';
  xaml += '      <Line X1="8" X2="8" Y1="6" Y2="6.1" Stroke="Black"'
          + '        StrokeThickness="12" StrokeEndLineCap="Triangle"/>';
  xaml += '    </Canvas>';
```

LISTING 7.4   Continued

```
xaml += '    <Canvas Name="thumb" Width="' + this.SMALLVALUE
         + '" Background="DarkGray">';
xaml += '      <Ellipse Name="thumbCircle" Width="12" Height="12"'
         + '    Canvas.Left="2" Fill="LightGray"/>';
xaml += '    </Canvas>';
xaml += '  </Canvas>';
xaml += '</Canvas>';

// Create the elements and add the passed-in content as a child of the root
this.canvas = content.GetHost().Content.CreateFromXaml(xaml, true);
this.canvas.Children.Add(content);

// Store the important elements in member variables
this.clip = this.canvas.FindName("clip");
this.scrollBar = this.canvas.FindName("scrollBar");
this.upArrow = this.canvas.FindName("upArrow");
this.downArrow = this.canvas.FindName("downArrow");
this.thumb = this.canvas.FindName("thumb");
this.thumbCircle = this.canvas.FindName("thumbCircle");
this.content = content;

// Move any Canvas.Left and Canvas.Top setting from the content
this.canvas["Canvas.Left"] = content["Canvas.Left"];
this.canvas["Canvas.Top"] = content["Canvas.Top"];
content["Canvas.Left"] = 0;
content["Canvas.Top"] = 0;

// Attach event handlers to the thumb
this.thumb.AddEventListener("MouseLeftButtonDown",
  delegate(this, this.onThumbMouseLeftButtonDown));
this.thumb.AddEventListener("MouseMove", delegate(this, this.onThumbMouseMove));
this.thumb.AddEventListener("MouseLeftButtonUp",
  delegate(this, this.onThumbMouseLeftButtonUp));

// Attach event handlers to the up and down arrows
this.upArrow.AddEventListener("MouseLeftButtonDown",
  delegate(this, this.onArrowMouseLeftButtonDown));
this.upArrow.AddEventListener("MouseLeftButtonUp",
  delegate(this, this.onArrowMouseUpOrLeave));
this.upArrow.AddEventListener("MouseLeave",
  delegate(this, this.onArrowMouseUpOrLeave));
this.downArrow.AddEventListener("MouseLeftButtonDown",
  delegate(this, this.onArrowMouseLeftButtonDown));
this.downArrow.AddEventListener("MouseLeftButtonUp",
  delegate(this, this.onArrowMouseUpOrLeave));
this.downArrow.AddEventListener("MouseLeave",
  delegate(this, this.onArrowMouseUpOrLeave));
```

7

LISTING 7.4   Continued

```
  // By default, set the root Canvas height to match
  // the content height (which means no scrolling)
  this.resize(content.Width, content.Height);
}

// Resize to the content's width and desired height
ScrollingCanvas.prototype.resize = function(height)
{
  // Resize the canvas and its clipping rectangle
  // (leaving room for the scrollbar)
  this.canvas.Width = this.content.Width + this.SMALLVALUE;
  this.canvas.Height = height;
  this.clip.Rect = "0,0," + this.canvas.Width + "," + this.canvas.Height;

  // Don't show the scrollbar if the content isn't taller than the canvas
  if (this.content.Height <= height)
  {
    this.scrollBar.Visibility = "Collapsed";
    return;
  }

  // Show, position and resize the scrollbar
  this.scrollBar.Visibility = "Visible";
  this.scrollBar["Canvas.Left"] = this.content.Width;
  this.scrollBar.Height = height;
  this.downArrow["Canvas.Top"] = height - this.SMALLVALUE;
  this.thumb.Height = Math.max(this.SMALLVALUE,
    (height - 2 * this.SMALLVALUE) * height / this.content.Height);
  this.thumbCircle["Canvas.Top"] = this.thumb.Height / 2
                                   - this.thumbCircle.Height / 2;

  this.maxThumbPosition = this.canvas.Height - this.SMALLVALUE
                          - this.thumb.Height;

  // Calculate the ratio of content scrolling distance to thumb scrolling distance
  this.ratio = (this.content.Height - height) /
               (height - 2 * this.SMALLVALUE - this.thumb.Height);

  // Reset the scrollbar
  this.scrollTo(0);
};

// Capture the mouse when pressing the thumb
ScrollingCanvas.prototype.onThumbMouseLeftButtonDown =
function(sender, mouseEventArgs)
{
  this.thumb.CaptureMouse();
  this.lastThumbPoint = mouseEventArgs.GetPosition(null);
  this.thumbDragging = true;
};
```

LISTING 7.4   Continued

```
// If pressed, move the thumb along with the mouse
ScrollingCanvas.prototype.onThumbMouseMove = function(sender, mouseEventArgs)
{
  if (this.thumbDragging)
  {
    var point = mouseEventArgs.GetPosition(null);
    this.scrollTo(this.thumb["Canvas.Top"] + point.Y - this.lastThumbPoint.Y);
    this.lastThumbPoint = point;
  }
};

// Release mouse capture when releasing the thumb
ScrollingCanvas.prototype.onThumbMouseLeftButtonUp =
function(sender, mouseEventArgs)
{
  this.thumb.ReleaseMouseCapture();
  this.thumbDragging = false;
};

// Move the content and thumb to the specified vertical position
ScrollingCanvas.prototype.scrollTo = function(thumbPosition)
{
  // Constrain the position to the bounds of the scrollbar
  thumbPosition = Math.max(thumbPosition, this.SMALLVALUE);
  thumbPosition = Math.min(thumbPosition, this.maxThumbPosition);

  if (this.thumb["Canvas.Top"] == thumbPosition)
  {
    // We're already at the desired position.
    // Just in case this is from a continuous scroll:
    this.stopContinuousScrolling();
  }
  else
  {
    // Move the thumb to the desired position
    this.thumb["Canvas.Top"] = thumbPosition;

    // Move the content to the corresponding position
    this.content["Canvas.Top"] = (this.SMALLVALUE - thumbPosition) * this.ratio;
  }
};

// Scroll continuously when pressing the up or down arrow
ScrollingCanvas.prototype.onArrowMouseLeftButtonDown =
function(sender, mouseEventArgs)
{
  this.startContinuousScrolling(sender.Name == "upArrow");
};
```

LISTING 7.4   Continued

```
// Stop scrolling continuously when releasing the up or down arrow
ScrollingCanvas.prototype.onArrowMouseUpOrLeave = function(sender, mouseEventArgs)
{
  this.stopContinuousScrolling();
};

// Begin continuous scrolling
ScrollingCanvas.prototype.startContinuousScrolling = function(up)
{
  var delta = this.SMALLVALUE;
  if (up)
    delta *= -1;

  // Call scroll every couple of milliseconds, adding the delta
  var scrollTo = delegate(this, this.scrollTo);
  var thumb = this.thumb;
  var callback = function() { scrollTo(thumb["Canvas.Top"] + delta); }
  this.handle = setInterval(callback, this.SMALLVALUE);
};

// End the continuous scrolling, if it is happening
ScrollingCanvas.prototype.stopContinuousScrolling = function()
{
  clearInterval(this.handle);
};

// Helper for attaching events to instance functions
function delegate(target, callback) {
  return function() { callback.apply(target, arguments); };
}
```

The first function in Listing 7.4 is the constructor for ScrollingCanvas, which performs several actions. (In JavaScript, you can create a constructor for a class simply by defining a global function with that name. Then, member functions can be defined by assigning functions as members of ClassName.prototype.) It dynamically constructs a new Canvas with the elements composing the scrollbar, adds the passed in content element as a child of this new Canvas, sets a number of instance members, attaches all the relevant event handlers, and gives the object an initial size (in case the consumer forgets to call resize).

One member variable—SMALLVALUE—is used throughout the code for a number of purposes: the width of the scrollbar, the width and height of the up and down arrow buttons, and even as the position and time offset for the continuous scrolling feature. (You can think of SMALLVALUE as a constant, which JavaScript doesn't have support for across all browsers.) The only unusual trick performed by the constructor is to remove any Canvas.Left and Canvas.Top settings from the passed-in content and apply it to the new Canvas parent instead. This is needed to make the new Canvas take the place of the content it now wraps. Note that ScrollingCanvas ignores any transforms that might have been applied to the child content, so the new parent Canvas and its scrollbar won't be scaled, translated, rotated, or skewed unless this is being done at a higher level in the tree of elements.

The resize function sizes and arranges everything based on the passed-in height desired for the new Canvas, as well as the current Width and Height of the child content. The RectangleGeometry used as Canvas's Clip is always kept in sync with the dimensions of the Canvas to ensure that the inner content doesn't leak outside its bounds. If the inner content isn't long enough to scroll, this function even hides the scrollbar altogether, which is a handy feature. Keep in mind, however, that resize must be manually called by the consumer whenever the size of the inner content has changed. No element-specific resizing event exists for ScrollingCanvas to take advantage of. Another gotcha is that this .Content.Width and this.Content.Height might not be the best way to get the size of the inner content. You could imagine the code special-casing a scrolling TextBlock as follows:

```
if (this.Content == "TextBlock")
{
  // Use this.Content.ActualWidth and this.Content.ActualHeight
}
else
{
  // Use this.Content.Width and this.Content.Height
}
```

The next three functions—onThumbMouseLeftButtonDown, onThumbMouseMove, and onThumbMouseLeftButtonUp—apply the standard drag-and-drop procedure shown in the preceding section to the scrollbar's thumb. The only difference is that the scrollTo function called inside onThumbMouseMove only pays attention to the Y coordinate of the mouse pointer. Along with mouse capture, this enables the user to scroll without worrying about keeping the mouse pointer on top of the scrollbar at all times. As with normal operating system scrollbars, you can freely move horizontally as long as you're still pressing the mouse button.

As written, the thumb dragging and dropping behavior suffers from the problem of losing mouse capture while thumbDragging is still true if the mouse pointer leaves the Silverlight control (as described in the preceding section). You could easily modify ScrollingCanvas to add the drop-on-MouseLeave technique, but keep in mind that this imposes additional requirements on the consumer of the ScrollingCanvas.

The scrollTo function first looks at the incoming value and constrains it to the bounds of the scrollbar, making it impossible to scroll too far. If there is a valid place to move the thumb, this function not only moves it, but also does the most important part of this entire class—it slides (scrolls) the content up or down the appropriate amount.

The next two functions are the event handlers for the up and down arrow buttons, which are small wrappers over the startContinuousScrolling and stopContinuousScrolling functions. Continuous scrolling starts when an arrow button is pressed, and it stops when the mouse button is released or the mouse pointer leaves the button's area, whichever comes first. (Mouse capture is not used in this case because it would be inconsistent with the behavior of operating system scrollbars.) Note that the same onArrowMouseUpOrLeave handler is used for four events: upArrow's MouseLeftButtonUp, upArrow's MouseLeave, downArrow's MouseLeftButtonUp, and downArrow's MouseLeave. You could go one step further and even attach the stopContinuousScrolling function directly to these events and avoid the intermediate function altogether.

The startContinuousScrolling and stopContinuousScrolling functions use a timer mechanism built into JavaScript that's discussed a bit further Chapter 9, "Animation." A built-in setInterval function is used to call scrollTo every 16 (SMALLVALUE) milliseconds, until clearInterval is called.

FAQ

? How do I get mouse wheel events?

Mouse wheel events, typically consumed as a handy shortcut for scrolling content, are not raised by Silverlight elements. You could attach a handler to the mouse wheel event raised by the HTML DOM, however. This could be added to the implementation of ScrollingCanvas, which would call scrollTo based on the data from the mouse wheel. (If you use multiple instances of ScrollingCanvas simultaneously, you'd also want to keep track of which instance the mouse pointer is currently over to avoid making the mouse wheel scroll all of them at once!)

The only headache with using the HTML DOM event is the inconsistency between browsers. In Internet Explorer, you must use the onmousewheel event, whose event object contains a wheelDelta property that expresses the amount of wheel roll in multiples of 120. In addition, a negative value means that the wheel was rolled toward the user, whereas a positive value means that the wheel was rolled away from the user. In other browsers, you must use the DOMMouseScroll event, whose event object contains a detail property that expresses the amount of wheel roll in multiples of 3. Furthermore, in these browsers, a negative value means that the wheel was rolled *away from* the user, and a positive value means that the wheel was rolled *toward* the user!

Using Silverlight's Stylus Support

Silverlight has special support for a pen digitizer, also known as a stylus, found on devices such as a Tablet PC. (This is sometimes referred to as "ink" support.) A stylus doesn't raise any unique events in Silverlight (unlike in WPF). By default, it appears to act just like a mouse. But just like the positional data sent to mouse event handlers, the mouseEventArgs object can reveal stylus-specific information if a stylus is indeed the source of the mouse events.

The mouseEventArgs object passed to handlers has two functions specific to a stylus. The first—GetStylusInfo—accepts no parameters and returns an object with two relevant properties:

▶ **DeviceType**, a string set to either Stylus, Mouse, or Touch, providing more information about the hardware generating the event. (Touch refers to a touch digitizer that acts like a stylus.)

- **IsInverted**, a Boolean revealing whether the stylus is being used as an eraser (with its back end against the screen). If the DeviceType is not Stylus, this is always false.

The second function—GetStylusPoints—must be passed a UI element. It returns a collection of objects, each with three relevant properties:

- **X**, the horizontal coordinate of the stylus point relative to the passed-in element.

- **Y**, the vertical coordinate of the stylus point relative to the passed-in element.

- **PressureFactor**, a value between 0 and 1 that indicates how much pressure was applied to the stylus when the point was registered. The higher the value, the more pressure was applied.

If the DeviceType is Mouse, GetStylusPoints always returns a collection with a single object. This single object has the same X and Y values you can get from GetPosition and a PressureFactor of 0.5. (A stylus might also behave this way because they do not all support pressure sensitivity.)

The richer information returned by devices with a DeviceType of Stylus or Touch is ideal for handwriting and drawing applications. When the stylus makes contact with the screen (or a finger makes contact with the touch digitizer), the MouseLeftButtonDown event is raised, the MouseMove event is raised as the stylus/finger is moved, and the MouseLeftButtonUp event is raised when the stylus/finger breaks contact. The idea is that inside MouseMove, you can add the appropriate shapes on the screen that record the movement.

> **WARNING**
>
> **GetStylusPoints must be passed a valid element instance!**
>
> GetStylusPoints is similar to the GetPosition function defined on the same mouseEventArgs object, in that the position returned can be reported as relative to the input element. However, unlike GetPosition, which accepts null for obtaining the position relative to the Silverlight control, you cannot pass null to GetStylusPoints.

> **FAQ**
>
> **? I can already create a handwriting or drawing application in Silverlight using normal mouse data, so what good is the stylus-specific information?**
>
> A stylus or touch device can give you two things that a normal mouse cannot: pressure sensitivity and higher resolution. Both of these things can make the writing or drawing much more natural than the result you would get with a mouse (or the result you would get from Flash, which does not have stylus support). Note that the higher-resolution and pressure-sensitive data is only available on Windows, however.
>
> The higher resolution explains why GetStylusPoints returns a *collection* of points (and pressures) and why it falls back to a single point when a mouse is used. In the time between two MouseMove events, a lot of rich motion might have been detected and recorded.

Representing Stylus Points in a Stroke

Rendering handwriting or drawings by dynamically creating the appropriate Paths on a Canvas is not a trivial undertaking, especially because each Path has a single StrokeThickness. Fortunately, for the convenience of easily displaying these things, Silverlight contains a Stroke object that can be used instead of a Path.

Stroke has a StylusPoints property that contains a collection of the same objects returned by mouseEventArgs's GetStylusPoints. Besides the normal collection functions such as Add, Insert, and Remove, this collection even defines an AddStylusPoints function that enables you to add an entire collection to the existing StylusPoints collection rather than adding the items one at a time. Therefore, a MouseMove event hander could continually append stylus points to a Stroke as follows:

```
var points = mouseEventArgs.GetStylusPoints(sender);
currentStroke.StylusPoints.AddStylusPoints(points);
```

Stroke also has a DrawingAttributes property that enables you to apply visual characteristics to the collection of points. DrawingAttributes is an object with Width, Height, Color, and OutlineColor properties. The Width and Height represent the size of the stroke when the PressureFactor of all points is 0.5 (the midpoint). The size of the stroke is scaled appropriately when the PressureFactor changes. Color and OutlineColor can be set to any value that a SolidColorBrush accepts. Setting the OutlineColor gives the stroke a border. This border is two pixels wide (when the content isn't scaled) and can't be customized.

Unlike Path, Stroke is not a UI element. This means that you can't add it to a Canvas and expect it to get rendered. (Adding a Stroke to a Canvas gives a parser error.) Instead, Silverlight provides an InkPresenter UI element that is capable of rendering Strokes.

> **TIP**
>
> By giving a Stroke asymmetrical values for Width and Height, you can simulate a variety of pens and markers!

Displaying Strokes with InkPresenter

The InkPresenter UI element is actually a superset of Canvas. You can add child UI elements to an InkPresenter and position them with Canvas.Left and Canvas.Top attached properties. But InkPresenter also defines a Strokes property that contains and automatically renders a collection of Stroke objects on top of any child UI elements it contains. All you need to do is collect the Strokes based on data given to the mouse events and add it to the InkPresenter's collection. Therefore, with an InkPresenter as follows, Listing 7.5 demonstrates how to render handwriting or drawings on the screen, whether the input device is a mouse, stylus, or touch device:

```
<InkPresenter Width="500" Height="500" Background="White"
  MouseLeftButtonDown="onMouseLeftButtonDown"
  MouseMove="onMouseMove" MouseLeftButtonUp="onMouseLeftButtonUp" />
```

LISTING 7.5   Turning Mouse Events on an `InkPresenter` into Rendered Ink

```
var currentStroke = null;
function onMouseLeftButtonDown(sender, mouseEventArgs)
{
  sender.CaptureMouse();
  var xaml = "<Stroke>";
    xaml += "  <Stroke.DrawingAttributes>";
    xaml += "    <DrawingAttributes Width='5' Height='5' Color='Blue'/>";
    xaml += "  </Stroke.DrawingAttributes>";
    xaml += "</Stroke>";

  // Create the initial stroke with its initial points
  currentStroke = sender.GetHost().Content.CreateFromXaml(xaml);
  currentStroke.StylusPoints.AddStylusPoints(
    mouseEventArgs.GetStylusPoints(sender));

  // Add the stroke to the InkPresenter
  sender.Strokes.Add(currentStroke);
}
function onMouseMove(sender, mouseEventArgs)
{
  if (currentStroke)
  {
    // Add the latest points to the current stroke
    currentStroke.stylusPoints.addStylusPoints(
      mouseEventArgs.getStylusPoints(sender));
  }
}
function onMouseLeftButtonUp(sender,args)
{
  // Stop adding to the current stroke.
  // The next MouseLeftButtonDown event will start a new stroke.
  sender.ReleaseMouseCapture();
  currentStroke = null;
}
```

Listing 7.5 is compatible with a mouse thanks to the behavior of `GetStylusPoints` described earlier. Figure 7.3 demonstrates how you might use `InkPresenter` to add annotations to an `Image`, which can be a child of the `InkPresenter` as follows:

```
<InkPresenter Width="500" Height="500" Background="White"
  MouseLeftButtonDown="onMouseLeftButtonDown"
  MouseMove="onMouseMove" MouseLeftButtonUp="onMouseLeftButtonUp">
  <Image Source="photo.jpg" Canvas.Top="200" Height="250"/>
</InkPresenter>
```

FIGURE 7.3   A creative ink annotation on top of
                        an image.

Both the Stroke object and
InkPresenter's Strokes collection
have two functions that enable more
sophisticated actions with their
content—GetBounds and HitTest.

GetBounds returns a Rect structure
revealing the bounding rectangle for the
Stroke(s). With this information, you
could provide a "sticky note" user interface, where the notes automatically size
to their content.

HitTest can be passed a collection of stylus points, and it tells you whether these points
intersect with the Stroke(s). The HitTest function defined on Stroke returns a Boolean.
The HitTest function defined on InkPresenter's Strokes collection returns the subset of
Stroke objects that intersect the input points (if any). One application of HitTest could
be the creation of a primitive eraser that erases entire Strokes when the mouse hits them.
For example, a handler for an InkPresenter's MouseMove could do the following:

```
var strokesToErase =
  sender.Strokes.HitTest(mouseEventArgs.GetStylusPoints(sender));
for (var i = 0; i < strokesToErase.Count; i++)
  sender.Strokes.Remove(strokesToErase.GetItem(i));
```

This behavior could even be triggered automatically for a stylus by calling
mouseEventArgs.GetStylusInfo and checking if IsInverted is true.

Keyboard Events

Silverlight 1.0 has limited keyboard support. On the surface, it seems pretty simple to use
because all UI elements have KeyDown and KeyUp events. However, there are a number of
pitfalls you can run into when attempting keyboard handling, and they are covered in
this section.

The Basics

Listing 7.6 shows the most basic use of KeyDown and KeyUp applied to the following XAML:

```
<Canvas xmlns="http://schemas.microsoft.com/client/2007">
  <TextBlock Name="eventInfo"/>
</Canvas>
```

LISTING 7.6   Demonstrating Both Keyboard Events

```
function createSilverlight()
{
  Silverlight.createObjectEx(
    {
      source: "Listing 7.6.xaml",
      parentElement: document.body,
      id: "silverlightControl",
      properties:
      { width: "100%", height: "100%", version: "1.0" },
      events: { onLoad: onLoad }
    }
  );
}

// Silverlight onLoad event handler
function onLoad(control, context, rootElement)
{
  rootElement.AddEventListener("KeyDown", onKeyDown);
  rootElement.AddEventListener("KeyUp", onKeyUp);

  // Save the eventInfo instance in a global variable used by the handlers
  eventInfo = rootElement.FindName("eventInfo");
}

function onKeyDown(sender, keyEventArgs)
{
  eventInfo.Text = "KeyDown";
}

function onKeyUp(sender, keyEventArgs)
{
  eventInfo.Text = "KeyUp";
}
```

> **WARNING**
>
> **Keyboard event handlers can only be attached to the root element!**
>
> Individual UI elements in the Silverlight control can never obtain keyboard focus; only the entire control can. Therefore, it makes no sense to ask for keys pressed on an Ellipse versus a TextBlock versus a parent Canvas, and so on (despite the fact that all these elements define the pair of keyboard events). To keep things simple, Silverlight raises an error if you attempt to attach a KeyDown or KeyUp handler to anything but the root object.

> **WARNING**
>
> **The Silverlight control must have focus to receive keystrokes!**
>
> The host browser and the user are the only ones who can give the control focus. For example, you can give the Silverlight control (or any control in a web page) focus by clicking on it or pressing Tab enough times. Although you can't steal focus as a developer, you can at least find out when the control has focus via the GotFocus and LostFocus events. Like the KeyDown and KeyUp events, these two events are defined on all UI elements, but handlers can only be attached on the root element.

> **WARNING**
>
> **Not all keystrokes are reported by the Silverlight control!**
>
> The host web browser ultimately decides what keystrokes get sent to any add-ons, and each web browser does this a bit differently. For example, you can get events for pressing the Tab key in Firefox, but not Internet Explorer. Neither browser sends events for Alt or F10 because it intercepts those for its own shortcuts. Sometimes, the ability to receive a keystroke depends on the combination of keys being pressed. For example, you can receive events for the Ctrl key and for the letter O, but not when they are pressed simultaneously because web browsers intercept that key combination to show a File Open dialog. And sometimes the ability to receive a keystroke depends on whether the event is KeyDown or KeyUp. For example, for Silverlight 1.0, you cannot get KeyDown events for the arrow keys (in Internet Explorer only), but you can still get KeyUp events for the arrow keys. This is simply a bug that should be fixed in the next version of Silverlight.
>
> The bottom line is that if keyboard events are a critical part of your Silverlight application, be sure to validate the behavior on all the target browsers and operating systems you care about.

Finding Out What Keys Were Pressed

The eventArgs parameter passed to keyboard event handlers (named keyEventArgs by convention) contains four properties:

▶ A numeric **Key** property that indicates what key was pressed or released

▶ A numeric **PlatformKeyCode** property that also indicates what key was pressed or released in an operating system–specific way

▶ A Boolean **Shift** property that is true if either Shift button on the keyboard is currently pressed (just like the mouseEventArgs property)

▶ A Boolean **Ctrl** property that is true if either Ctrl button on the keyboard is currently pressed (just like the mouseEventArgs property)

Table 7.2 shows the various values you can receive from Key and, for convenience, PlatformKeyCode on Windows and Mac OS X. (The PlatformKeyCode values for any operating system match what can be found in that operating system's documentation.)

TABLE 7.2   Silverlight 1.0 Key Values, Contrasted with PlatformKeyCode on Two Operating Systems

Physical Key	Key	PlatformKeyCode (Windows)	PlatformKeyCode (Mac OS X)
Backspace	1	8	51
Tab	2	9	48
Enter	3	13	36
Shift	4	16	56
Ctrl	5	17	59
Alt	6	18	58
Caps Lock	7	20	57
Esc	8	27	53
Spacebar	9	32	49
Page Up	10	33	116
Page Down	11	34	121
End	12	35	119
Home	13	36	115
Left Arrow	14	37	123
Up Arrow	15	38	126
Right Arrow	16	39	124
Down Arrow	17	40	125
Insert	18	45	114
Delete	19	46	117
0	20	48	29
1	21	49	18
2	22	50	19
3	23	51	20
4	24	52	21
5	25	53	23
6	26	54	22

TABLE 7.2   Continued

Physical Key	Key	PlatformKeyCode (Windows)	PlatformKeyCode (Mac OS X)
7	27	55	26
8	28	56	28
9	29	57	25
A	30	65	0
B	31	66	11
C	32	67	8
D	33	68	2
E	34	69	14
F	35	70	3
G	36	71	5
H	37	72	4
I	38	73	34
J	39	74	38
K	40	75	40
L	41	76	37
M	42	77	46
N	43	78	45
O	44	79	31
P	45	80	35
Q	46	81	12
R	47	82	15
S	48	83	1
T	49	84	17
U	50	85	32
V	51	86	9
W	52	87	13
X	53	88	7
Y	54	89	16
Z	55	90	6
F1	56	112	122
F2	57	113	120
F3	58	114	99
F4	59	115	118
F5	60	116	96
F6	61	117	97
F7	62	118	98
F8	63	119	100
F9	64	120	101
F10	65	121	109
F11	66	122	103

TABLE 7.2   Continued

Physical Key	Key	PlatformKeyCode (Windows)	PlatformKeyCode (Mac OS X)
F12	67	123	111
0 (numeric keypad only)	68	96	82
1 (numeric keypad only)	69	97	83
2 (numeric keypad only)	70	98	84
3 (numeric keypad only)	71	99	85
4 (numeric keypad only)	72	100	86
5 (numeric keypad only)	73	101	87
6 (numeric keypad only)	74	102	88
7 (numeric keypad only)	75	103	89
8 (numeric keypad only)	76	104	91
9 (numeric keypad only)	77	105	92
* (numeric keypad only)	78	106	67
+ (numeric keypad only)	79	107	69
- (numeric keypad only)	80	109	78
. (numeric keypad only)	81	110	65
/ (numeric keypad only)	82	111	75
Unknown Key	255	(many values)	(many values)

Because the Key value is consistent across operating systems, you should try to use it whenever possible. But the values represented by Key are only a subset of keys available on any individual operating system, so PlatformKeyCode is useful for determining whether keys outside this subset were pressed or released. For example, Macintosh keyboards have keys that Windows keyboards lack, such as F13, F14, F15, and F16. Windows keyboards have keys that Macintosh keyboards lack, such as Scroll Lock or the Windows key. If you only look at the value of Key for any of these keystrokes, they would all appear as 255 (unknown) and would be indistinguishable from each other.

Using Full-Screen Mode

Silverlight's capability to make your content full screen is relevant for this chapter because full-screen mode can only be activated within a Silverlight input event handler. This limitation is in place for security reasons and ensures that only the user has the power to initiate full-screen mode. It would be extremely annoying if browsing to a web page could take over your screen without your consent!

Switching to full-screen mode is as simple as setting the Silverlight control's Content.FullScreen property to true (inside a Silverlight input event handler), and switching back is as simple as setting it to false. For example, the following KeyDown event handler switches the control to full-screen mode when the user presses the letter F:

```
function onKeyDown(sender, keyEventArgs)
{
  // Enter full-screen mode when the user presses 'F'
```

```
  if (keyEventArgs.Key == 35)
    sender.GetHost().Content.FullScreen = true;
}
```

Note that once the control is in full-screen mode, it does not raise any more keyboard events (but mouse events are still raised). This is again for security reasons, as full-screen content is more likely to trick a user into entering private information. The only valid keystroke once in full-screen mode is the Esc key, which automatically exits full-screen mode. Also note that full-screen mode cannot be initiated from an HTML input event handler, such as when clicking an HTML button.

Silverlight's full-screen mode is different from what the browser calls full-screen mode. Besides working in all supported browsers and operating systems, Silverlight's full-screen mode makes the content take up absolutely every pixel on the screen (on the current monitor only, even if multiple monitors are available). The user is also given a message for a few seconds explaining how to exit full-screen mode (and showing the domain serving the content) every time it is activated. This message is overlaid on top of the content, and is shown in Figure 7.4.

FIGURE 7.4   The notification that full-screen mode has begun.

When the control switches in or out of full-screen mode, a corresponding OnFullScreenChange event is raised. You can attach a handler by directly assigning a function reference to the control's Content property, for example:

```
// Silverlight onLoad event handler
function onLoad(control, context, rootElement)
{
  control.Content.OnFullScreenChange = myHandler;
}
```

The OnFullScreenChange handler is sent a sender parameter, which is always the root element.

The main reason for attaching a handler to OnFullScreenChange is to resize your content to fit the new dimensions, using techniques similar to the ones shown in the preceding chapter. If you don't do this, your content will likely look silly and occupy just the top-left corner of the screen. Note that neither the HTML resize event nor the Silverlight control's OnResize event gets raised when switching in or out of full-screen mode. Therefore, properly resizing content in the face of both normal browser resizing and resizing coming from full-screen mode requires handling OnFullScreenChange in addition to one of the standard resizing events. In addition, you must use the control's Content.ActualWidth and Content.ActualHeight properties to discover the control's dimensions (the dimensions of the screen) in full-screen mode. These values have no relation to the dimensions of the host HTML document.

WARNING

You can't mix and match HTML content with full-screen Silverlight content!

You can use full-screen mode with either windowed or windowless Silverlight content, but the control always behaves in a windowed fashion when in full-screen mode. This means that any HTML elements that might have been overlaid are not visible in full-screen mode, a transparent control background appears as black, and a translucent control background is mixed with black. Also, note that popping up a new window (even a JavaScript `alert`) immediately exits full-screen mode.

TIP

For maximum performance, when you switch to full-screen mode, you should hide (or temporarily remove) any elements that will not be seen in this mode. This is actually a good performance tip in general, as fewer elements in the scene means less work for the Silverlight add-on.

Conclusion

Silverlight's input events make it possible to create interactive content that leverages the basic functionality of the mouse and keyboard. There are several shortcomings, such as the lack of richer mouse events (double-click, the mouse wheel, and so on) and the inconsistencies in keyboard events across browsers and platforms (despite the Silverlight team's best efforts). On the positive side, some missing mouse events can be simulated, or the corresponding HTML DOM events can be used instead.

Furthermore, there are some areas where Silverlight input events are more helpful than the ones in HTML, such as having platform-neutral values for keyboard keys, or special information if a stylus (or other high-resolution pressure-sensitive device) is used rather than a mouse. Fortunately, because the stylus/touch support was designed to look like a mouse to your JavaScript code (and vice versa), it is hard to write code that depends on a specific input device and would therefore break if that device was not present.

CHAPTER 8

Downloading Content on Demand

Silverlight includes a special downloader object that can fetch all sorts of content from your web server, such as XAML files, JavaScript files, font files, images, videos, or even all these inside a .ZIP file. This enables you to easily delay the retrieval of content until it is needed, which helps you create a more responsive user experience. Or, if nothing else, you can provide a sexy progress indicator while all the content downloads rather than relying on the default browser experience.

The downloader issues HTTP GET requests that don't refresh the current web page, much like the XmlHttpRequest object that has become the foundation for Asynchronous JavaScript and XML (AJAX). If you've used the XmlHttpRequest object that browsers provide to JavaScript, using the Silverlight downloader will be a familiar experience because it was modeled after the object.

Initiating a Download

To initiate a download, you must create the downloader object with a call to the Silverlight control's CreateObject function, optionally attach some event handlers, and call the downloader's Open and Send functions. The following JavaScript demonstrates how to initiate a download to a secondary XAML file (MoreXaml.xaml) inside the onLoad event handler for the primary XAML content:

```
// Silverlight onLoad event handler
function onLoad(control, context, rootElement)
```

```
{
  var downloader = control.CreateObject("downloader");
  downloader.AddEventListener("Completed", onCompleted);
  downloader.Open("GET", "MoreXaml.xaml");
  downloader.Send();
}
```

For Silverlight 1.0, "downloader" (case-insensitive) is the only valid parameter for CreateObject. Future versions of Silverlight might include additional objects you can create with this mechanism. The downloader defines a Completed event that will be raised when the download successfully completes. This code uses the AddEventListener function discussed in the preceding chapter to attach an onCompleted handler defined in the next section.

The downloader's Open and Send functions are simplified versions of XmlHttpRequest's open and send functions. The first parameter must always be set to the string "GET", referring to the HTTP verb GET. The second parameter is the URL of the file you want to download, relative to the HTML page hosting the JavaScript. The Send function sends the HTTP GET request, which is always performed asynchronously. That is why you should listen for the Completed event if you want to perform an action as soon as the file download is complete. The downloader also has an Abort function for stopping the download, so you can support a user interface with a cancel button.

WARNING

The URL passed to the downloader's Open function has several limitations!

The URL passed to Open must be a relative URL, although you could always start it with a forward slash if you want to reference something relative to the domain root. The result of this limitation is that you can only use the Silverlight downloader to download content from the same domain (and same protocol) that served the current web page. This is consistent with the policy that browsers enforce with the XmlHttpRequest object and Silverlight enforces for its XAML source, although these other cases do support absolute URLs as long as the domain matches.

Also, a web page sitting on your local hard drive can't use the downloader to retrieve content via normal file system paths. Instead, you must host the content on a web server (even if it is just localhost).

Using the Downloaded Content

When the download is complete, your Completed event handler is called (if you attached one), and the downloader itself is passed as the first parameter. The downloader has a property called ResponseText that contains the actual downloaded content represented as a string. (In the preceding example, that would be the content of MoreXaml.xaml.)

If the control's current XAML contained a Canvas as the root element, and if you wanted to add the entire downloaded XAML content as a new child to this Canvas, you could use the following implementation of a Completed event handler:

```
function onCompleted(sender, eventArgs)
{
  // Grab the downloaded XAML string
  var xaml = sender.ResponseText;
  // Get a reference to the Silverlight control
  var control = sender.GetHost();
  // Load and parse the downloaded XAML string
  var newContent = control.Content.CreateFromXaml(xaml);
  // Add the downloaded content to the root Canvas
  control.Content.Root.Children.Add(newContent);
}
```

The downloader object has a Status property (and corresponding StatusText property) that represents the HTTP status code returned from the underlying HTTP GET request. Because the Completed event handler is only called after a successful download, there are only two expected status codes: 200 (with StatusText set to "OK") and 204 (with StatusText set to "No content"). The downloader also has a URI property set to whatever URL was passed to the Open call. This is convenient for determining which download has completed if you're handling more than one from the same event handler.

As with any network request, a download might fail unexpectedly. You can attach a handler to the downloader's DownloadFailed event and handle the failure in a custom way. DownloadFailed event handlers are passed the downloader as the sender and the same errorEventArgs parameter passed to the ImageFailed event mentioned in Chapter 5, "Brushes and Images." By default, the error would be handled by the default onError event handler attached to the control (such as the default_error_handler function discussed in Chapter 1, "Getting Started").

8

TIP

Although you can parse and load downloaded XAML in two easy steps inside a Completed event handler (retrieving the ResponseText and then sending it to CreateFromXaml), the Silverlight control's Content property defines another XAML-parsing function optimized specifically for downloaded XAML. This function is called CreateFromXamlDownloader, and it accepts the entire downloader object rather than a string. Therefore, instead of writing the following code inside a Completed event handler

```
var xaml = sender.ResponseText;
var newContent = sender.GetHost().Content.CreateFromXaml(xaml);
```

you should write the following:

```
var newContent = sender.GetHost().Content.CreateFromXamlDownloader(sender, "");
```

Continues

> **TIP**
>
> **Continued**
>
> This is more efficient than using `CreateFromXaml` because it avoids copying the XAML content into a temporary string. The second parameter to `CreateFromXamlDownloader` is only relevant for downloading packages, which are described in the next section.

When downloading binary content (font files, images, or videos), you shouldn't use the `ResponseText` property on the downloader object. Instead, much like the `CreateFromXamlDownloader` mechanism, UI elements that know how to display text (`TextBlock`), images (`Image` and `ImageBrush`), and videos (`MediaElement`) define a `SetSource` (or `SetFontSource`) function that accepts the downloader object and a part name. Chapter 4, "Text," demonstrated this with the `TextBlock` element.

> **TIP**
>
> For the best performance, you should detach all downloader event handlers and then set the downloader instance to `null` when you're done with it (inside the `Completed` event handler, for example).

Downloading Multiple Items Simultaneously in a `.ZIP` File

The downloader supports retrieving a *package* containing multiple parts and (most importantly) selectively retrieving those parts after the download has finished. You can take advantage of this package support by compressing your files into a `.ZIP` file (using a tool such as WinZip or the compressed folder functionality in Windows).

Initiating a download of a `.ZIP` file is no different than initiating a download of any other file; simply give the appropriate URL to the downloader's `Open` function. The difference is in the consumption of the downloaded data. Rather than using the `ResponseText` property to retrieve the downloaded content, you should call the downloader's **Get**`ResponseText` function. This accepts a "part name" parameter, enabling you to specify which part of the package you want to retrieve. For `.ZIP` files, the "part name" is simply the filename inside the `.ZIP` file. Therefore, if you downloaded a `.ZIP` file containing two XAML files and two JavaScript files, you could retrieve them inside a `Completed` event handler as follows:

```
function onCompleted(sender, eventArgs)
{
  var xaml1 = sender.GetResponseText("1.xaml");
  var xaml2 = sender.GetResponseText("2.xaml");
  var script1 = sender.GetResponseText("1.js");
  var script2 = sender.GetResponseText("2.js");
```

```
  // Do something with this content
  ...
}
```

The second parameter of CreateFromXamlDownloader is the same "part name" you can give to GetResponseText (or an empty string if you didn't download a package), so you can call it as follows to efficiently parse and load XAML that was downloaded inside a .ZIP file:

```
var newContent = sender.GetHost().Content.CreateFromXamlDownloader(
  sender, "1.xaml");
```

The various SetSource and SetFontSource functions also accept a "part name" parameter. Therefore, to use binary content inside a .ZIP file, be sure to pass the filename as the second parameter.

Silverlight handles uncompressing the content, so the efficiency gained by combining and compressing multiple files in a single .ZIP file is practically abstracted away to your JavaScript code. (This is crucial because the ability to download a .ZIP file wouldn't be very interesting if you didn't have a way to uncompress it!)

> **TIP**
>
> Your .ZIP file can have any file extension and still work with the Silverlight downloader, unless it contains font files. Downloaded fonts inside a package can only be applied to a TextBlock if the package extension is .ZIP. This is simply a bug in Silverlight 1.0.

Displaying a Progress Bar

Because the downloader does its work asynchronously, you are free to show some sort of "loading" user interface while users wait for the download to complete. These days, graphics that make no commitment about how much progress remains are pretty popular, such as the spinning blue wait cursor in Windows Vista or the series of pulsing dots on websites such as expedia.com. You could certainly show such a graphic (sometimes called an *indeterminate* progress bar) after calling Send, and then hide it after your Completed event handler is called. But Silverlight makes it possible for you to go a step further and provide a *determinate* progress bar, thanks to an event and a property that tells you exactly how much of the download remains.

This event is called DownloadProgressChanged, and it is called throughout the download process, whenever progress changes by at least .05%. The downloader's relevant property is called DownloadProgress, which is a number between 0 and 1—where 0 means that no progress has been made and 1 means that the download is finished.

A Simple Progress Bar

The following two listings take advantage of the DownloadProgressChanged event to show a custom progress bar before the main XAML content is loaded and rendered. Listing 8.1 contains the initial "loading" user interface with a simple progress bar. Listing 8.2

contains the code needed to download content, update the progress bar, and then replace the UI with the downloaded XAML when complete.

LISTING 8.1   Loading.xaml—The Initial "Loading" User Interface

```
<Canvas xmlns="http://schemas.microsoft.com/client/2007">
  <!-- The background: -->
  <Rectangle Fill="LightGray" Width="100" Height="22"/>
  <!-- The growing bar: -->
  <Rectangle Name="progressBar" Fill="Lime" Width="0" Height="22"/>
  <!-- Some text: -->
  <TextBlock Name="progressBarText">0%</TextBlock>
</Canvas>
```

LISTING 8.2   Code to Handle the Download and Update the Progress Bar

```
function createSilverlight()
{
  Silverlight.createObjectEx(
    {
      source: "Loading.xaml",
      parentElement: document.body,
      id: "silverlightControl",
      properties: { width: "100%", height: "100%", version: "1.0" },
      events: { onLoad: onLoad }
    }
  );
}
// Silverlight onLoad event handler
function onLoad(control, context, rootElement)
{
  // Start the download of bigFile.zip
  var downloader = control.CreateObject("downloader");
  downloader.AddEventListener("DownloadProgressChanged", onProgressChanged);
  downloader.AddEventListener("Completed", onCompleted);
  downloader.Open("GET", "bigFile.zip");
  downloader.Send();
}
// Handler for updating the progress bar
function onProgressChanged(sender, eventArgs)
{
  var percentComplete = sender.DownloadProgress * 100;
  sender.FindName("progressBar").Width = percentComplete;
  sender.FindName("progressBarText").Text = Math.floor(percentComplete) + "%";
}
// Handler for successful completion of download
```

LISTING 8.2   Continued

```
function onCompleted(sender, eventArgs)
{
  var control = sender.GetHost();
  var root = control.Content.Root;
  // Parse and load XAML from inside the .ZIP file
  var newContent = control.Content.CreateFromXamlDownloader(
    sender, "Main.xaml");
  // Remove the progress bar XAML content from the root Canvas
  root.Children.Clear();
  // Add the downloaded content to the root Canvas
  root.Children.Add(newContent);
}
```

The progress bar is created with two Rectangles: a static one for the background and a dynamically changing one for the foreground. A TextBlock is also used to show the percentage complete in a numeric fashion. The two elements that need to be updated from JavaScript are given names.

In the corresponding JavaScript, the handler for the DownloadProgressChanged event is pretty simple thanks to the downloader's DownloadProgress property. The downloader is passed as the first parameter to this handler, just as with the Completed event. Because the progress bar's width is 100, multiplying the DownloadProgress value by 100 not only gives the percent complete, but also the desired width of the progressBar Rectangle. (Math.floor is used to round down the potentially fractional value when displayed as text, but this value is fine as is for Width.)

The onCompleted handler retrieves, parses, and loads the XAML content inside the .ZIP file (assumed to be in a file called Main.xaml), and then it replaces the progress bar with the "real" user interface in two easy steps. First, it clears all children from the root Canvas, and then it adds the new content (which must have a single root of its own) as a single child to the existing Canvas.

The result of running this code is demonstrated with a few snapshots in Figure 8.1.

FIGURE 8.1   The progress bar updates as the content gets downloaded.

If you use the technique from Chapter 5 to get a gradient with a crisp line, you could accomplish the same visual effect from Figure 8.1 with only one Rectangle rather than two. The idea is to adjust the Offset of GradientStops as progress is made. The following XAML accomplishes this:

```
<Canvas xmlns="http://schemas.microsoft.com/client/2007">
  <!-- Only one Rectangle: -->
```

```
  <Rectangle Width="100" Height="22">
    <Rectangle.Fill>
      <LinearGradientBrush EndPoint="1,0">
        <GradientStop Color="Aqua" Offset="0"/>
        <GradientStop Name="middleStop1" Color="Aqua" Offset="0"/>
        <GradientStop Name="middleStop2" Color="LightGray" Offset="0"/>
        <GradientStop Color="LightGray" Offset="1"/>
      </LinearGradientBrush>
    </Rectangle.Fill>
  </Rectangle>
  <!-- Some text: -->
  <TextBlock Name="progressBarText">0%</TextBlock>
</Canvas>
```

if it is used with Listing 8.2 and the following update to onProgressChanged:

```
// Handler for updating the progress bar
function onProgressChanged(sender, eventArgs)
{
  var percentComplete = sender.DownloadProgress * 100;
  sender.FindName("middleStop1").Offset = sender.DownloadProgress;
  sender.FindName("middleStop2").Offset = sender.DownloadProgress;
  sender.FindName("progressBarText").Text = Math.floor(percentComplete) + "%";
}
```

The crisp line in the gradient, enabled by middleStop1 and middleStop2, moves from left to right as the Offset of these elements is set to the current value of the downloader's DownloadProgress property. The raw property value can be used directly because gradients operate on the same range of 0 to 1.

Progress Bar Customizations

The progress bar from Figure 8.1 is very plain and simple, but you can use the same techniques to create really innovative progress indicators that match the design of your site. For example, the following XAML can be used with Listing 8.2 and the updated implementation of onProgressChanged that updates the two GradientStop Offsets:

```
<Canvas xmlns="http://schemas.microsoft.com/client/2007">
  <Ellipse Width="300" Height="300" Stroke="Lime">
    <Ellipse.Fill>
      <RadialGradientBrush>
        <GradientStop Color="Green" Offset="0"/>
        <GradientStop Name="middleStop1" Color="Lime" Offset="0"/>
        <GradientStop Name="middleStop2" Color="White" Offset="0"/>
        <GradientStop Color="White" Offset="1"/>
      </RadialGradientBrush>
    </Ellipse.Fill>
  </Ellipse>
```

```
  </Ellipse>
  <!-- Some text: -->
  <TextBlock Name="progressBarText" FontSize="20" Foreground="White"
    Canvas.Left="128" Canvas.Top="135">0%</TextBlock>
</Canvas>
```

By switching the `Rectangle` to an `Ellipse` and the `LinearGradientBrush` to a `RadialGradientBrush` (with different colors), you get a vastly different effect from Figure 8.1, shown in Figure 8.2.

FIGURE 8.2   The customized progress bar updates as the content gets downloaded.

Depending on the effect you want, you could remove the extra `GradientStops` that enable the crisp line:

```
<Canvas xmlns="http://schemas.microsoft.com/client/2007">
  <Ellipse Width="300" Height="300" Stroke="LightGray">
    <Ellipse.Fill>
      <RadialGradientBrush>
        <GradientStop Color="Brown" Offset="0"/>
        <GradientStop Name="endPoint" Color="White" Offset="0"/>
      </RadialGradientBrush>
    </Ellipse.Fill>
  </Ellipse>
  <!-- Some text: -->
  <TextBlock Name="progressBarText" FontSize="20" Foreground="White"
    Canvas.Left="128" Canvas.Top="135">0%</TextBlock>
</Canvas>
```

and update a single `Offset` with the current `DownloadProgress` value:

```
// Handler for updating the progress bar
function onProgressChanged(sender, eventArgs)
{
  var percentComplete = sender.DownloadProgress * 100;
  sender.FindName("endPoint").Offset = sender.DownloadProgress;
```

```
    sender.FindName("progressBarText").Text = Math.floor(percentComplete) + "%";
}
```

This produces the result in Figure 8.3.

FIGURE 8.3   Another look for a customized progress bar, created by tweaking the GradientStops and colors.

Another simple idea for a customized progress bar would be to make the dynamic gradient become the Foreground brush of a single TextBlock:

```
<TextBlock Name="progressBarText" FontSize="100">
  <TextBlock.Foreground>
    <LinearGradientBrush EndPoint="0,1">
      <GradientStop Color="Purple" Offset="0"/>
      <GradientStop Color="Purple" Offset="0"/>
      <GradientStop Color="LightGray" Offset="0"/>
      <GradientStop Color="LightGray" Offset="1"/>
    </LinearGradientBrush>
  </TextBlock.Foreground>
</TextBlock>
```

The following implementation of onProgressChanged moves the horizontal crisp line in the gradient from top to bottom:

```
// Handler for updating the progress bar
function onProgressChanged(sender, eventArgs)
{
  var percentComplete = sender.DownloadProgress * 100;
  var textBlock = sender.FindName("progressBarText");
  textBlock.Foreground.GradientStops.GetItem(1).Offset = sender.DownloadProgress;
  textBlock.Foreground.GradientStops.GetItem(2).Offset = sender.DownloadProgress;
  textBlock.Text = Math.floor(percentComplete) + "%";
}
```

The result is shown in Figure 8.4. Note that this example retrieves each GradientStop by calling GetItem on the GradientStops collection rather than via FindName. Silverlight currently has a bug that can cause the setting of a TextBlock's Text property to fail when its Foreground is either set to a brush with a Name or a brush containing an element (such as a GradientStop) with a Name.

0% **50% 100%**

FIGURE 8.4   The TextBlock's Foreground serves as the progress bar.

Note that starting and ending points of the gradient extend above and below the text that is actually getting displayed. This is a result of the TextBlock leaving room for characters with ascending or descending strokes (such as É or y). Therefore, without additional tweaks, this TextBlock-based progress bar looks almost empty at 25% and completely full at 75%.

Conclusion

Silverlight's downloader object makes it easy to manage large content effectively. Although using Silverlight's downloader is optional, it is a good idea to become acquainted with it. Something as simple as downloading content on demand can turn an otherwise unusable application into an application that appears to be extremely responsive. Improvements in raw performance and responsiveness that usually result from using the downloader can be tracked down to several potential factors:

- ▶ Less content is loaded up front.

- ▶ Downloads are potentially smaller than normal HTTP GET requests. (This would be true if you use the .ZIP file support *and* if your web server doesn't already compress the content it serves.)

- ▶ Multiple HTTP GET requests can be consolidated into one (if you use the .ZIP file support).

CHAPTER 9

Animation

Silverlight's animation functionality makes it very straightforward to add dynamic effects to your content. It's also one of the most obvious features in Silverlight to abuse! But rather than worrying about a future of websites filled with bouncing and spinning text, think instead of all the *subtle* ways in which animation can be put to good use. Certainly you've come across an Adobe Flash–enabled website with a slick animation that left a good impression, or you've watched a baseball game or newscast on TV in which scrolling text or animated transitions enhanced the viewing experience. Animation might not be appropriate for every project created with Silverlight, but many can benefit from its judicious use.

When exposed via design tools such as Microsoft Expression Blend, Silverlight's animation support provides capabilities much like Adobe Flash. But because it's a core part of the Silverlight platform with fairly straightforward elements, you can easily create a wide range of animations without the help of such a tool. Indeed, this chapter demonstrates several different animation techniques with nothing more than short snippets of XAML and JavaScript.

This chapter begins by looking at what it would mean to animate elements without any special support from Silverlight. It then examines Silverlight's animation elements and the many ways to use and customize them. The chapter then concludes by examining a more powerful form of animation that uses keyframes.

Introducing Animations

When most people think about animation, they think of a cartoon-like mechanism, where movement is simulated by displaying images in rapid succession. In Silverlight, animation has a more specific definition: varying the value of a property over time. This could be related to motion, such as making an element grow by increasing its Width or rotate by updating the Angle of its RotateTransform, or it could be something like varying the value of a color.

This section begins by examining the options for performing this work manually (without the Silverlight-specific support that is the focus of this chapter). It then introduces Silverlight's elements that can do almost all the animation work for you.

Performing Animation "By Hand"

The classic way to implement such an animation scheme is to set up a timer and a callback function that is periodically called back based on the frequency of the timer. Inside the callback function, you can manually update the target property (doing a little math to determine the current value based on the elapsed time or a counter) until it reaches the final value. At that point, you could stop the timer.

Of course, nothing is stopping you from following this classic approach with Silverlight. The HTML DOM defines two pairs of functions that can be used by JavaScript to get timer functionality:

▶ **setInterval**, which calls the function you specify (or evaluates the string you specify) at a given interval until you call **clearInterval**.

▶ **setTimeout**, which calls the function you specify (or evaluates the string you specify) *once* after the specified time has elapsed, unless you call **clearTimeout** first.

With these functions, you can animate Silverlight elements the same way you could animate HTML elements. (Chapter 7, "Responding to Input Events," used setInterval and clearInterval to animate the scrollbar thumb inside ScrollingCanvas.) For example, let's say that we have the following Rectangle, whose Width we want to grow from 50 to 100 over the course of one second:

```
<Canvas xmlns="http://schemas.microsoft.com/client/2007">
  <Rectangle Name="rectangle" Width="50" Height="50" Fill="Red" Stroke="Black"
    StrokeThickness="5"/>
</Canvas>
```

Listing 9.1 uses setInterval and clearInterval to make this happen.

LISTING 9.1   Animating Manually with setInterval and clearInterval

```
function createSilverlight()
{
  Silverlight.createObjectEx(
```

LISTING 9.1   Continued

```
    {
      source: "Figure 9.1.xaml",
      parentElement: document.body,
      id: "silverlightControl",
      properties:
      { width: "100%", height: "100%", version: "1.0" },
      events: { onLoad: onLoad }
    }
  );
}
// Silverlight onLoad event handler
function onLoad(control, context, rootElement)
{
  rectangle = control.content.findName("rectangle");
  count = 0;
  // Call updateWidth every 100 milliseconds
  handle = setInterval(updateWidth, 100);
}
function updateWidth()
{
  if (count == 10)
  {
    // The animation is complete
    clearInterval(handle);
  }
  else
  {
    // Increase the Width by 5 pixels
    rectangle.Width += 5;
    count++;
  }
}
```

In the onLoad event handler, setInterval is used to call the updateWidth function every 100 milliseconds. The value returned by setInterval is a handle that must be passed to clearInterval if you want to stop the callbacks. All three variables in onLoad (rectangle, count, and handle) are implicitly declared globally (because they are never declared with the var keyword) so that they can be accessed by the updateWidth function.

Inside updateWidth, count is used to ensure that the function is called only 10 times. Each of those 10 times, it increases the Rectangle's Width property by 5, for a total increase of 50 pixels. And because each call is spaced 100 milliseconds apart, the animation from the Rectangle's initial Width of 50 to its final Width of 100 takes one second. (Note that the first call is delayed by 100 milliseconds, however. If you want the animation to start immediately, you could simply add a direct call to updateWidth immediately before the call to setInterval.) The result of the animation is shown in Figure 9.1. The animation is a little choppy, but you could make it smoother by decreasing the 100 millisecond interval.

Beginning of animation   Halfway through animation   End of animation
(Width = 50)   (Width = 75)   (Width = 100)

FIGURE 9.1   Manually animating the Width of a Rectangle using setInterval.

DIGGING DEEPER

setInterval Versus setTimeout

Because setTimeout only calls the specified function once after the specified delay, here is how the preceding JavaScript code could be updated to use setTimeout and produce the same results:

```
// Silverlight onLoad event handler
function onLoad(control, context, rootElement)
{
 rectangle = control.content.findName("rectangle");
 count = 0;
 // Call updateWidth 100 milliseconds from now
 setTimeout(updateWidth, 100);
}
function updateWidth()
{
 if (count == 10)
 {
   // The animation is complete. Do nothing.
 }
 else
 {
   // Increase the Width by 5 pixels
   rectangle.Width += 5;
   // Call updateWidth again, 100 milliseconds from now
   setTimeout(updateWidth, 100);
   count++;
 }
}
```

In this case, choosing one approach over the other is primarily a matter of personal preference. (There can be a slight timing difference between the two approaches, however. With setInterval, updateWidth is called every 100 milliseconds. With setTimeout, updateWidth is called every 100 milliseconds *plus* the time it takes updateWidth to execute.)

Performing Animation with Silverlight Support

Using `setInterval` or `setTimeout` is a reasonable way to implement animations. For most animations, however, the designers of Silverlight wanted the creation process to be simpler and more declarative—one that could be specified by a designer using a tool such as Expression Blend. So, Silverlight has several elements that enable you to describe and apply an animation without doing the manual work to perform it. These elements are extremely useful when you know how you want your animation to behave for large amounts of time in advance.

The main animation elements are

- **DoubleAnimation**, which can vary the value of a numeric property. The "Double" refers to the `double` data type that's common in languages other than JavaScript; it doesn't mean that the animation will happen twice. (The name was chosen for consistency with WPF.)

- **ColorAnimation**, which can vary the value of a color property. This does *not* include properties such as `Foreground`, `Background`, `Fill`, and `Stroke` (which accept brushes), but rather properties on the various color brushes covered in Chapter 5, "Brushes and Images."

- **PointAnimation**, which can vary the value of a `Point` property. `Point` properties can be found in a few places, such as the `Center` property on `RadialGradientBrush` and `EllipseGeometry`, the `RenderTransformOrigin` property on all UI elements, or various properties on `LineSegment`, `ArcSegment`, and more.

The only distinguishing feature of each of these elements is the data type they operate on. The choice of which animation to use is entirely based on the type of the property you want to animate. Besides being easier to use, Silverlight's animation elements provide better performance than manual animation with `setInterval` or `setTimeout`.

Using an Animation

The most commonly used animation is `DoubleAnimation` because it can animate many interesting properties: `Width`, `Height`, `Opacity`, `ScaleX`, `ScaleY`, `Angle`, and so on. (Note that Silverlight animation elements can only animate properties defined on Silverlight elements.)

Using `DoubleAnimation`, we can perform the same `Width` growing animation depicted in Figure 9.1 without custom JavaScript. To get the same behavior, we can declare a `DoubleAnimation` element in XAML as follows:

```
<DoubleAnimation From="50" To="100" Duration="0:0:1"/>
```

This states, in a pretty straightforward fashion, "animate a numeric property from 50 to 100 over the course of one second." The only trick is putting this element in the right place so that it operates on the correct element (our `Rectangle`) and its correct property (`Width`) at the correct time (when it has loaded). Here is one way that the `DoubleAnimation` can be applied to the XAML file containing the red `Rectangle`:

```
<Canvas xmlns="http://schemas.microsoft.com/client/2007">
  <Rectangle Name="rectangle" Width="50" Height="50" Fill="Red" Stroke="Black"
    StrokeThickness="5">
    <Rectangle.Triggers>
      <EventTrigger RoutedEvent="Rectangle.Loaded">
        <EventTrigger.Actions>
          <BeginStoryboard>
            <Storyboard Storyboard.TargetProperty="Width"
              Storyboard.TargetName="rectangle">
              <DoubleAnimation From="50" To="100" Duration="0:0:1"/>
            </Storyboard>
          </BeginStoryboard>
        </EventTrigger.Actions>
      </EventTrigger>
    </Rectangle.Triggers>
  </Rectangle>
</Canvas>
```

With this addition, the XAML file produces the same result as the example from Figure 9.1 but much smoother *and without any JavaScript* (other than the call to `Silverlight.createObjectEx`, which could also be avoided by directly using the `OBJECT` or `EMBED` element).

Having the `DoubleAnimation` embedded inside five layers of tags looks a bit insane, but fortunately this is not the only way to use an animation. (The alternative is covered in the "Interacting with Animations from JavaScript" section later in this chapter.) In addition, these elements are essentially boilerplate and rarely need to be changed. Here's a quick explanation of the extra elements, from the outside in:

▶ **EventTrigger**—This object being added to the `Rectangle`'s `Triggers` collection provides a way to declaratively initiate an action when a given event occurs. (All UI elements have a `Triggers` property.) In WPF (and future versions of Silverlight), you can specify one of several events via the `RoutedEvent` property. In Silverlight 1.0, however, only the `Loaded` event is supported.

▶ **BeginStoryboard**—This is the single action added to the `EventTrigger`'s collection of actions. `BeginStoryboard` is the only action Silverlight 1.0 supports, so you can simply think of this element as the glue that binds a `Storyboard` to an `EventTrigger`.

▶ **Storyboard**—This is the most important of the three objects. It connects one or more animations to a specific element and a specific property via its `TargetName` and `TargetProperty` attached properties. `Storyboard` and its properties are examined in depth in the "More About `Storyboards`" section later in this chapter.

Although a `Storyboard` can contain multiple `Animations`, `BeginStoryboard` can only contain one `Storyboard`. If you want to attach multiple `Storyboards` to the same element, you can accomplish this by adding multiple `BeginStoryboard` elements to the `EventTrigger`'s `Actions` collection.

Before looking at additional ways to use an animation, let's look at a few important characteristics of these animation elements.

Linear Interpolation

It's important to note that `DoubleAnimation`, `ColorAnimation`, and `PointAnimation` take care of smoothly changing the target property value over time via *linear interpolation*. In other words, for the previously defined one-second animation, the value of `Width` is `55` when 0.1 seconds have elapsed (5% progress in both the value and time elapsed), `75` when 0.5 seconds have elapsed (50% progress in both the value and time elapsed), and so on. Internally, a function is being called at regular intervals, performing the calculations that you would have to do if performing an animation the "raw" way.

Figuring out how to apply an animation to get the desired results can take a little practice. For example, if you want an element to fade in, it doesn't make sense to animate its `Visibility` property because there's no middle ground between `Collapsed` and `Visible`. (In addition, `Visibility` is not a number, color, or `Point`, so it simply cannot be animated.) Instead, you should animate its `Opacity` property from `0` to `1`.

WARNING

`DoubleAnimation` cannot be used on integer properties!

It's a subtle distinction for JavaScript because all numeric data types look the same; some Silverlight properties accept fractional values (doubles), whereas others only accept integers. An example of an integer property is `Canvas.ZIndex`. Directly setting it to a value such as 1.5 would fail, so applying a `DoubleAnimation` to this property also fails. (The linear interpolation would undoubtedly choose a fractional value at some point in time.) To animate such a value, you need to update it manually based on a timer (such as the `setInterval/setTimeout` approach described earlier in this chapter).

WARNING

Avoid animating the size of text!

It is possible to animate `FontSize` on `TextBlock` or `Glyphs` with a `DoubleAnimation`, or animate the properties of a `ScaleTransform` applied to such elements (directly or via a parent). However, such an animation is likely to exhibit poorer performance than other animations. Silverlight smoothes text whenever it is rendered, so animated text gets smoothed on every frame. This additional work can cause frames to be skipped.

The only way to avoid this behavior and still get the effect of animated text is to convert the text into `Paths`, as described in Chapter 4, "Text."

Controlling Duration

The `Duration` property on the animation elements accepts a string of the format `days.hours:minutes:seconds.fraction`, although you can omit pieces of the specification. That's why the value `0:0:1` used earlier means one second, as does the more verbose `0.0:0:1.0`. If you omit `Duration` altogether, one second is assumed.

WARNING

Be careful when specifying a `Duration` value!

The type converter for `Duration` accepts shortcuts in its syntax, so you don't need to specify every piece of `days.hours:minutes:seconds.fraction`. However, the behavior is not what you might expect. The string `"2"` means two *days*, not two seconds! The string `"2.5"` means two *days* and five *hours*! And the string `"0:2"` means two *minutes*. Given that most animations are no more than a few seconds long, the typical syntax used is `hours:minutes:seconds` or `hours:minutes:seconds.fraction`. So, two seconds can be expressed as `"0:0:2"`, and half a second can be expressed as `"0:0:0.5"` or `"0:0:.5"`.

Flexibility with `From` and `To`

Specifying the `From` property of an animation is optional. If you omit it, the animation begins with the current value of the target property, whatever that might be. Therefore, the previous XAML file can be rewritten as

```
<Canvas xmlns="http://schemas.microsoft.com/client/2007">
  <Rectangle Name="rectangle" Width="50" Height="50" Fill="Red" Stroke="Black"
    StrokeThickness="5">
    <Rectangle.Triggers>
      <EventTrigger RoutedEvent="Rectangle.Loaded">
        <EventTrigger.Actions>
          <BeginStoryboard>
            <Storyboard Storyboard.TargetProperty="Width"
              Storyboard.TargetName="rectangle">
              <!-- No From specified: -->
              <DoubleAnimation To="100" Duration="0:0:1"/>
            </Storyboard>
          </BeginStoryboard>
        </EventTrigger.Actions>
      </EventTrigger>
    </Rectangle.Triggers>
  </Rectangle>
</Canvas>
```

This is a handy way to avoid duplicating the same value in multiple places. If the `Rectangle` is given a `Width` greater than `100`, this same animation would *shrink* the `Width` rather than grow it. And if the explicit `Width` setting on the `Rectangle` were removed, the animation would use a starting value of `0`.

> **TIP**
>
> Omitting an explicit `From` setting is important for getting smooth animations, especially when an animation is initiated in response to a repeatable user action. For example, if the animation to grow a `Rectangle`'s `Width` from 50 to 100 is started whenever the `Rectangle` is clicked, rapid clicks would make the `Width` jump back to 50 each time. By omitting `From`, however, subsequent clicks make the animation continue from its current animated value, keeping the visual smoothness of the effect. Similarly, if you have an element grow on `MouseEnter` and then shrink on `MouseLeave`, omitting `From` on both animations prevents the size of the element from jumping if the mouse pointer leaves the element before it's done growing, or if the mouse pointer reenters the element before it's done shrinking.

Specifying the `To` property is also optional. If you omit the `From` *and* `To` from an animation, it won't do anything; however, if you have an explicit `From` without a `To`, the animation will interpolate the value from `From` to whatever the current property setting is. The following animation makes the `Rectangle`'s `Width` grow from 0 to 50:

```
<Canvas xmlns="http://schemas.microsoft.com/client/2007">
  <Rectangle Name="rectangle" Width="50" Height="50" Fill="Red" Stroke="Black"
    StrokeThickness="5">
    <Rectangle.Triggers>
      <EventTrigger RoutedEvent="Rectangle.Loaded">
        <EventTrigger.Actions>
          <BeginStoryboard>
            <Storyboard Storyboard.TargetProperty="Width"
              Storyboard.TargetName="rectangle">
              <!-- No To specified: -->
              <DoubleAnimation From="0" Duration="0:0:1"/>
            </Storyboard>
          </BeginStoryboard>
        </EventTrigger.Actions>
      </EventTrigger>
    </Rectangle.Triggers>
  </Rectangle>
</Canvas>
```

Each animation also has a `By` property that can be set instead of the `To` property. The value of `By` is added to `From` (or the current property value if no `From` is specified) to get the resulting `To`. The following animation means "animate the value *by* 100 (to 150)" instead of "animate the value *to* 100":

```
<DoubleAnimation From="50" By="100" Duration="0:0:1"/>
```

Using `By` without `From` is a flexible way to express "animate the value from its current value to 100 units larger":

```
<DoubleAnimation By="100" Duration="0:0:1"/>
```

Negative values are also supported for shrinking the current value:

```
<DoubleAnimation By="-100" Duration="0:0:1"/>
```

> **TIP**
>
> Giving an element a `ScaleTransform` and then animating its `ScaleX` and `ScaleY` properties is often a more flexible alternative to directly animating an element's `Width` and `Height`. By animating `ScaleX` and `ScaleY`, you can change the element size by a percentage rather than a fixed number of units.

Interacting with Animations from JavaScript

`Storyboards` expose some members to make writing JavaScript that interacts with animations fairly straightforward. Because `EventTriggers` are so limited in Silverlight 1.0, most animation scenarios require writing a little bit of JavaScript to get the desired results.

Functions for Controlling a Storyboard

`Storyboard` defines a handful of functions that enable JavaScript to control the animation(s) it contains much like an audio or video file: `Begin`, `Stop`, `Pause`, and `Resume`. (`Resume` plays an animation from the point it was paused, whereas `Begin` always plays the animation from the very beginning.) These functions are vital for triggering animations when various events happen, such as mouse movement or clicks. (If Silverlight 1.0 supported events other than `Loaded` in an `EventTrigger`, you would not need to call these functions for simple event handling.)

To initiate an animation in response to any event (or at any other arbitrary time), you should follow this two-step approach instead of the `EventTrigger` mechanism:

> **LOOKING FORWARD**
>
> As with WPF, future versions of Silverlight will support additional events in an `EventTrigger`. This eliminates the need to write procedural code simply to trigger animations in response to events.

1. Place a named `Storyboard` inside the `Resources` collection of any element (in the same namescope as the element you want to animate).

2. Retrieve the `Storyboard` from JavaScript using `FindName`, and then call `Begin` whenever you want the `Storyboard` to begin.

All UI elements have a `Resources` collection property. In Silverlight 1.0, this `Resources` collection can only contain `Storyboards`. (In future versions of Silverlight, `Resources` will be able to hold other objects as well.) `Storyboards` placed inside a `Resources` collection do not begin automatically. They sit idle, ready for JavaScript code to interact with them.

For example, suppose that we want the red Rectangle from previous examples to grow in Width when the mouse pointer hovers over it and shrink back to normal when the mouse pointer leaves. Although conceptually this involves two animations—growing and shrinking—we can reuse the same animation object. Therefore, one way to enable this is as follows:

```
<Canvas xmlns="http://schemas.microsoft.com/client/2007">
  <Rectangle Name="rectangle" Width="50" Height="50" Fill="Red" Stroke="Black"
    StrokeThickness="5">
    <Rectangle.Resources>
      <Storyboard Name="storyboard"
        Storyboard.TargetProperty="Width"
        Storyboard.TargetName="rectangle">
        <DoubleAnimation Name="animation" Duration="0:0:1"/>
      </Storyboard>
    </Rectangle.Resources>
  </Rectangle>
</Canvas>
```

Notice that the DoubleAnimation doesn't specify a From or a To value. This would normally be a problem, but in this example, JavaScript is going to set a To value before beginning the parent Storyboard. Here is what the corresponding JavaScript looks like:

```
// Silverlight onLoad event handler
function onLoad(control, context, rootElement)
{
  storyboard = control.Content.FindName("storyboard");
  animation = control.Content.FindName("animation");

  var rectangle = control.Content.FindName("rectangle");
  rectangle.AddEventListener("MouseEnter", onMouseEnter);
  rectangle.AddEventListener("MouseLeave", onMouseLeave);
}
function onMouseEnter()
{
  animation.To = 100;
  storyboard.Begin();
}
function onMouseLeave()
{
  animation.To = 50;
  storyboard.Begin();
}
```

Note the animation is never given a From value to prevent the Width of the Rectangle from jumping if the mouse pointer enters or leaves before a running animation completes.

The Completed Event

If you want to perform some custom work as soon as an animation has finished, Storyboard's Completed event gives you this capability. With the preceding XAML file, the following JavaScript initiates the shrink animation as soon as the grow animation completes, followed by the grow animation when the shrink animation completes, and so on, to give a never ending "throbbing" effect:

```
// Silverlight onLoad event handler
function onLoad(control, context, rootElement)
{
  storyboard = control.Content.FindName("storyboard");
  animation = control.Content.FindName("animation");
  storyboard.addEventListener("Completed", onCompleted);

  // Start by growing:
  animation.To = 100;
  storyboard.Begin();
}
function onCompleted()
{
  if (animation.To == 100)
  {
    // Done growing, so start shrinking:
    animation.To = 50;
    storyboard.Begin();
  }
  else
  {
    // Done shrinking, so start growing:
    animation.To = 100;
    storyboard.Begin();
  }
}
```

Tweaking the Animation Timeline

You've seen the core properties of animation elements: From, To, and By for setting the initial and ending values, as well as Duration for controlling the timeline. But a lot more properties can alter an animation's timeline in interesting ways.

As with the By property, some of these properties might look like silly tricks that could easily be accomplished manually with a little bit of math or a little bit of code. That is true, but the main point of all these properties is to enable a lot of easy-to-code tweaks purely from XAML.

BeginTime

If you don't want an animation to begin immediately on load (or whenever the containing Storyboard's Begin function is called), you can insert a delay by setting BeginTime with the same syntax accepted by Duration:

```
<DoubleAnimation BeginTime="0:0:5" From="50" By="100" Duration="0:0:1"/>
```

Besides being potentially useful in isolation, setting BeginTime can be useful for specifying a sequence of animations that start one after the other.

You can even set BeginTime to a negative value:

```
<DoubleAnimation BeginTime="-0:0:0.5" From="50" By="100" Duration="0:0:1"/>
```

This starts the animation immediately, but at 0.5 seconds into the timeline (as if the animation really started 0.5 seconds previously). Therefore, the preceding animation is equivalent to one with From set to 75, To set to 100, and Duration set to 0.5 seconds.

SpeedRatio

The SpeedRatio property is a multiplier applied to Duration. It's set to 1 by default, but you can set it to any whole or fractional value greater than 0:

```
<DoubleAnimation SpeedRatio="2" BeginTime="0:0:5" From="50" By="100"
  Duration="0:0:1"/>
```

A value less than 1 slows down the animation, and a value greater than 1 speeds it up. SpeedRatio does not affect BeginTime; the preceding animation still has a five-second delay, but the transition from 50 to 100 takes only half a second rather than a whole second.

AutoReverse

If AutoReverse is set to true, the animation "plays backward" as soon as it completes. The reversal takes the same amount of time as the forward progress. For example, the following animation makes the value go from 50 to 100 in the first second, and then from 100 back to 50 over the course of another second (for a total duration of two seconds):

```
<DoubleAnimation AutoReverse="true" From="50" By="100" Duration="0:0:1"/>
```

When using AutoReverse, the Completed event is only raised after the reversal completes (in this case, two seconds after the animation begins).

SpeedRatio affects the speed of *both* the forward and backward animations. Therefore, giving the preceding animation a SpeedRatio of 2 would make the entire animation run for one second, and giving it a SpeedRatio of 0.5 would make it run for four seconds. Note that any delay specified via BeginTime does *not* delay the reversal; it always happens immediately after the normal part of the animation completes.

RepeatBehavior

By setting RepeatBehavior, you can do one of the following:

▶ Make the animation repeat itself a certain number of times, regardless of its duration

▶ Make the animation repeat itself until a certain amount of time has elapsed

To repeat the animation a certain number of times, you can set RepeatBehavior to a number followed by "x" (for example, "2x" or "3x"). The number is treated as a multiplier, so it represents the number of times the animation should run. For example, the following animation is performed twice in a row:

```
<DoubleAnimation RepeatBehavior="2x" AutoReverse="true" From="50" By="100"
  Duration="0:0:1"/>
```

If AutoReverse is true, the reversal is repeated as well. So, the preceding animation goes from 50 to 100 to 50 to 100 to 50 over the course of four seconds. If BeginTime is set to introduce a delay, that delay is *not* repeated. Note that the number used for RepeatBehavior can even be fractional (such as 2.5x). And as with AutoReverse, the Completed event is only raised after all the repetitions have completed.

To repeat the animation until a certain amount of time has elapsed, you should be able to specify a time-based RepeatBehavior with the same syntax as Duration and BeginTime. However, Silverlight currently has a bug causing time-based RepeatBehavior to be ignored unless it is shorter than the natural duration. For example, the following animation is correctly cut off early:

```
<DoubleAnimation RepeatBehavior="0:0:0.5" AutoReverse="true" From="50" By="100"
  Duration="0:0:1"/>
```

In half a second, the animation only has a chance for the value to go from 50 to 75. Note that the time-based RepeatBehavior is not scaled by SpeedRatio; if you set SpeedRatio to two in the preceding animation, the value animates from 50 to 100 during the half-second.

TIP

You can make an animation repeat indefinitely by setting RepeatBehavior to Forever instead of a numeric value:

```
<DoubleAnimation RepeatBehavior="Forever" AutoReverse="true" From="50" By="100"
  Duration="0:0:1"/>
```

The combination of these RepeatBehavior and AutoReverse settings accomplishes the same "throbbing" effect performed in the previous section, but without the need for any code to listen for the Completed event and to manually start another animation. (When using a RepeatBehavior of Forever, the Completed event *never* gets raised.)

DIGGING DEEPER

The Total Timeline Length of an Animation

With all the different adjustments that can be made to an animation with properties such as BeginTime, SpeedRatio, AutoReverse, and RepeatBehavior, it can be hard to keep track of how long it will take an animation to finish after it is initiated. Its Duration value certainly isn't adequate for describing the true length of time. Instead, the following formula describes an animation's true duration:

$$\text{Total Timeline Length} = \text{BeginTime} + \left(\frac{\text{Duration} * (\text{AutoReverse}?2:1)}{\text{SpeedRatio}} * \text{RepeatBehavior}\right)$$

This only applies if RepeatBehavior is not specified as a time-based value.

FillBehavior

By default, when an animation completes, the target property remains at the final animated value unless some other mechanism later changes the value. This is typically the desired behavior, but if you want the property to jump back to its pre-animated value after the animation completes, you can set FillBehavior to Stop (rather than its default value of HoldEnd). Note that Silverlight currently has a bug when you attempt to use FillBehavior and RepeatBehavior on the same animation. Currently, FillBehavior is always Stop when RepeatBehavior is used, and it can't be changed.

More About Storyboards

Storyboards have a few subtleties and extra features that haven't been covered yet. We'll cover them in this section and also take the opportunity to show some different and creative ways to apply animations to Silverlight content.

Specifying the Target Property

In all the XAML so far, Storyboard's TargetProperty attached property has been set to the name of a property (Width) directly on the target object. But TargetProperty supports more complicated expressions (known as *property paths*), such as a property with a chain of subproperties.

The following Rectangle has a LinearGradientBrush with three GradientStops as a Fill. It uses a ColorAnimation to make the middle Color repeatedly animate from black to white and back. (The idea of animating a Color might sound strange, but internally it has floating-point values representing each of the color channels, so ColorAnimation can interpolate those values the same way DoubleAnimation does for its single value.) To animate the middle Color of the LinearGradientBrush, the Storyboard uses a complex TargetProperty expression:

6

```
<Rectangle Name="rectangle" Width="200" Height="200">
  <Rectangle.Fill>
    <LinearGradientBrush>
      <LinearGradientBrush.GradientStops>
        <GradientStop Color="Blue" Offset="0"/>
        <GradientStop Color="Black" Offset="0.5"/>
        <GradientStop Color="Blue" Offset="1"/>
      </LinearGradientBrush.GradientStops>
    </LinearGradientBrush>
  </Rectangle.Fill>
  <Rectangle.Resources>
    <Storyboard Name="rectangleStoryboard" Storyboard.TargetName="rectangle"
      Storyboard.TargetProperty=
      "(Shape.Fill).(GradientBrush.GradientStops)[1].(GradientStop.Color)">
      <ColorAnimation From="Black" To="White" Duration="0:0:2"
        AutoReverse="True" RepeatBehavior="Forever"/>
    </Storyboard>
  </Rectangle.Resources>
</Rectangle>
```

The syntax for `TargetProperty` is basically a chain of properties qualified by their element name, wrapped in parentheses, and delimited with periods. The syntax supports indexing into a collection, which is why the `[1]` accomplishes getting the middle element in the `GradientStops` collection. This `Rectangle` animates whenever the `Storyboard`'s `Begin` function is called, as shown in Figure 9.2.

FIGURE 9.2   Animating the middle `Color` in a `LinearGradientBrush`.

If coming up with complex `TargetProperty` expressions is too difficult, you could alternatively name the element containing the final property and refer to that as the `TargetName` instead of a parent element. For example, the preceding XAML could be rewritten as follows:

```
<Rectangle Name="rectangle" Width="200" Height="200">
  <Rectangle.Fill>
```

```
    <LinearGradientBrush>
      <LinearGradientBrush.GradientStops>
        <GradientStop Color="Blue" Offset="0"/>
        <GradientStop Name="animatingGradientStop" Color="Black" Offset="0.5"/>
        <GradientStop Color="Blue" Offset="1"/>
      </LinearGradientBrush.GradientStops>
    </LinearGradientBrush>
  </Rectangle.Fill>
  <Rectangle.Resources>
    <Storyboard Name="rectangleStoryboard"
      Storyboard.TargetName="animatingGradientStop"
      Storyboard.TargetProperty="Color">
      <ColorAnimation From="Black" To="White" Duration="0:0:2"
        AutoReverse="True" RepeatBehavior="Forever"/>
    </Storyboard>
  </Rectangle.Resources>
</Rectangle>
```

Another interesting effect would be to attach a `DoubleAnimation` to a `GradientStop`'s `Offset` property and give the brush an animated "gleam" by making the highlight move from 0 to 1. If you want to animate *both* `Color` and `Offset` simultaneously, you can add two `Storyboards` to the `Rectangle`'s `Resources` collection as follows, and then call `Begin` on both `Storyboards` when you want both to begin:

```
<Rectangle.Resources>
  <Storyboard Name="rectangleStoryboard1"
    Storyboard.TargetName="animatingGradientStop"
    Storyboard.TargetProperty="Color">
    <ColorAnimation From="Black" To="White" Duration="0:0:2"
      AutoReverse="True" RepeatBehavior="Forever"/>
  </Storyboard>
  <Storyboard Name="rectangleStoryboard2"
    Storyboard.TargetName="animatingGradientStop"
    Storyboard.TargetProperty="Offset">
    <DoubleAnimation From="0" To="1" Duration="0:0:2"
      AutoReverse="True" RepeatBehavior="Forever"/>
  </Storyboard>
</Rectangle.Resources>
```

However, Silverlight provides a mechanism for animating different properties within the same `Storyboard`. First, a `Storyboard` can contain multiple animations. `Storyboard`'s content property is `Children`, a collection. Second, because `TargetProperty` is an attached property, it can be applied to `Storyboard`'s children. This can be done instead of setting it on the `Storyboard` or in addition to setting it on the `Storyboard`. In the latter case, the animation setting overrides the `Storyboard` setting.

Therefore, the preceding XAML could be rewritten as follows:

```
<Rectangle.Resources>
  <Storyboard Name="rectangleStoryboard"
    Storyboard.TargetName="animatingGradientStop">
    <ColorAnimation Storyboard.TargetProperty="Color" From="Black" To="White"
      Duration="0:0:2" AutoReverse="True" RepeatBehavior="Forever"/>
    <DoubleAnimation Storyboard.TargetProperty="Offset" From="0" To="1"
      Duration="0:0:2" AutoReverse="True" RepeatBehavior="Forever" />
  </Storyboard>
</Rectangle.Resources>
```

This single Storyboard contains two animations, with each one targeting a different property on the target object. This XAML is not only more concise, but also enables you to call Begin on only one Storyboard to start the animations. Both animations start simultaneously, but if you want a Storyboard to contain animations that begin at different times, you can simply give each animation a different BeginTime value.

Specifying the Target Object

Storyboard's TargetName attached property can be set to the name of *any* element in the same namescope. If FindName can find the element, it can also be used as the TargetName.

Here's a fun example that points TargetName to a different element. It "morphs" one picture into another by animating the opacity of the second picture that sits on top of the first:

```
<Canvas xmlns="http://schemas.microsoft.com/client/2007">
  <Canvas.Resources>
    <Storyboard Name="storyboard" Storyboard.TargetName="jim2"
      Storyboard.TargetProperty="Opacity">
      <DoubleAnimation From="1" To="0" Duration="0:0:4"
        AutoReverse="True" RepeatBehavior="Forever"/>
    </Storyboard>
  </Canvas.Resources>
  <Image Name="jim1" Source="jim1.png"/>
  <Image Name="jim2" Source="jim2.png"/>
</Canvas>
```

Jim, the subject of these photos, shaved his impressive beard and got a long overdue haircut, but took before and after photos that are eerily similar. The result of this animation is shown in Figure 9.3.

Opacity = 1   Opacity = 0.5   Opacity = 0

FIGURE 9.3   Animating an Image's Opacity to morph between two similar photos.

In this example, pointing TargetName to a different element is a little contrived because the Storyboard could have been placed directly in jim2's Resources collection rather than the parent Canvas's collection. But in larger examples (such as perhaps a slideshow of Images), it can be desirable to accumulate animations in a single location.

Also, just like TargetProperty, TargetName can be applied to individual children of a Storyboard. The following Storyboard contains two animations, each operating on a different target element and target property:

```
<Canvas xmlns="http://schemas.microsoft.com/client/2007">
  <Canvas.Resources>
    <Storyboard Name="storyboard">
      <DoubleAnimation From="1" To="0.1" Duration="0:0:4"
        Storyboard.TargetName="jim2" Storyboard.TargetProperty="Opacity"
        AutoReverse="True" RepeatBehavior="Forever" />
      <DoubleAnimation From="0" To="300" Duration="0:0:4"
        Storyboard.TargetName="jim1" Storyboard.TargetProperty="(Canvas.Left)"
        AutoReverse="True" RepeatBehavior="Forever" />
    </Storyboard>
  </Canvas.Resources>
  <Image Name="jim1" Source="jim1.png" />
  <Image Name="jim2" Source="jim2.png" />
</Canvas>
```

The result is shown in Figure 9.4.

> **WARNING**
>
> **Attached properties must be wrapped in parentheses when used as a Storyboard's TargetProperty!**
>
> Notice that in the XAML for Figure 9.4, Canvas.Left is placed inside parentheses when used as the value of TargetProperty. Similar to the more complicated property paths, any expression involving a period for TargetProperty must use parentheses. The string "Canvas.Left" does not work, nor does the simpler string "Left" (because the target Image element does not have it own property named Left).

Initial appearance

At 2 seconds

At 4 seconds

FIGURE 9.4   Animating two distinct target elements from the same Storyboard.

Treating a Storyboard Like an Animation

A Storyboard is more than just a simple container that associates one or more animations with one or more target objects and their properties. Storyboard and the animation elements share the same timeline-related properties discussed earlier: Duration, BeginTime, SpeedRatio, AutoReverse, RepeatBehavior and FillBehavior.

Listing 9.2 contains a Storyboard that fades one TextBlock in and out at a time, for an effect somewhat like watching a movie trailer. The Storyboard itself is marked with a

`RepeatBehavior` to make the entire sequence of animation repeat indefinitely. This animation is contained within an `EventTrigger` just to drive home the point that all this can be done without any custom JavaScript. Figure 9.5 shows how this listing is rendered at three different spots of the sequence.

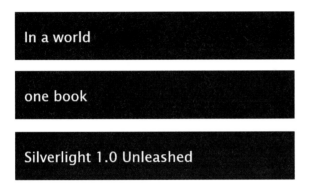

FIGURE 9.5   Snapshots of the movie-trailer-like title sequence.

LISTING 9.2   A Storyboard Containing Several Animations

```
<Canvas xmlns="http://schemas.microsoft.com/client/2007"
  Background="Black" Width="600" Height="100">
  <Canvas.Triggers>
    <EventTrigger RoutedEvent="Canvas.Loaded">
      <BeginStoryboard>
        <Storyboard Storyboard.TargetProperty="Opacity" RepeatBehavior="Forever">
          <DoubleAnimation Storyboard.TargetName="title1" BeginTime="0:0:2"
            From="0" To="1" Duration="0:0:2" AutoReverse="True"/>
          <DoubleAnimation Storyboard.TargetName="title2" BeginTime="0:0:6"
            From="0" To="1" Duration="0:0:2" AutoReverse="True"/>
          <DoubleAnimation Storyboard.TargetName="title3" BeginTime="0:0:10"
            From="0" To="1" Duration="0:0:2" AutoReverse="True"/>
          <DoubleAnimation Storyboard.TargetName="title4" BeginTime="0:0:14"
            From="0" To="1" Duration="0:0:2" AutoReverse="True"/>
          <DoubleAnimation Storyboard.TargetName="title5" BeginTime="0:0:18"
            From="0" To="1" Duration="0:0:2" AutoReverse="True"/>
        </Storyboard>
      </BeginStoryboard>
    </EventTrigger>
  </Canvas.Triggers>
  <Canvas Canvas.Left="20" Canvas.Top="30">
    <TextBlock Opacity="0" Name="title1" Foreground="White" FontSize="30">
      In a world</TextBlock>
    <TextBlock Opacity="0" Name="title2" Foreground="White" FontSize="30">
```

LISTING 9.2   Continued

```
      where rich content must be created</TextBlock>
    <TextBlock Opacity="0" Name="title3" Foreground="White" FontSize="30">
      one book</TextBlock>
    <TextBlock Opacity="0" Name="title4" Foreground="White" FontSize="30">
      will explain it all...</TextBlock>
    <TextBlock Opacity="0" Name="title5" Foreground="White" FontSize="30">
      Silverlight 1.0 Unleashed</TextBlock>
  </Canvas>
</Canvas>
```

Setting the timeline-related properties on `Storyboard` affects the entire set of child animations, although in a slightly different way than setting the same property individually on
all children. For example, if Listing 9.2 set `RepeatBehavior="Forever"` on every child
animation rather than the `Storyboard` itself, it would wreak havoc. The first title would
fade in and out as expected, but then at 6 seconds, *both* `title1` and `title2` would fade in
and out together. At 10 seconds, `title1`, `title2`, and `title3` would fade in and out simultaneously. And so on.

Similarly, setting `SpeedRatio="2"` on each `DoubleAnimation` would make each fade take
one second rather than two, but the final animation would still start 18 seconds after the
animation starts. On the other hand,
setting
`SpeedRatio="2"` on the `Storyboard`
would speed up the entire animation by
a factor of two, including the
`BeginTimes`. Therefore, the final animation would start 9 seconds after the
animation starts. Setting `Duration` to a
time shorter than the natural duration
can cut off the entire sequence of
animations early.

> **TIP**
>
> Storyboards not only share several proper-
> ties with animations, but both elements also
> define a `Completed` event. Therefore, you
> can act upon individual animations finishing
> even when they are part of a `Storyboard`
> containing other animations that could still
> be running.

DIGGING DEEPER

Using Empty `Storyboards` as Simple Timers

With Storyboard's Duration property and Completed event, you can create a simple timer
without having to use the `setInterval` or `setTimeout` functions described at the beginning
of the chapter. This could look as follows in XAML:

```
<!-- Call onCompleted in 100 milliseconds: -->
<Storyboard Duration="0:0:0.1" Completed="onCompleted"/>
```

with the following implementation of onCompleted:

```
function onCompleted(sender, eventArgs)
{
```

Continued

```
// Arbitrary logic can go here:
...
// Call onCompleted again in another 100 milliseconds:
// (sender is the Storyboard)
sender.Begin();
}
```

This is generally more precise and reliable than setInterval or setTimeout and has the benefit of tying in with the Silverlight control's maxFramerate property value. In fact, if you change the Duration to 0, this technique turns into a per-frame callback, similar to Flash's enterFrame feature.

Keyframe Animations

The normal animation elements only support linear interpolation from one value to another. If you want to represent a more complicated animation, you can specify *keyframes*, which provide specific values at specific times. To take advantage of keyframes, you must use a separate keyframe-enabled animation element. Instead of using DoubleAnimation, ColorAnimation, or PointAnimation, you must use the companion element DoubleAnimationUsingKeyFrames, ColorAnimationUsingKeyFrames, or PointAnimationUsingKeyFrames.

The keyframe animation elements have the same properties and events as their counterparts, except the From, To, and By properties. Instead, they have a KeyFrames collection that can hold keyframe instances specific to the data type being animated. Silverlight has three types of keyframes, which this section examines.

Linear Keyframes

Listing 9.3 uses DoubleAnimationUsingKeyFrames to help move an Image of a house fly in a zigzag pattern, as illustrated in Figure 9.6. The motion is accomplished by animating the Canvas.Left and Canvas.Top attached properties.

FIGURE 9.6   Zigzag motion is easy to create with a keyframe animation.

LISTING 9.3 The Zigzag Animation for Figure 9.6

```
<Canvas xmlns="http://schemas.microsoft.com/client/2007">
  <Image Name="fly" Source="fly.png">
    <Image.Triggers>
      <EventTrigger RoutedEvent="Image.Loaded">
        <EventTrigger.Actions>
          <BeginStoryboard>
            <Storyboard Storyboard.TargetName="fly">
              <DoubleAnimation Storyboard.TargetProperty="(Canvas.Left)"
                From="0" To="500" Duration="0:0:3"/>
              <DoubleAnimationUsingKeyFrames
                Storyboard.TargetProperty="(Canvas.Top)" Duration="0:0:3">
                <LinearDoubleKeyFrame Value="0" KeyTime="0:0:0"/>
                <LinearDoubleKeyFrame Value="200" KeyTime="0:0:1"/>
                <LinearDoubleKeyFrame Value="0" KeyTime="0:0:2"/>
                <LinearDoubleKeyFrame Value="200" KeyTime="0:0:3"/>
              </DoubleAnimationUsingKeyFrames>
            </Storyboard>
          </BeginStoryboard>
        </EventTrigger.Actions>
      </EventTrigger>
    </Image.Triggers>
  </Image>
</Canvas>
```

The fly's motion consists of two animations that begin in parallel when the image loads. One is a simple `DoubleAnimation` that increases its horizontal position linearly from 0 to 500. The other is the keyframe-enabled animation, which oscillates the vertical position from 0 to 200; then back to 0; then back to 200.

Each keyframe instance (`LinearDoubleKeyFrame`) in Listing 9.3 gives a specific value and a time for that value to be applied. Silverlight still needs to calculate intermediate values between these "key times," however. Because each keyframe is represented with an instance of *Linear*DoubleKeyFrame, the intermediate values are derived from simple linear interpolation. For example, at 0.5, 1.5, and 2.5 seconds, the calculated value is 100.

But `DoubleAnimationUsingKeyFrames`'s `KeyFrames` collection can contain other types of keyframe objects. In addition to `LinearDoubleKeyFrame`, it can contain instances of `SplineDoubleKeyFrame` and `DiscreteDoubleKeyFrame`. (These three types of keyframes exist for colors and `Points` as well.)

Spline Keyframes

The `SplineDoubleKeyFrame`, `SplineColorKeyFrame`, and `SplinePointKeyFrame` elements enable animations with nonlinear interpolation, which are often more lifelike than simple linear animations. Each of these objects can be used just like its linear counterpart, so updating `DoubleAnimationUsingKeyFrames` from Listing 9.3, as follows, produces the exact same result:

```
<DoubleAnimationUsingKeyFrames
  Storyboard.TargetProperty="(Canvas.Top)" Duration="0:0:3">
  <SplineDoubleKeyFrame Value="0" KeyTime="0:0:0"/>
  <SplineDoubleKeyFrame Value="200" KeyTime="0:0:1"/>
  <SplineDoubleKeyFrame Value="0" KeyTime="0:0:2"/>
  <SplineDoubleKeyFrame Value="200" KeyTime="0:0:3"/>
</DoubleAnimationUsingKeyFrames>
```

The spline keyframe elements have an additional `KeySpline` property that differentiates themselves from the linear elements. `KeySpline` can be set to an instance of a `KeySpline` object, which describes the desired motion as a cubic Bézier curve. `KeySpline` has two properties of type `Point` that represent the curve's control points. (The start point of the curve is always `0`, and the end point is always `1`.) A type converter enables you to specify a `KeySpline` in XAML as a simple list of two points. For example, the following update changes the fly's motion from the simple zigzag in Figure 9.6 to the more complicated motion in Figure 9.7:

```
<DoubleAnimationUsingKeyFrames
  Storyboard.TargetProperty="(Canvas.Top)" Duration="0:0:3">
  <SplineDoubleKeyFrame KeySpline="0,1 1,0" Value="0" KeyTime="0:0:0"/>
  <SplineDoubleKeyFrame KeySpline="0,1 1,0" Value="200" KeyTime="0:0:1"/>
  <SplineDoubleKeyFrame KeySpline="0,1 1,0" Value="0" KeyTime="0:0:2"/>
  <SplineDoubleKeyFrame KeySpline="0,1 1,0" Value="200" KeyTime="0:0:3"/>
</DoubleAnimationUsingKeyFrames>
```

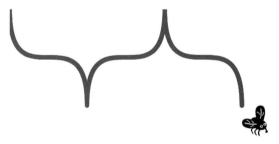

FIGURE 9.7   With `KeySpline` specified, the interpolation between keyframes is now based on cubic Bézier curves.

Finding the right value for `KeySpline` that gives the desired effect can be tricky, and it almost certainly requires the use of a design tool such as Expression Blend. But several free tools can be found online that help you visualize Bézier curves based on the specified control points.

Discrete Keyframes

A discrete keyframe simply indicates that no interpolation should be done from the previous keyframe. Updating DoubleAnimationUsingKeyFrames from Listing 9.3, as follows, produces the motion illustrated in Figure 9.8:

```
<DoubleAnimationUsingKeyFrames
  Storyboard.TargetProperty="(Canvas.Top)" Duration="0:0:3">
  <DiscreteDoubleKeyFrame Value="0" KeyTime="0:0:0"/>
  <DiscreteDoubleKeyFrame Value="200" KeyTime="0:0:1"/>
  <DiscreteDoubleKeyFrame Value="0" KeyTime="0:0:2"/>
  <DiscreteDoubleKeyFrame Value="200" KeyTime="0:0:3"/>
</DoubleAnimationUsingKeyFrames>
```

FIGURE 9.8   Discrete keyframes make the fly's vertical position jump from one key value to the next with no interpolation.

Of course, all three types of keyframes can be mixed into the same animation. The following mixture makes the fly follow the path shown in Figure 9.9:

```
<DoubleAnimationUsingKeyFrames
  Storyboard.TargetProperty="(Canvas.Top)" Duration="0:0:3">
  <DiscreteDoubleKeyFrame Value="0" KeyTime="0:0:0"/>
  <LinearDoubleKeyFrame Value="200" KeyTime="0:0:1"/>
  <DiscreteDoubleKeyFrame Value="0" KeyTime="0:0:2"/>
  <SplineDoubleKeyFrame KeySpline="0,1,1,0" Value="200" KeyTime="0:0:3"/>
</DoubleAnimationUsingKeyFrames>
```

Because the first keyframe's time is at the very beginning, its type is actually irrelevant. Each frame only indicates how interpolation is done *before* that frame.

FIGURE 9.9   Mixing all three types of keyframes into a single animation.

Conclusion

With animation, you can do something as simple as a subtle rollover effect or as complex as an animated cartoon. Storyboards, which are necessary to attach animations to other elements, help to orchestrate a complex series of animations.

The same could be said for other areas of Silverlight, but going overboard with animation can harm the usability and accessibility of your content. Another factor to consider is the performance implication of animation. Too much animation could make otherwise useful content become unusable on a less-powerful computer. Lowering the Silverlight control's maxFramerate can improve performance, but at the expense of losing smoothness in your animations. Finding the right balance depends on the nature of your content and will likely involve some trial and error.

CHAPTER 10

Audio and Video

Silverlight's support for audio and video is one of its key features in version 1.0. You can get outstanding video quality with Silverlight and make it go full screen—up to 720p high-definition quality on a reasonably-equipped computer—although its performance greatly depends on the computer viewing it. Video can be seamlessly intermixed with any other Silverlight content and transformed just like any other element.

Fortunately, due to the hard work that the Silverlight team had to do behind-the-scenes to enable this rich media functionality on all supported operating systems, taking advantage of this support is actually very straightforward. This chapter is all about what you can do with MediaElement, the versatile element that hosts all audio and video in Silverlight. After looking at what you can do with MediaElement in XAML and in JavaScript, this chapter explains how Expression Encoder can save you enormous amounts of time and effort and help you produce a truly professional result.

FAQ

What audio and video formats are supported by Silverlight?

Silverlight 1.0 supports five video formats and four audio formats. The following table lists the video formats:

Video Format	Standard Four-Character Code (FourCC)
Windows Media Video 9 Advanced Profile (VC-1 compliant)	WMVC1
Windows Media Video 9 Advanced Profile (not VC-1 compliant)	WMVA
Windows Media Video 9	WMV3
Windows Media Video 8	WMV2
Windows Media Video 7	WMV1

VC-1 is a widely supported video format standardized by the Society of Motion Picture and Television Engineers. It has three profiles—Simple, Main, and Advanced. Windows Media Video 9 Advanced Profile is Microsoft's implementation of the VC-1 Advanced Profile specification. The older Windows Media Video 9 (WMV3) format has three profiles—Simple, Main, and Complex—and all but the latter are compliant with the corresponding VC-1 profiles.

The four supported audio formats are Windows Media Audio (WMA) 7, 8, and 9, as well as MP3. Not *every* MP3 file can be played, however. Like most MP3 players, only bit rates up to 320kbps are supported.

Note that several Windows Media formats are not supported by Silverlight, such as WMA Voice (a format optimized for speech) or WMA Professional (which can support 7.1 channel surround sound instead of the mono/stereo support of standard WMA). In addition, Windows Media Video that uses MP3 audio is not supported, despite the fact that these two formats are supported independently!

If you have existing audio or video in an unsupported format, it shouldn't be hard to transcode it into a supported one using any number of existing audio/video tools.

FAQ

What's the difference between audio and video in Silverlight versus audio and video in WPF?

Both WPF and Silverlight have a MediaElement element for embedding media in a user interface, and WPF supports all the formats that Silverlight does. Because audio and video is such a core scenario for Silverlight 1.0, the Silverlight MediaElement has been given extra capabilities that the WPF MediaElement does not have, whether it's something sophisticated, such as the capability to retrieve metadata or timeline markers, or something simple, such as an AutoPlay property. The VideoBrush described in Chapter 5, "Brushes and Images," is also unique to Silverlight, although you can accomplish the same effect in WPF with the more general-purpose VisualBrush.

Continued

Although the exposed functionality is very similar between the two technologies, the underlying implementation is much different. WPF's audio and video support is built on top of Windows Media Player, but Silverlight's is not. Depending on Windows Media Player was not an option for Silverlight due to its cross-platform support and requirement for being a small download.

Playing Audio and Video with MediaElement

MediaElement, seen briefly in previous chapters, is designed for playing audio and video, whether it's a normal media file that needs to be downloaded or streaming media. This section examines the various ways to retrieve and display content with MediaElement.

FAQ

Does Silverlight support Digital Rights Management (DRM)?

Silverlight 1.0 does not, but the next version of Silverlight should support Microsoft's PlayReady technology for providing DRM capabilities.

The Source Property

You can set MediaElement's Source property to the URL of an audio or video file, and it plays automatically as soon as the content is loaded. Therefore, annoying users of your web page with automatic background music (similar to Internet Explorer's BGSOUND element) is as simple as loading XAML content such as the following:

```
<MediaElement xmlns="http://schemas.microsoft.com/client/2007"
  Source="song.wma"/>
```

Or, playing a video automatically in a rectangular region is as simple as

```
<MediaElement xmlns="http://schemas.microsoft.com/client/2007"
  Source="video.wmv"/>
```

As with the Source on Image or ImageBrush, MediaElement's Source can be an absolute URL pointing to any domain or a relative URL (relative to the host HTML file). And if you have the media file in the same directory as an HTML file on the local file system, you can point the Source to that file using just the filename. The content renders at its natural size by default.

MediaElement supports three protocols for the URL: HTTP, HTTPS, or MMS (Microsoft Media Services). HTTPS can only be used if the hosting page is served via HTTPS, and HTTP or MMS can only be used if the hosting page is served via HTTP. The Source can also be pointed to an Advanced Stream Redirector (ASX) playlist, which is a simple XML file that combines multiple media files into a single entity. For example, the following ASX file combines two videos into a single source:

```
<asx version="3.0">
  <title>My Playlist</title>
  <entry>
    <title>Movie #1</title>
    <ref href="first.wmv"/>
  </entry>
  <entry>
    <title>Movie #2</title>
    <ref href="second.wmv"/>
  </entry>
</asx>
```

If you point MediaElement's Source to this file, first.wmv starts playing and then second.wmv plays as soon as first.wmv finishes. (You can also open ASX files with Windows Media Player and watch the entire sequence, jump to later movies in the list, and so on.) Examining the format of ASX files is outside the scope of this book, but there are many online resources describing all the options.

Visual Effects

To use video in a nonrectangular region, you could either paint a shape with a VideoBrush that points to a named MediaElement, as shown in Chapter 5, or you could just use a single MediaElement but set its Clip property to an arbitrary geometry, using the techniques from Chapter 3, "Shapes, Lines, and Curves." Because MediaElement is a UI element, you can not only set its Width, Height, and Clip, but also set its Opacity or OpacityMask, give it any number of RenderTransforms, use Canvas.ZIndex on it, and so on.

The flexibility of video in Silverlight can seem unusual to people used to dealing with video as a "black box," but it really can be treated just as any other shape, image, or text. The following XAML, rendered in Figure 10.1, places two instances of a video on top of each other, both half-transparent, both clipped with a circle, and one rotated 180°:

```
<Canvas xmlns="http://schemas.microsoft.com/client/2007">
  <MediaElement Source="playtime.wmv" Opacity="0.5"
    Canvas.Left="300" Canvas.Top="300">
    <MediaElement.Clip>
      <EllipseGeometry Center="120,120" RadiusX="120" RadiusY="120"/>
    </MediaElement.Clip>
    <MediaElement.RenderTransform>
      <RotateTransform Angle="180"/>
    </MediaElement.RenderTransform>
  </MediaElement>
  <MediaElement Source="playtime.wmv" Opacity="0.5">
    <MediaElement.Clip>
      <EllipseGeometry Center="120,120" RadiusX="120" RadiusY="120"/>
    </MediaElement.Clip>
  </MediaElement>
</Canvas>
```

FIGURE 10.1 Clipped, rotated, and half-transparent video inside two `MediaElement`s.

Audio-Specific Features

`MediaElement` has a few features for controlling audio, whether it's audio-only content or the audio that's part of a video:

- You can set the `Volume` property to any value from `0` to `1`. The default value is `0.5`.

- You can mute the audio by setting its `IsMuted` property to `true`.

- You can shift the balance toward the left or right speaker by setting its `Balance` property to a value between `-1` and `1`. `-1` means that all the audio is sent to the left speaker; `0` (the default) means that all the audio is sent to both speakers; and `1` means that all the audio is sent to the right speaker.

- If the media has multiple audio tracks, you can select a different one by setting the `AudioStreamIndex` property (whose default value is `0`). The `AudioStreamCount` property tells you how many tracks exist.

Video-Specific Features

`MediaElement` has three properties specific to video: `NaturalVideoWidth`, `NaturalVideoHeight`, and `Stretch`. `NaturalVideoWidth` and `NaturalVideoHeight`, which give the original dimensions of the video (or `0` for audio), can be helpful for making decisions on how to display the video. If you don't give `MediaElement` an explicit `Width` and `Height`, it is given these dimensions.

10

If you give `MediaElement` an explicit `Width` and `Height` that don't match the natural values, `Stretch` controls how the video fills the space. `Stretch` works the same way as on shapes, `Image`, `ImageBrush`, and `VideoBrush`. Figure 10.2 demonstrates the four `Stretch` values with the following XAML:

```
<Canvas xmlns="http://schemas.microsoft.com/client/2007">
  <Rectangle Width="150" Height="150" Fill="Red" Canvas.Left="160"/>
  <MediaElement Stretch="None" Width="150" Height="150" Source="playtime.wmv"/>
  <MediaElement Stretch="Uniform" Width="150" Height="150" Source="playtime.wmv"
    Canvas.Left="160"/>
  <MediaElement Stretch="UniformToFill" Width="150" Height="150"
    Source="playtime.wmv" Canvas.Top="160"/>
  <MediaElement Stretch="Fill" Width="150" Height="150" Source="playtime.wmv"
    Canvas.Top="160" Canvas.Left="160"/>
</Canvas>
```

The `Rectangle` is there just to help demonstrate the `Stretch` of `Uniform`, as it's the only setting in which the entire 150x150 region is not filled with video.

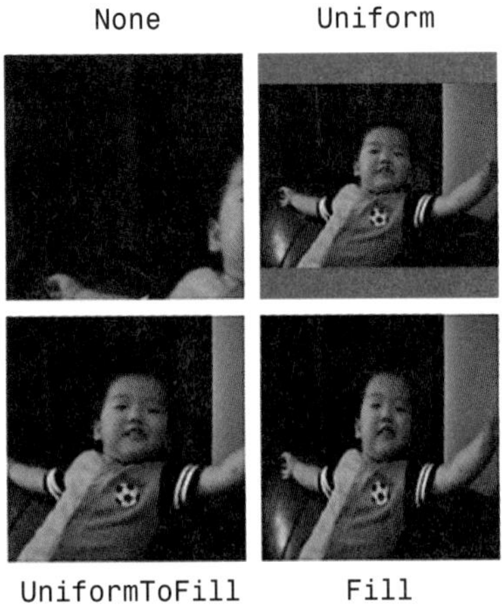

Progressive Download Versus Streaming

Silverlight supports both HTTP-based *progressive download* and *streaming* of audio and video files. This happens automatically when you set the `Source` of a `MediaElement`, and the choice of one versus the other is determined by the URL and the media it points to. If the `Source` uses the HTTP or HTTPS protocol, Silverlight attempts to perform a progressive download but falls back to streaming if that fails. However, if the `Source` uses the MMS protocol, Silverlight attempts to stream the file but falls back to progressive download on failure.

Progressive download simply means that although the media file is downloaded to the client via a standard HTTP GET request, playback can begin fairly instantly. Users can rewind and fast forward the media at any time, but only within the subset of content that has already been downloaded.

FIGURE 10.2 `MediaElement` with four different `Stretch` settings.

> **TIP**
>
> For maximum performance, you should avoid setting an explicit `Width` or `Height` on `MediaElement`. If its natural size is not desirable, you should explore the possibility of re-encoding the video file(s) with the ideal size.

Streaming, on the other hand, refers to an efficient protocol that keeps an active connection between the client and server. This enables users to rewind and fast forward to *any* part of the content at any time. Most importantly (for the content providers, anyway), streaming is often much less expensive than a progressive download because only the portions of media actually viewed or heard (plus a little bit of buffer, controlled by `MediaElement`'s `BufferingTime` property) are delivered by the server. Compare this to progressive download, for which the file is retrieved as quickly as the web server can send the bytes. Note that Silverlight's streaming support requires Windows Server.

Much like Silverlight's generic downloader object, `MediaElement` contains a `DownloadProgressChanged` event and corresponding `DownloadProgress` property that enables you to customize your interaction with the progressive download process. You could implement a user interface similar to sites such as YouTube, for example, which show a background progress bar that makes it easy to compare the amount of video downloaded to the current position in the video. `DownloadProgressChanged` is raised whenever download progress changes by at least .05 percent from the time the download begins to the time it is complete. The `DownloadProgress` property starts at 0 and ends at 1.

For streaming media, the `DownloadProgressChanged` event is raised only once (with `DownloadProgress` set to 1) when the media is opened and buffered. Rather than using the

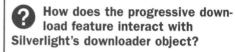

FAQ

? How does the progressive download feature interact with Silverlight's downloader object?

The explicit downloading enabled by Silverlight's downloader object is separate from the implicit downloading done by `MediaElement`. `MediaElement` does contain a `SetSource` function (just like `Image` and `ImageBrush`) that enables it to work with explicitly downloaded audio or video files. However, unless you want to download the media simultaneously with other files in a .ZIP file, or unless you want to guarantee that the entire media file has been downloaded before playback begins, there's no reason to choose explicit downloading over the implicit progressive downloading.

DIGGING DEEPER

Selecting a Stream in a Multiple Bit Rate File

Progressive download and streaming differ in how they handle a multiple bit rate (MBR) file. An MBR file contains multiple encodings of the same content, each with a different bit rate. The idea is to provide a tailored experience depending on the bandwidth available. Streaming honors this and selects the appropriate stream based on current conditions. Progressive download, however, always uses the stream with the highest bit rate.

`DownloadProgressChanged` event and the `DownloadProgress` property, the relevant event and property for streaming media is the `BufferingProgressChanged` event and the `BufferingProgress` property. They work the same way as the download event and property.

10

Controlling Audio and Video with JavaScript

`MediaElement` has a number of functions, properties, and events that make it possible for JavaScript to interact with audio or video in very rich ways. The functionality provided by these members range from the obvious (such as `Play` and `Stop` functions) to the not-so-obvious (such as the `Attributes` or `Markers` properties).

Changing the Media's State

JavaScript can call MediaElement's Play and Stop functions, as well as Pause if the read-only CanPause property is true. (Silverlight sets CanPause to false when the MediaElement contains streaming media, which doesn't support pausing. When CanPause is false, calls to Pause fail silently.) Calls to these functions are always asynchronous, so if you called Stop immediately after Play, none of the content would be played.

A single instance of MediaElement can play multiple audio or video files, but only one at a time (either by swapping the Source or pointing the Source to an ASX playlist). You can play multiple audio or video files simultaneously, but to do that, you need a separate instance of MediaElement for each file.

A CurrentState property tracks the state of the media, and a corresponding CurrentStateChanged event is raised whenever its value changes. The values for CurrentState are Opening, Buffering, Playing, Paused, Stopped, Closed, and Error.

As mentioned at the beginning of the chapter, content in a MediaElement plays automatically as soon as it is loaded. This might not always be desirable, of course. You might want instances of MediaElement to contain sound effects to be used in response to specific user actions, such as clicking or hovering over an element. There are a few options for preventing the automatic playing behavior. For example, you could call Stop in a Silverlight onLoad event handler, or you could wait to set the Source of the MediaElement until you're ready for the media to be played. But the best option is to take advantage of MediaElement's AutoPlay property, which is set to true by default. Simply set it to false, and the media won't be played until you call the Play function.

Basic Media Events

MediaElement has all the standard UI element events (such as MouseEnter, MouseLeftButtonDown, and so on), and it has a number of specialized events mentioned throughout this chapter. Three core media-related events that are good to be aware of are MediaOpened, MediaEnded, and MediaFailed.

The MediaOpened event is especially useful because some of MediaElement's properties are not valid until this event is raised. These properties are AudioStreamIndex and AudioStreamCount, NaturalVideoWidth and NaturalVideoHeight, NaturalDuration, CanPause, and Markers. If you need to interact with any of these properties, you should handle the MediaOpened event and use them inside this event handler.

The MediaFailed event provides a way to provide special error-handling logic specific to MediaElement. By default, any failures are bubbled up to the Silverlight control's onError handler.

Positioning the Audio or Video

MediaElement defines two properties that make it easy to jump to arbitrary

> **TIP**
>
> To create continuously looping background audio or video, you can handle the MediaEnded event and call Stop (to reset the position to the beginning) then Play inside of it.

parts of audio or video content or to implement a user interface that allows users to do this. Its `Position` property always returns the current spot in the media, whether it's playing, paused, or stopped. `Position` can also be set to a new value to change the current position (if the media format supports seeking). `Position` accepts the same syntax as an animation's `Duration` for representing time. Therefore, to set the `Position` to 10 seconds from the beginning, you would set it to the string `"0:0:10"`. Attempting to set the `Position` to a negative time or a time greater than the duration of the media is treated the same as setting the `Position` to zero.

The string syntax for setting `Position` is enabled by a type converter, so when you retrieve the value of `Position`, you don't get the same string back. Instead, you get an object with a numeric `Seconds` field. This makes it easier to do math, but if you want to display this value, you'll probably want to do a bit of work to format it nicely. For example:

```
var seconds = mediaElement.Position.Seconds;
// Display the value as mm:ss
var timeDisplay = Math.floor(seconds / 60) + ":" + (seconds % 60 < 10 ? "0" : "") +
    Math.floor(seconds % 60);
```

If you need to know what the duration of the media is, `MediaElement` has a `NaturalDuration` property that returns this length. Like `Position`, the information is returned as an object with a `Seconds` field, so doing math with the two properties is straightforward. Note that for streaming media, `NaturalDuration` is always `null` because the exact length is unknown (perhaps even to the server, as with live broadcasts). Also, if the `Source` is an ASX playlist, `NaturalDuration` and `Position` are associated with the current media only and get reset as each new item in the playlist begins.

Using Timeline Markers

Sometimes audio or video files have built-in *timeline markers* that contain custom infor-mation associated with specific points in time. An example of this would be markers that designate when a new chapter begins in a movie or even closed captioning text. (You can easily embed timeline markers in your own content, too, thanks to tools such as Expression Encoder.) Silverlight's `MediaElement` provides an easy way to retrieve these Windows Media–based timeline markers so that you can provide a custom, perhaps inter-active, experience.

Windows Media defines two main types of timeline markers—one is just called a *marker*, and one is called a *script command*. They are essentially the same thing—just a way to associate custom text with time-based positions—but their intent is different. Script commands are suggestions for the host to run custom code at that point, whereas markers tend to convey static data. Technically, the only difference is that a marker has one text value, whereas a script command has two text values (a *type* and a *command*, sometimes called a *param*).

`MediaElement` hides the difference between these types of timeline markers and exposes them via a single `Markers` property. This property is a collection of marker objects with three properties:

10

- ▸ **Time**—The position (relative to the beginning of the media) of the marker.

- ▸ **Text**—The main text value from the marker.

- ▸ **Type**—The type of the marker, if it's a script command. (If it's not a script command, Type is set to the same value as Text.)

You can retrieve and process all markers as soon as the media is opened, which can be useful for showing a display of all chapters. For other types of markers that might be easier to process on-demand, you can leverage MediaElement's MarkerReached event. MarkerReached is raised whenever MediaElement's Position matches the Time of a marker during playback. The sender passed to a MarkerReached event handler is the MediaElement, and the eventArgs object is the marker (with the Time, Text, and Type properties).

> ## WARNING
>
> **Some markers are only accessible via the MarkerReached event!**
>
> Windows Media supports timeline markers encoded as a separate stream, rather than embedded in the media file's header. This low-level detail normally wouldn't matter, but MediaElement treats these separate-stream markers differently. MediaElement raises the MarkerReached event for separate-stream markers as expected, but they are never placed in its Markers collection.

> ## FAQ
>
>  **How can I get metadata associated with audio or video, such as Album Artist or Genre?**
>
> MediaElement has a read-only Attributes property that gives a collection of metadata objects, each with a Name property and a Value property. This only exposes ASX metadata, however. Retrieving embedded metadata is not supported.
>
> To get all the ASX metadata associated with audio or video content, you could loop through the collection as follows, assuming that element is set to an instance of a MediaElement:
>
> ```
> for (var i = 0; i < element.Attributes.Count; i++)
> {
>    var attribute = element.Attributes.GetItem(i);
>    // Do something with attribute.Name and attribute.Value here!
> }
> ```
>
> Because Attributes is a read-only collection, it has Count and GetItem functions but no Add or Remove functions. However, it has a special GetItemByName function that enables direct retrieval of a specific attribute. For example:
>
> ```
> var attribute = element.Attributes.GetItemByName("Genre");
> ```
>
> If the attribute does not exist, GetItemByName returns null.

Building a Media Player User Interface

With all the functionality that MediaElement provides, you could build a fairly sophisticated Silverlight-based media player that rivals the core functionality of a program such as Windows Media Player. If you leverage Expression Encoder, discussed in the next section, you won't need to implement a media player from scratch. But to give you an idea of how it can be done, Listings 10.1

FIGURE 10.3 A basic hand-crafted Silverlight media player.

and 10.2 show all the XAML and JavaScript necessary to construct the very simple media player pictured in Figure 10.3.

LISTING 10.1 XAML for a Simple Media Player

```
<Canvas xmlns="http://schemas.microsoft.com/client/2007">
  <MediaElement Source="playtime.wmv"
    MediaOpened="onMediaOpened" MediaEnded="onMediaEnded"/>

  <!-- The Play Button -->
  <Canvas MouseLeftButtonDown="onPlayClicked">
    <Rectangle Height="25" Width="50" Stroke="White" Fill="#66FFFFFF"/>
    <TextBlock Canvas.Left="7" Canvas.Top="2" Foreground="White">PLAY</TextBlock>
  </Canvas>

  <!-- The Stop Button -->
  <Canvas MouseLeftButtonDown="onStopClicked" Canvas.Left="55">
    <Rectangle Height="25" Width="50" Stroke="White" Fill="#66FFFFFF"/>
    <TextBlock Canvas.Left="6" Canvas.Top="2" Foreground="White">STOP</TextBlock>
  </Canvas>

  <!-- The Pause Button -->
  <Canvas MouseLeftButtonDown="onPauseClicked" Canvas.Left="110">
    <Rectangle Height="25" Width="50" Stroke="White" Fill="#66FFFFFF"/>
    <TextBlock Canvas.Left="2" Canvas.Top="2" Foreground="White">PAUSE
    </TextBlock>
  </Canvas>

  <!-- The Current Position -->
  <TextBlock Name="positionText" Canvas.Left="2" Canvas.Top="26"
    Foreground="White"/>
</Canvas>
```

The Canvas contains five children: the MediaElement, a TextBlock for displaying the current position and total duration, and three "buttons" for playing, stopping, and pausing. Each button is just a Canvas with a TextBlock and a background Rectangle.

LISTING 10.2 JavaScript for the Simple Media Player

```
function onMediaOpened(sender, args)
{
  mediaElement = sender;
  positionText = sender.findName("positionText");
  // Start updating the position text every second
  handle = setInterval(updatePosition, 1000);
}
function onMediaEnded(sender, args)
{
  // Stop updating the position text
  clearInterval(handle);
}
function updatePosition()
{
  // Format both the Position and NaturalDuration for display
  positionText.Text = formatSeconds(mediaElement.Position.Seconds) + " | " +
    formatSeconds(mediaElement.NaturalDuration.Seconds);
}
function formatSeconds(seconds)
{
  // Convert seconds into mm:ss
  return Math.floor(seconds / 60) + ":" + (seconds % 60 < 10 ? "0" : "") +
    Math.floor(seconds % 60);
}
function onPlayClicked(sender, args)
{
  mediaElement.Play();
}
function onStopClicked(sender, args)
{
  mediaElement.Stop();
}
function onPauseClicked(sender, args)
{
  mediaElement.Pause();
}
```

The handler for MediaElement's MediaOpened event kicks off a timer that updates the
positionText TextBlock every second. (The "empty Storyboard" technique from the
preceding chapter would be more precise and reliable, but setInterval and
clearInterval are used here for simplicity.) It also stores a few items in global variables to
be used by other functions. The MediaEnded event handler simply clears the timer. The
updatePosition function that's called every second displays the values of Position and
NaturalDuration with the help of the formatSeconds function that turns the raw number

of seconds into a readable display. Finally, the three button event handlers do nothing more than call the corresponding `Play`, `Stop`, and `Pause` functions on `MediaElement`. That's all there is to it.

Using Expression Encoder

Microsoft's Expression Encoder is a new tool that enables audio and video professionals to create stunning media content to use with Silverlight. The core job of Expression Encoder is to import an audio or video file, and then export it in a different format. It has a number of features to help you choose an encoding and make the right trade-offs between a large number of settings, such as an amazing A/B compare feature that compares your chosen settings in real-time. It also has a command-line interface for doing batch (or even server-side) processing.

But it allows you to do much more than the core task of encoding. You can do basic stitching and trimming; you can add timeline markers and take advantage of special support for chapter thumbnails; you can add metadata; you can include live sources (such as a web cam or DV cam); and you can even switch between multiple sources (live or prerecorded) during a live broadcast, as if you're running your own television studio.

Another extremely handy feature is the ability to produce not just audio or video content, but a fully functioning Silverlight-based media player complete with buttons for playing, stopping, pausing, rewinding, fast forwarding, muting, and so on. It even provides a thumbnail-based chapter selection user interface, and full-screen video playback simply by double-clicking the video. And, it comes with a long list of professionally designed skins, three of which are shown in Figure 10.4. The output of the tool is a functioning HTML page with all the corresponding JavaScript and XAML files (plus the media file, of course). The skins are entirely vector based, and are set up to resize to fill the page while maintaining the aspect ratio. Several of them even have slick animations for showing and hiding pieces of the user interface.

10

FIGURE 10.4 Three built-in skins for the Silverlight media player produced by Expression Encoder.

Therefore, Expression Encoder can save an enormous amount of time, especially for straightforward user-controlled media playback. If that is your goal, you might not even need to know anything else covered in this chapter! But even if you want to do something more advanced that requires custom XAML and/or JavaScript, having Expression Encoder spit out its XAML and JavaScript and then using that as a starting point is an excellent strategy.

FAQ

 What's the difference between Expression Encoder, Windows Media Encoder, and Windows Movie Maker?

All these tools can be used to produce video supported by Silverlight. Windows Movie Maker is for casual movie production and focuses more on glitzy transitions and editing effects rather than supporting a rich set of formats. The two "Encoder" tools are aimed for professionals and are more powerful, except that they omit the visual effects and transitions. (The assumption is that the Hollywood studios or other professionals using these encoding tools already have better editing and special effects tools than what Microsoft provides.)

As for Windows Media Encoder versus Expression Encoder, the quality of their encoding is the same because they use the exact same codecs. Each tool has features that the other lacks, but Expression Encoder is a much richer tool in terms of both feature set and ease of use. And unlike Windows Media Encoder, Expression Encoder has many Silverlight-specific features built in, such as encoder profiles compatible with Silverlight Streaming by Windows Live, direct publishing to the Silverlight Streaming site, and the ready-to-use media player templates built with XAML and JavaScript. Note that Windows Media Encoder is a free utility, but Expression Encoder is not.

Conclusion

Silverlight's audio and video support, together with a powerful tool such as Expression Encoder, makes it very easy to create compelling multimedia content on the Web. If you combine that with the highly scalable distribution provided by Silverlight Streaming by Windows Live, you've got a complete solution for delivering multimedia (intermixed with other Silverlight content) that is truly first class. It almost couldn't get any easier!

Even if you don't take advantage of additional tools and services, the core functionality of MediaElement is compelling by itself. With a number of ways to control the audio or video, and the ability to break outside of a rigid rectangle (as with using the Windows Media Player ActiveX control), the things you can accomplish with multimedia are pretty much limited by your imagination!

Index

Numbers

A

How can we make this index more useful? Email us at indexes@samspublishing.com

H

I

How can we make this index more useful? Email us at indexes@samspublishing.com

How can we make this index more useful? Email us at indexes@samspublishing.com

U

How can we make this index more useful? Email us at indexes@samspublishing.com

Y-Z